11 Public and Community Services

The Career Information Center includes:

Administration, Business, and Office / 1

Agribusiness, Environment, and Natural Resources / 2

Communications and the Arts / 3

Construction / 4

Consumer, Homemaking, and Personal Services / 5

Engineering, Science, and Technology / 6

Health / 7

Hospitality and Recreation / 8

Manufacturing / 9

Marketing and Distribution / 10

Public and Community Services / 11

Transportation / 12

Employment Trends and Master Index / 13

11 Public and Community Services

career information center

Sixth Edition

MACMILLAN LIBRARY REFERENCE USA
Simon & Schuster Macmillan
NEW YORK

Prentice Hall International
LONDON   MEXICO CITY   NEW DELHI   SINGAPORE   SYDNEY   TORONTO

Editorial Staff

Editorial Directors, Richard Lidz and Linda Perrin

Project Director, Suzanne J. Murdico

Editorial Assistant, Andrew Scoblionko

Writers, Debra Goldentyer, Bruce Goldstone, William Harless, Jonathan M. Leeds, Nancy J. Nielsen, Judith Peacock, Donna Singer

Copy Editor, Patricia Ciaccio

Photo Research Coordinator, Sara Matthews

Researchers/Bibliographers, Amy B. Lewis, Andrew Scoblionko

Production Supervisors, Amy Davis, William A. Murray

Electronic Production, Lisa Evans-Skopas, Cynthia C. Feldner

Art and Design, Maxson Crandall

Acknowledgments: It would be impossible to acknowledge the many people who gave their help, their time, and their experience to this project. However, we especially want to thank all the people at unions and trade and professional associations for their help in providing information and photographs. We also wish to thank the U.S. Department of Labor, Bureau of Labor Statistics, for their cooperation and for providing up-to-date statistics, salary information, and employment projections for all the job profiles.

 Developed and produced by Visual Education Corp., Princeton, New Jersey

Macmillan Library Reference USA
Simon & Schuster Macmillan
866 Third Avenue
New York, NY 10022

ISSN 1082-703X

ISBN 0028974727 (set)

ISBN 0028974840 (volume 11)

Printed in the United States of America

printing number
1 2 3 4 5 6 7 8 9 10

This paper meets the requirements of ANSI/NISO Z39.48-1992 (Permanence of Paper).

Career Information Center
Editorial Advisory Board

Contents

Job Summary Chart   vii

Foreword   x

Using the Career Information Center   xi

Career Information Center Occupational Profiles   xiii

Looking into Public and Community Services   1

Getting into Public and Community Services   15

Jobs Requiring No Specialized Training   37

Jobs Requiring Some Specialized Training/Experience   69

Jobs Requiring Advanced Training/Experience   87

Further Reading and Resources   147
    General Career Information—Books   147
    General Career Information—Audiovisual Materials   156
    General Career Information—Computer Software   158
    Career and Vocational Information on Public and Community
       Services   160

Directory of Institutions Offering Career Training   167

Index   189

Photographic Credits   193

Job Summary Chart

Job	Salary	Education/Training	Employment Outlook	Page
Jobs Requiring No Specialized Training				
Armed Services Career	Average—$28,000	Varies—see profile	Very good	37
Border Patrol Agent	Starting—$18,000 to $20,000	High school	Fair	39
Building Custodian	Average—$13,500 to $14,400	None	Good	41
Corrections Officer	Varies—see profile	Varies—see profile	Excellent	42
Electric Power Service Worker	Varies—see profile	High school plus training	Fair	44
Electric Power Transmission and Distribution Worker	Varies—see profile	High school plus training	Fair	46
Federal Government Worker	Varies—see profile	Varies—see profile	Fair	48
Fire Fighter	Average—$25,900 to $42,800	None	Fair	50
Geriatric Aide	Average—$11,000 to $18,000	None	Excellent	52
Highway Maintenance Worker	Average—$18,000 to $23,000	None	Very good	54
Meter Reader	Average—$19,500 to $23,000	None	Poor	55
Police Officer	Starting—$18,000 to $22,000 Average—$24,500 to $41,200	None	Fair	57
Postal Service Worker	Starting—$23,700 Average—$32,800	None	Poor	58
Power Plant Worker	Average—$26,500 to $41,000	None	Fair	60
Refuse Worker	Average—$18,000 to $24,000	None	Good	62
Security Guard	Varies—see profile	None	Excellent	64
State Police Officer	Starting—$20,000 Average—$24,500 to $41,200	High school	Fair	66
Jobs Requiring Some Specialized Training/Experience				
Crime Laboratory Technician	Average—$20,000 to $29,000	High school	Very good	69
Day Care Worker	Average—$210 to $320 a week	High school	Excellent	70
Detective	Average—$24,500 to $41,200	High school	Fair	72
Institutional Child Care Worker	Varies—see profile	High school	Very good	74
Institutional Housekeeper	Average—$210 to $375 a week	Varies—see profile	Good	76

Job	Salary	Education/ Training	Employment Outlook	Page
Legal Assistant, Corporate	Starting—$22,000 to $26,000 Average—$25,000 to $32,000	High school plus training	Excellent	77
Paralegal Aide	Starting—$21,000 to $25,000 Average—$26,000 to $30,000	Varies—see profile	Excellent	79
Shorthand Reporter	Average—$19,200 to $28,100	High school	Good	80
Teacher's Aide	Average—$8 to $8.50 an hour	Varies—see profile	Very good	82
Youth Organization Worker	Average—$14,000 to $16,000	High school	Fair	84

Jobs Requiring Advanced Training/Experience

Job	Salary	Education/ Training	Employment Outlook	Page
Adult Education Worker	Average—$18,700 to $38,800	College	Very good	87
City Manager	Varies—see profile	College	Fair	88
College Student Personnel Worker	Varies—see profile	College	Fair	90
Criminologist	Starting—$23,000 to $28,000 Average—$40,000 to $50,000	Advanced degree	Fair	92
Customs Worker	Average—$36,000 to $40,000	High school plus training	Fair	94
FBI Special Agent	Starting—$30,600 Average—$47,900 to $56,600	College plus training	Poor	95
Foreign Service Worker	Varies—see profile	Varies—see profile	Poor	97
Fund Raiser	Varies—see profile	College	Good	99
Government Inspector and Examiner	Varies—see profile	Varies—see profile	Very good	101
Internal Revenue Service Worker	Starting—$21,000 to $27,000	College	Good	102
Lawyer	Varies—see profile	Advanced degree	Good	104
Lawyer, Corporate	Average—$50,000 to $80,000	Advanced degree	Good	106
Lawyer, Public Service	Varies—see profile	Advanced degree	Very good	107
Librarian, Public	Varies—see profile	Advanced degree	Fair	109
Librarian, School	Starting—$25,400 to $27,400 Average—$34,000 to $42,000	College plus training	Varies— see profile	111
Librarian, Special	Average—$29,200 to $31,800	Varies—see profile	Good	113
Marriage and Family Counselor	Starting—$25,000 to $30,000	College	Good	115
Parole Officer	Starting—$20,000 to $30,000	College plus training	Good	117
Political Consultant	Varies—see profile	College	Very good	118
Probation Officer	Starting—$20,000 to $30,000	College plus training	Good	120

Job	Salary	Education/Training	Employment Outlook	Page
Rehabilitation Counselor	Starting—$18,000 to $25,000	College plus training	Very good	122
Religious Vocation	Varies—see profile	Varies—see profile	Varies—see profile	123
School Administrator	Average—$49,200 to $58,800	College plus training	Fair	125
School Counselor	Starting—$24,000 Average—$38,500 to $42,500	College plus training	Very good	127
School Media Specialist	Average—$27,400 to $37,900	Advanced degree	Fair	129
Social Worker	Starting—$20,000 to $30,000 Average—$25,600 to $41,400	Advanced degree	Very good	131
Teacher, College	Varies—see profile	Advanced degree	Varies—see profile	133
Teacher, Elementary and Preschool	Average—$32,000 to $38,000	College plus training	Good	135
Teacher, Secondary School	Average—$33,000 to $39,000	College plus training	Very good	138
Teacher, Vocational Education	Average—$24,000 to $34,000	High school plus training	Very good	140
Urban and Regional Planner	Varies—see profile	Advanced degree	Fair	141
Vocational Counselor	Starting—$20,000 to $23,000 Average—$24,000 to $41,500	College	Very good	143

Foreword

The sixth edition of the *Career Information Center* mirrors the ongoing changes in the job market caused by new technological and economic developments. These developments continue to change what Americans do in the workplace and how they do it. People have a critical need for up-to-date information to help them make career decisions.

The *Career Information Center* is an individualized resource for people of all ages and at all stages of career development. It has been recognized as an excellent reference for librarians, counselors, educators, and other providers of job information. It is ideally suited for use in libraries, career resource centers, and guidance offices, as well as in adult education centers and other facilities where people seek information about job opportunities, careers, and their own potential in the work force.

This sixth edition updates the features that made the earlier editions so useful.

- A Job Summary Chart, a quick reference guide, appears in the front section of each volume to help readers get the basic facts and compare the jobs described in the volume.
- Each volume of the *Career Information Center* begins with an overview of the job market in that field. These "Looking into . . ." sections have been completely revised and updated. They also include new graphs, charts, and boxes providing information such as industry snapshots and the fastest-growing and top-dollar jobs in the field.
- Each volume has a section called "Getting into . . . ," which contains useful information on entering the particular field. It offers self-evaluation and decision-making help; and it relates possible job choices to individual interests, abilities, and work characteristics. There is also practical information on job hunting, using classified ads, preparing resumes, and handling interviews. "Getting into . . ." also includes a section on employee rights.
- Each volume has a listing of all job profiles in the series and the volumes in which they appear, making access to profiles in other volumes easy.
- *Career Information Center* contains more than 648 occupational profiles in which over 3,000

jobs are discussed. Each profile describes work characteristics, education and training requirements, job entry, advancement possibilities and employment outlook, working conditions, and earnings and benefits.

- Job Summary Boxes, provided for each occupational profile, highlight the education or training required, salary range, and employment outlook. High-growth jobs are identified by means of an eye-catching logo.
- Volume 13 has been revised to reflect career concerns of the 1990s and employment trends through the year 2005. This volume includes updated articles on benefits, employment law, health in the workplace, job search strategies, job training, and job opportunities at home. This sixth edition also contains two completely new articles on adjusting to job loss and identifying opportunities for retraining.
- Volume 13 has been expanded with the addition of 35 new occupational profiles. These profiles contain complete, up-to-date descriptions of jobs not discussed in earlier editions of the *Career Information Center*.
- More than 750 photographs appear in the *Career Information Center,* including many new photos. Each profile is illustrated with a photo, providing a visual glimpse of life on the job. Special care has been taken to select photos that give the reader a sense of what it feels like to be in a specific field or job.
- Updated bibliographies in each volume include recommended readings in specific job areas. Additional titles for the vocational counselor are included in Volumes 1 and 13.
- Each volume also contains a comprehensive directory of accredited occupational education and vocational training facilities listed by occupational area and grouped by state. Directory materials are generated from the IPEDS (Integrated Postsecondary Education Data System) database of the U.S. Department of Education.

The *Career Information Center* recognizes the importance not only of job selection, but also of job holding, coping, and applied life skills. No other career information publication deals with work attitudes so comprehensively.

Using the Career Information Center

The *Career Information Center* is designed to meet the needs of many people—students, people just entering or reentering the job market, those dissatisfied with present jobs, those without jobs—anyone of any age who is not sure what to do for a living. The *Career Information Center* is for people who want help in making career choices. It combines the comprehensiveness of an encyclopedia with the format and readability of a magazine. Counselors, librarians, teachers, and other professionals will also find it a useful guidance and reference tool.

The *Career Information Center* is organized by occupational interest area rather than by alphabetical order. Jobs that have something in common are grouped together. In that way people who do not know exactly what job they want can read about a number of related jobs. The *Career Information Center* classifies jobs that have something in common into clusters. The classification system is adapted from the 20-cluster organization used by the U.S. Department of Labor into a more manageable 12-cluster system. Each volume of the *Career Information Center* explores one of these occupational clusters.

To use the *Career Information Center*, first select the volume that treats the occupational area that interests you most. Because there are many ways to group occupations, you may not find a particular job in the volume in which you look for it. In that case, check the central listing of all the profiles, which is located in the front of each volume (1 through 12). This listing will direct you to the number of the volume in which each profile appears. Volume 13 also includes a comprehensive index of all the jobs in the volumes.

After selecting a volume or volumes, investigate the sections that you feel would be most helpful. It isn't necessary to read these volumes from cover to cover. The books are arranged so that you can go directly to the specific information you want. Here is a description of the sections included in each book.

Job Summary Chart—This chart presents in tabular form the basic data from each profile: salary, education and training, employment outlook, and the page on which you can find the job profile.

Looking into . . .—An overview of the occupational cluster, which describes the opportunities, characteristics, and trends in that particular field.

Getting into . . .—A how-to guide designed to help you decide what jobs may be most satisfying to you and what strategies you can use to get the right job. You'll learn, for example, how to write an effective resume, how to complete an application form, what to expect in an interview, how to use networking, and what to do if someone has discriminated against you.

Job Summary Box—This box gives the most important facts about the job: education and training required, salary, and job outlook.

Education and Training indicates whether the job requires no education, high school, college, advanced degree, voc/tech school, license, or training.

Salary Range is given as an approximate yearly wage unless "a week" or "an hour" is noted. These are average salaries that may vary significantly from region to region.

Employment Outlook is based on Bureau of Labor Statistics' projections through the year 2005. The ratings are defined as follows: *poor* means there is a projected employment decrease of 1 percent or more; *fair* means there is a projected employment increase of 0 to 13 percent; *good* means there is a projected employment increase of 14 to 26 percent; *very good* means there is a projected employment increase of 27 to 40 percent; and *excellent* means there is a projected employment increase of 41 percent or more.

Finally, the job outlook is determined by the projected change in employment plus other factors. For example, a job with *excellent* projected employment growth in which many more people are entering the field than there are jobs available will have an outlook that is *good* rather than *excellent*.

For all categories, the phrase "varies—see profile" means the reader must consult the profile for the information, which is too extensive to include in the Job Summary Box.

An eye-catching logo appears in the upper right corner of some Job Summary Boxes to highlight jobs with high growth potential:

Jobs Requiring No Specialized Training, Jobs Requiring Some Specialized Training/Experience, Jobs Requiring Advanced Training/ Experience—These sections, organized by level of training required to get the job, are made up of the occupational profiles for each volume. Each profile explores a number of related jobs and covers seven major points: description of the job, the education and training requirements, ways to get the job, advancement possibilities and employment outlook, the working conditions, the earnings and benefits, and places to go for more information.

Jobs Requiring No Specialized Training includes jobs that require no education or previous work experience beyond high school.

Jobs Requiring Some Specialized Training/Experience includes jobs that require one, two, or three years of vocational training, college, or work experience beyond high school.

Jobs Requiring Advanced Training/Experience includes jobs that require a bachelor's or advanced degree and/or equivalent work experience in that field.

Further Reading and Resources—A selected bibliography that includes the most recent books and audiovisual materials on general career information, how-to books on such topics as resume writing and preparing for tests, useful computer software, and specific references for each volume. In addition, there are special sections of readings for the career counselor in Volumes 1 and 13.

Directory of Institutions Offering Career Training—A listing, organized first by career area, then by state, of the schools that offer occupational training beyond high school. For jobs requiring a bachelor's degree or an advanced degree, check a library for college catalogs and appropriate directories.

Index at end of each volume—This index serves not only to cross-reference all the jobs in the volume but also to show related jobs in the field. For example, under the entry LICENSED PRACTICAL NURSE, you will find Home Health Aide, Nurse's Aide and Orderly, and Ward Clerk. In addition, the "profile includes" part of an entry lists other jobs that are mentioned in the profile, in this case Licensed Vocational Nurse and Registered Nurse.

Volume 13, Employment Trends with Master Index—This volume includes several features that will help both the job seeker and the career counselor. A useful correlation guide provides the DOT (*Dictionary of Occupational Titles*) number of each of the job profiles in the *Career Information Center*. There is also a special section on career information for Canada. The updated and revised "Employment Trends" section contains articles on health in the workplace; employment projections through the year 2005; job search strategies; employment trends for women, minorities, immigrants, older workers, and the physically challenged; employment demographics; employment law; benefits programs; training; and employment opportunities at home. This section also contains two completely new articles on adjusting to job loss and identifying opportunities for retraining. All articles have been written by authorities in these fields. The articles provide job seekers and career professionals with an overview of current employment issues, career opportunities, and outlooks. In addition, this volume contains 35 job profiles that are new to this edition of the *Career Information Center*. Finally, there is a master index to all the jobs included in all 13 volumes.

The *Career Information Center*, then, is exactly what it says—a center of the most useful and pertinent information needed to explore and choose from the wide range of job and career possibilities. The *Career Information Center* provides people with a solid foundation of information for getting a satisfying job or rewarding career.

Career Information Center Occupational Profiles*

Accountant, 1
Accountant, Certified Public, 1
Actor, 3
Actuary, 1
Acupuncturist, 7
Administrative Assistant, 1
Admitting Clerk, 7
Adult Education Worker, 11
Advertising Account Executive, 10
Advertising Copywriter, 3
Advertising Manager, 10
Aerospace Engineer, 6
The Aerospace Industry, 9
Aerospace Technician, 6
Agricultural Engineer, 2
Agricultural Supply Sales Worker, 2
Agricultural Technician, 2
Agronomist, 2
AIDS Counselor, 7
Air Pollution Control Technician, 2
Air Traffic Controller, 12
Air-Conditioning and Heating
    Technician, 4
Air-Conditioning Engineer, 6
Air-Conditioning, Heating, and
    Refrigeration Mechanic, 4
Aircraft Mechanic, 12
Airline Baggage and Freight
    Handler, 12
Airline Dispatcher, 12
Airline Flight Attendant, 12
Airline Reservations Agent, 12
Airline Ticket Agent, 12
Airplane Pilot, 12
Airport Manager, 12
Airport Utility Worker, 12
All-Round Machinist, 9
The Aluminum and Copper
    Industry, 9
Ambulance Driver, 7
Anatomist, 6
Animal Caretaker, 8
Announcer, 3
Anthropologist, 6
The Apparel Industry, 9
Appliance Service Worker, 5
Appraiser, 5
Archaeologist, 6
Architect, 4
Architectural Drafter, 4
Architectural Model Maker, 4
Armed Service Career, 11
Art Director, 3
Art and Music Therapist, 7
Artificial Intelligence Specialist, 6
Artist, 3
Assembler, 9
Astronomer, 6

Athletic Coach, 8
Athletic Trainer, 8
Auctioneer, 10
Auditor, 1
Auto Body Repairer, 12
Auto Parts Counter Worker, 10
Auto Sales Worker, 10
Automated Manufacturing Manager,
    9
Automobile Driving Instructor, 12
Automotive Exhaust Emissions
    Technician, 13
The Automotive Industry, 9
Automotive Mechanic, 12
Avionics Technician, 12

Bank Clerk, 1
Bank Officer, 1
Bank Teller, 1
Barber and Hairstylist, 5
Bartender, 8
Bicycle Mechanic, 12
Biochemist, 6
Biological Technician, 6
Biologist, 6
Biomedical Engineer, 6
Biomedical Equipment Technician, 7
Blacksmith and Forge Shop Worker, 9
Blood Bank Technologist, 13
Boat Motor Mechanic, 12
Boiler Tender, 9
Boilermaking Worker, 9
Bookbinder, 3
Bookkeeper, 1
Border Patrol Agent, 11
Botanist, 6
Bowling Pin Mechanic, 8
Bricklayer, 4
Bridal Consultant, 5
Broadcast Technician, 3
Brokerage Clerk, 13
Building Custodian, 11
Building Inspector, 4
Business Home Economist, 5
Business Machine Operator, 1

Cable Television Engineer, 3
Cable Television Technician, 3
CAD Specialist, 6
Cafeteria Attendant, 8
CAM Operator, 13
Camera Operator, 3
Candy, Soft Drink, and Ice Cream
    Manufacturing Worker, 2
Car Rental Agent, 12
Car Wash Worker, 12
Cardiac-Monitor Technician/
    Perfusionist, 13

Carpenter, 4
Cartographer, 13
Cartoonist, 3
Cashier, 10
Casino Worker, 13
Caterer, 8
Cement Mason, 4
Ceramic Engineer, 6
The Ceramics Industry, 9
Chauffeur, 5
Cheese Industry Worker, 2
Chemical Engineer, 6
Chemical Technician, 6
Chemist, 6
Child Care Worker, Private, 5
Chiropractor, 7
Choreographer, 13
City Manager, 11
Civil Engineer, 4
Civil Engineering Technician, 4
Claim Adjuster, 1
Claim Examiner, 1
College Student Personnel Worker,
    11
College/University Administrator, 13
Commercial Artist, 3
Companion, 5
Comparison Shopper, 10
Compensation Specialist, 1
Composer, 3
Composing Room Worker, 3
Composite Technician, 9
Computer Artist, 3
Computer Consultant, 1
Computer Database Manager, 1
Computer Operator, 1
Computer Programmer, 1
Computer Servicer, 1
Computer Software Documentation
    Writer, 1
Construction Electrician, 4
Construction Equipment Dealer, 4
Construction Equipment Mechanic,
    4
Construction Laborer, 4
Construction Millwright, 4
Construction Supervisor, 4
Consumer Advocate, 5
Consumer Credit Counselor, 5
Controller, 1
Convention Specialist, 8
Cook and Chef, 8
Cooperative Extension Service
    Worker, 2
Corrections Officer, 11
Correspondence Clerk, 1
Cosmetologist, 5
Court Clerk, 13

*Occupational Profiles and Volume Number

Craftsperson, 3
Credit Checker, 1
Credit Collector, 1
Credit Officer, 1
Crime Laboratory Technician, 11
Criminologist, 11
Crop Scientist, 2
Cruise Director, 8
Custom Tailor and Dressmaker, 5
Custom Upholsterer, 5
Customs Worker, 11

Dairy Industry Worker, 2
Dancer, 3
Darkroom Technician, 3
Data Entry Keyer, 1
Data Processing Manager, 1
Day Care Worker, 11
Demographer, 6
Demolition Worker, 4
Dental and Medical Secretary, 7
Dental Assistant, 7
Dental Hygienist, 7
Dental Laboratory Technician, 7
Dentist, 7
Desktop Publisher, 3
Detective, 11
Dialysis Technician, 7
Diesel Mechanic, 12
Dietetic Technician, 5
Dietitian and Nutritionist, 5
Dining Room Attendant, 8
Direct Market Broker, 10
Direct Sales Worker, 10
Director, 3
Dishwasher, 8
Display Worker, 13
Distribution Manager, 10
Diver, 2
Divorce Mediator, 5
Dock Worker, 12
Doorkeeper, 8
Drafter and Design Technician, 6
The Drug Industry, 9
Dry Cleaning Worker, 5
Drywall Installer and Finisher, 4

Economist, 6
Editor, Book, 3
Editor, Copy, 3
Editor, Magazine, 3
Editor, Newspaper, 3
EEG and EKG Technician, 7
Electric Power Service Worker, 11
Electric Power Transmission and
    Distribution Worker, 11
Electrical Technician, 6
Electrical/Electronics Engineer, 6
Electrologist, 5
Electromechanical Technician, 6
The Electronics Industry, 9
Electronics Technician, 6
Electroplater, 9
Elevator Constructor and Repair
    Worker, 4
Embalmer, 5

Emergency Medical Technician, 7
Employee Benefits Manager, 1
Employment Agent, 1
Employment Counselor, 1
Energy Conservation Technician,
    4
Entomologist, 6
Environmental Technician, 2
Environmentalist, 2
Epidemiologist, 13
Equipment Rental and Leasing
    Service Agent, 10
Ergonomist, 6
Estimator, 4
Executive Search Recruiter, 1
Expediter, 4

Farm Laborer, 2
Farm Manager, 2
Farm Office Worker, 2
Farmer, Cotton, Tobacco, and
    Peanut, 2
Farmer, Dairy , 2
Farmer, Fruit, 2
Farmer, Grain, 2
Farmer, Livestock, 2
Farmer, Poultry, 2
Farmer, Vegetable, 2
Fast Food Franchise Worker, 8
FBI Special Agent, 11
Federal Government Worker, 11
Fiction Writer, 3
File Clerk, 1
Film Editor, 3
Financial Analyst, 1
Financial Planner, 1
Fire Fighter, 11
Fire Protection Engineer, 6
Fish Culture Technician, 2
Fisher, 2
Fitness Instructor, 8
Fleet Manager, 13
Flight Engineer, 12
Flight Information Coordinator and
    Radio Operator, 12
Flight Instructor, 12
Floor Covering Installer, 4
Floral Designer, 5
Fluid Power Technician, 6
Food and Beverage Manager, 8
Food Broker, 10
Food Canning and Freezing Worker,
    2
Food Processing Technician, 2
Food Scientist, 2
Foreign Service Worker, 11
Forensic Scientist, 6
Forester, 2
Forestry Products Technician, 2
Forestry Technician, 2
The Foundry Industry, 9
Fund Raiser, 11
Funeral Director, 5
The Furniture Industry, 9

Gardener and Grounds Keeper, 5
Gas Station Attendant, 12

General Manager, 1
Genetic Engineering Research
    Assistant, 6
Genetic Engineering Research
    Scientist, 6
Geographer, 2
Geologist, 2
Geophysicist, 2
Geriatric Aide, 11
Geriatric Social Worker, 7
The Glass Industry, 9
Glazier, 4
Government Inspector and
    Examiner, 11
Graphic Designer, 13
Gunsmith, 6

Hazardous Waste Management
    Technician, 2
Head Waiter and Waitress, 8
Heavy Construction Contractor, 4
Heavy Equipment Operator, 4
Highway Contractor, 4
Highway Engineer, 4
Highway Inspector, 4
Highway Maintenance Worker, 11
Historian, 6
Home Caterer, 5
Home Economics Teacher, 5
Home Health Aide, 7
Homemaker, 5
Horse Industry Worker, 2
Horticulturist, 2
Hospice Worker, 7
Hospital Administrator, 7
Hospitality Cashier, 8
Hotel Bellhop and Porter, 8
Hotel Desk Clerk, 8
Hotel Executive Housekeeper, 8
Hotel Houseworker, 8
Hotel Manager, 8
Housekeeper, Domestic, 5
Hydraulic Maintenance Technician,
    9
Hydrologist, 2

Import and Export Worker, 10
The Industrial Chemical Industry, 9
Industrial Designer, 9
Industrial Engineer, 9
Industrial Hygienist, 6
Industrial Laser Machine Operator,
    9
Industrial Machinery Repairer, 9
Industrial Upholsterer, 9
Information Marketing Specialist, 10
Inhalation Therapist, 7
Institutional Child Care Worker, 11
Institutional Housekeeper, 11
Instructional Designer, 3
Instrument Maker, 9
Instrument Repairer, 9
Instrumentation Technician, 6
Insulation Worker, 4
Insurance Agent and Broker, 10
Integrated Circuit Technician, 13

Intercity Bus Driver, 12
Interior Designer, 5
Internal Revenue Service Worker, 11
Interviewing Clerk, 13
Investment Banker, 1
The Iron and Steel Industry, 9
Iron and Steel Worker, 4

Jeweler, 5
Journalist, 3
Judge, 13

Labor Relations Specialist, 9
Laboratory Animal Care Worker, 7
Landscape Architect, 4
Laser and Fiber Optics Engineer, 6
Laser and Fiber Optics Technician, 6
Lather, 4
Laundry Worker, 5
Lawyer, 11
Lawyer, Corporate, 11
Lawyer, Public Service, 11
The Leather and Shoe Industries, 9
Legal Assistant, Corporate, 11
Librarian, Public, 11
Librarian, School, 11
Librarian, Special, 11
Licensed Practical Nurse, 7
Lifeguard, 8
Lighting Technician, 3
Linguist, 6
Literary and Theatrical Agent, 3
Lithographic Worker, 3
Local Transit Operator, 12
Local Truck Driver, 12
Locksmith, 5
Locomotive Firer, 12
Logger, 2
Long-Haul Truck Driver, 12
Lumbermill Worker, 2

Machine Tool Operator, 9
Mail Clerk, 1
Mail Service Worker, 1
Maintenance Electrician, 4
Management Information Systems (MIS) Professional, 1
Manufactured Home Assembler and Installer, 4
Manufacturers' Sales Worker, 10
Manufacturing Engineer, 9
Marble, Tile, and Terrazzo Worker, 4
Marine Engineer, 2
Marine Services Technician, 12
Marketing Director, 10
Marketing Research Worker, 10
Marriage and Family Counselor, 11
Massage Therapist, 5
Mathematician, 6
Meat Packing Worker, 2
Mechanical Engineer, 6
Mechanical Engineering Technician, 6

Media Buyer, 10
Media Time Sales Worker, 10
Medical Assistant, 7
Medical Illustrator, 7
Medical Laboratory Technologist, 7
Medical Laboratory Worker, 7
Medical Physicist, 7
Medical Record Administrator, 7
Medical Record Technician/Clerk, 7
Meeting Planner, 13
Menu Planner, 8
Merchant Marine Captain, 12
Merchant Marine Engineer and Chief Engineer, 12
Merchant Marine Purser, 12
Merchant Marine Radio Officer, 12
Merchant Marine Steward and Cook, 12
Messenger Service Worker, 1
Metallurgical Engineer, 6
Metallurgical Technician, 6
Meter Reader, 11
Meteorologist, 2
Microbiologist, 6
Miner, Coal, 2
Miner, Metal, 2
Mining Engineer, 2
Mining Technician, 2
Model, 3
Motion Picture Projectionist, 8
Motorcycle Mechanic, 12
Mover, 12
Museum Curator, 8
Museum Worker, 8
Music Teacher, 13
Music Video Producer, 3
Musician, 3

Nanny, 5
Naval Architect, 2
Nuclear Engineer, 6
Nuclear Medicine Technologist, 13
Nuclear Technician, 6
Numerical Control Machine Operator, 9
Nurse Anesthetist, 7
Nurse's Aide/Orderly, 7
Nurse-Midwife, 7
Nursery Worker, 2

Occupational Therapist, 7
Occupational Therapy Assistant, 7
Ocean Technician, 2
Oceanographer, 2
Office Clerk, 1
The Office Machine and Computer Industry, 9
Office Machine Servicer, 1
Office Manager, 1
Office Planner, 1
Operating Room Technician, 7
Operations Research Analyst, 1
Ophthalmologist, 7
Optician, 7
Optometric Assistant, 7
Optometrist, 7

Ordinary and Able Seaman, 12
Orthoptist, 7
Osteopathic Physician, 7
Outdoor Guide, 8
Outplacement Consultant, 1

The Packaging Industry, 9
The Paint, Varnish, and Lacquer Industry, 9
Painter and Paperhanger, 4
Pantry Supervisor, 8
The Paper Industry, 9
Paralegal Aide, 11
Park Ranger, 8
Parking Analyst, 12
Parking Attendant, 12
Parole Officer, 11
Party Planner, 13
Pastry Chef and Baker, 8
Pathologist, 6
Payroll Clerk, 1
Personal Excercise Trainer, 5
Personal Service Worker, 5
Personal Shopper, 5
Personnel Administrator, 1
Personnel Clerk, 1
Personnel Recruiter, 1
Pest Control Worker, 5
Pet Care Worker, 5
Petroleum and Natural Gas Exploration and Production Worker, 2
Petroleum Engineer, 2
The Petroleum Refining Industry, 9
Pharmaceutical Detail Representative, 7
Pharmaceutical Technician, 6
Pharmacist, 7
Pharmacologist, 7
Photo Researcher, 13
Photoengraver, 3
Photographer, 3
Physical Therapist, 7
Physical Therapy Assistant, 7
Physician, 7
Physician Assistant, 7
Physicist, 6
Piano and Organ Tuner and Technician, 5
Plasterer, 4
The Plastics Industry, 9
Platemaker, 3
Plumber and Pipe Fitter, 4
Podiatrist, 7
Police Officer, 11
Political Consultant, 11
Political Scientist, 6
Postal Service Worker, 11
Power Plant Worker, 11
Power Tool Repairer, 4
Power Truck Operator, 12
Printing Press Operator, 3
Probation Officer, 11
Producer, 3
Product Manager, 13
Production Designer, 3

Production Manager, 9
Production Painter, 9
Production, Planning, and
    Expediting Clerk, 13
Production Supervisor, 9
Professional Athlete, 8
Professional Organizer, 13
Proofreader, 3
Property/Facilities Manager, 13
Prosthetist/Orthotist, 7
Psychiatric Aide/Technician, 13
Psychiatrist, 7
Psychologist, 7
Public Health Educator, 13
Public Relations Manager, 3
Public Relations Worker, 3
Purchasing Agent, 10

Quality Control Engineer, 9
Quality Control Inspector, 9
Quality Control Manager, 6

Radio and Television Newscaster, 13
Radiologic Technologist, 7
Railroad Braker, 12
Railroad Clerk, 12
Railroad Conductor, 12
Railroad Engineer, 12
Railroad Maintenance Worker, 12
Railroad Signaler and Signal
    Maintainer, 12
Railroad Station Agent, 12
Railroad Telegrapher, Telephoner,
    and Tower Operator, 12
Railroad Track Worker, 12
Range Manager, 2
Real Estate Appraiser, 10
Real Estate Developer, 13
Real Estate Sales Worker and
    Broker, 10
Receptionist, 1
Recreation Worker, 8
Recreational Therapist, 7
Refuse Worker, 11
Registered Nurse, 7
Rehabilitation Counselor, 11
Religious Vocation, 11
Reprographic Worker, 3
Research Home Economist, 5
Restaurant Host/Hostess, 8
Restaurant Manager, 8
Restaurant Steward, 8
Resume Writer, 1
Retail Butcher, 10
Retail Buyer, 10
Retail Store Sales Worker, 10
Rigger, 4
Robotics Engineer, 6
Robotics Technician, 6
Roofer, 4
Route Delivery Worker, 12
The Rubber Industry, 9
Rug and Carpet Cleaner, 5

Safety Engineer, 6
Sales Demonstrator, 10

Sales Manager, 10
Sanitary Engineer, 2
School Administrator, 11
School Counselor, 11
School Media Specialist, 11
Scriptwriter, 3
Secretary, 1
Securities Broker, 1
Security Guard, 11
Semiconductor Processor, 13
Septic Tank Installer, 4
Sheet Metal Worker, 4
The Shipbuilding Industry, 9
Shipping and Receiving Clerk, 10
Shoe Repairer, 5
Short Order Cook, 8
Shorthand Reporter, 11
Sign Language and Oral Interpreter,
    3
Singer, 3
Small Animal Breeder, 2
Small Business Owner, 10
Social Director, 8
Social Worker, 11
Sociologist, 6
Soil Scientist, 2
Solar Energy Technician, 4
Sound Technician, 3
Special Service Bus Driver, 12
Specification Writer, 4
Speech Pathologist/Audiologist, 7
Sports Instructor, 13
Stadium Manager, 8
Stadium Worker, 8
Stagehand, 3
State Police Officer, 11
Stationary Engineer, 9
Statistical Clerk, 1
Statistician, 1
Stenographer/Transcriber, 1
Stock Clerk, 10
Stonemason, 4
Store Manager, 10
The Structural Clay Products
    Industry, 9
Substance Abuse Counselor, 7
Supermarket Worker, 10
Surgeon, 13
Surveyor, 4
Surveyor's Helper, 4
Swimming Instructor, 8
Swimming Pool Servicer, 5
Systems Analyst, 1
Systems Engineer, 6

Tape Librarian, 1
Tax Preparer, 1
Taxi Driver, 12
Teacher, College, 11
Teacher, Elementary and Preschool,
    11
Teacher, Secondary School, 11
Teacher, Vocational Education, 11
Teacher's Aide, 11
Technical Writer, 3
Telecommunications Specialist, 3

Telemarketing Specialist, 10
Telephone Central Office Design
    Engineer, 3
Telephone Central Office
    Supervisor, 3
Telephone Central Office
    Technician, 3
Telephone Design Engineer, 3
Telephone Line Workers and Cable
    Splicer, 3
Telephone Operator, 3
Telephone Service Representative, 3
Telephone Service Technician, 3
Television and Radio Service
    Technician, 3
Textile Designer, 3
The Textile Industry, 9
Theater and Movie House Manager,
    8
Ticket Taker, 8
Tire Changer/Repairer, 13
Title Examiner, 10
Tobacco Industry Worker, 2
Tool and Die Maker, 9
Tour Escort, 8
Tow Truck Operator, 12
Trade Show Manager, 10
Traffic Engineer, 12
Traffic Manager, 12
Training Specialist, 1
Translator and Interpreter, 3
Transportation Engineer, 12
Travel Agent, Corporate, 8
Travel Agent, Incentive, 8
Travel Agent, Wholesale and Retail,
    8
Truck and Bus Dispatcher, 12
Truck Terminal Manager, 12

Underwriter, 1
Union Business Agent, 1
Urban and Regional Planner, 11
Usher, 8

Vending Machine Route Worker, 10
Veterinarian, 2
Vocational Counselor, 11

Waiter and Waitress, 8
Ward Clerk, 7
Warehouse Worker, 10
Wastewater Treatment Plant
    Operator, 13
Watch Repairer, 5
Water Resources Engineer, 2
Water Well Driller, 4
Welder, 4
Wholesale Sales Worker, 10
Wildlife Manager, 2
Window Cleaner, 5
Wood Scientist and Technologist, 2
Word Processor, 1

Youth Organization Worker, 11

Zoo Administrator, 8
Zoologist, 6

Looking into Public and Community Services

In 1992, San Juan Bautista, a small community in California, teetered on the edge of bankruptcy. The city council was forced to lay off the town's 6 full-time and 12 part-time employees. The local newspaper predicted that the community would soon collapse without these workers. Fortunately, citizen volunteers stepped forward to fill the gap. They carted away trash, swept the streets, read water meters, sent out utility bills, answered phones at city hall, filled potholes, cleared storm drains, shelved library books, and performed many other tasks to keep the town running until the fiscal crisis had passed.

The citizen volunteers of San Juan Bautista performed the role of public-sector workers. The people who work in the public sector help to keep communities running smoothly and efficiently. Public and community service employees ensure that schoolchildren learn, taxes are collected, water and electricity are available in homes, trash is removed and disposed of properly, and people are safe. The majority of public-sector workers are employed by federal, state, and local governments.

Public and community service jobs often have parallels in private business, but there are important differences. One difference is in the way both sectors measure success. Private-sector businesses generally measure success by their profits. Public-sector organizations measure success by results. For example, if a student learns to read or use a computer, the teacher has been successful. A second difference is that public and community services are often created to deal with specific conditions or problems, such as transportation for the elderly.

The Government and Public Services

As far back as colonial times, there were public and community services. New England towns, for example, collected taxes to support public elementary schools, which were established to ensure that all children would be able to read the Bible. In addition, colonial settlements often accepted responsibility for the welfare of poor people in the community.

Despite these early examples of public services, Americans long resisted government intervention in their lives. One of the major issues leading to the Declaration of Independence was the colonies' objection to paying taxes to Great Britain without having any representation in the British Parliament, which decided how the tax revenues would be spent. Once the citizens of the 13 original colonies had won their independence, they certainly were not going to give it up to another distant government. Under the U.S. Constitution, the power to tax was divided between state and federal governments.

Division of Powers

To ensure against a powerful central government, the representatives of the new nation formed a central governing body that would govern the nation under laws set down in the U.S. Constitution. Many agreed with Thomas Jefferson that "that government governs best which governs least." Central government powers were kept in check by dividing the federal government into three branches—executive, legislative, and judicial—and then limiting the powers of each by a series of constitutional checks and balances.

Another factor in limiting the powers of the federal government (and, by extension, the number of government workers) was the idea of delegated and reserved powers. As listed in the Constitution, the delegated, or assigned, powers of the federal government include the powers "to lay and collect taxes . . . to borrow money . . . to coin money . . . to regulate commerce with foreign nations, and among several states . . . to raise and support armies . . . to provide and maintain a navy." The signers of the Constitution clearly intended the federal government to exercise authority only over matters of common concern to the people of all the states. The states reserved for themselves control over any matters that had not been expressly delegated to the federal government or excluded from state control. Among the states' reserved powers were control over transportation within the state, matters of marriage and divorce, and public education.

These constitutional provisions discouraged the growth of the central government. Throughout most of the nation's early history, the small number of government workers reflected this belief. Local governments provided schools and law enforcement; counties and states built and maintained roads and established court systems. The federal government took care of defense, diplomacy, and other matters of national concern. Private groups, religious organizations, or the family itself took care of welfare and public assistance functions.

The Civil War, however, brought about significant changes, including the end of rural, agricultural America. In the years after the war, cities grew rapidly as Americans moved away from the farms and as waves of immigrants poured into the United States. Problems that were once handled privately were magnified in the crowded cities. Crime, poverty, and disease became more visible as urban populations became more concentrated, and the responsibility for those problems was gradually assumed by local governments.

As many of these problems outgrew the resources of local government, the federal government also became involved. What the federal government could do, however, was limited by its difficulty in raising the money necessary to hire and pay employees. It was not until 1913, when the 16th Amendment to the Constitution was passed instituting a federal income tax, that the federal government could raise enough money to expand its services.

The Establishment of the Civil Service System

Once the government had the money to hire people, it was able to fill the jobs with qualified individuals under a civil service system started in the 1880s. This system had been designed to correct long-standing abuses in appointing federal employees. Before this, federal government was staffed according to the spoils system. Under the spoils system, those elected to federal office appointed their own friends and political allies to federal jobs after dismissing the previous office holder's appointees. This system failed to recognize the need for qualified, trained government employees and resulted in an entirely new group of federal employees every time a new party was elected to office.

The abuses of the spoils system eventually became serious enough to attract congressional attention. In 1883 Congress established a bipartisan civil service commission to prepare and administer competitive examinations given to applicants for government jobs. Several states also passed civil service laws and began to fill jobs through civil service examinations. These laws put into effect the idea that merit and suitability are the criteria for hiring someone for public service.

An Explosion of Civil Service Employees

No single event changed the civil service system more than the Great Depression of the 1930s. In this period of record unemployment and devastating poverty, the federal government began to hire people to provide jobs as well as services. Federal employees in public works programs built and maintained roads and post offices and worked on soil conservation projects. Others painted murals on public buildings and wrote travel guides. Because federal revenues fell during the Depression, the government had to resort to deficit spending; that is, it had to borrow money to pay its employees and to meet its financial obligations. The government had been in debt in the past, usually during wartime, but it had never made borrowing money a tool to offset economic recession. The idea was that deficit spending would help fuel the economy and that repaying the debt would be less burdensome when the economy improved.

Deficit spending, a radical departure in the 1930s, has become an enduring feature of economic policy. As the government has grown larger, so has the national debt. In the 1980s and early 1990s a soaring budget deficit contributed to renewed discussions about the proper role of government in providing community services and renewed demands for government cutbacks. Many political leaders, for instance, called for religious and community organizations, families, and volunteers to assume more responsibility for community services, especially care of the poor, elderly, and disabled.

Today, politicians debate which is better equipped to manage community services: federal government or state and local government.

Today, politicians debate which is better equipped to manage community services: federal government or state and local government. Some leaders favor returning tax money to the states in the form of block grants, believing that states understand the needs of their residents better than do the politicians in faraway Washington, DC. Other leaders fear that without federal control, states will spend money in indiscriminate and wasteful fashion.

Much has been discussed about "reinventing" and "reengineering" government to make it more cost-efficient and responsive to citizens' problems. This includes "downsizing" government, especially at the federal level, and "decentralizing" government, or moving the center

of government away from Washington, DC. The outcome of all these discussions will affect not only the types and number of jobs available on the federal level, but also those on the state and local levels and even some jobs in the private sector.

Careers in the Public Sector

As noted previously, the public sector employs people in a wide range of occupations that are also found in the private sector. These occupations include engineers, physicians, secretaries, accountants, mechanics, and construction trade workers. On the other hand, occupations such as legislators, revenue agents, city planners, and drill sergeants are unique to the public sector.

Federal Government

According to the U.S. Bureau of Labor Statistics, the federal government employed close to 3 million civilian workers in 1993. Although employees work in the legislative, judicial, and executive branches, the overwhelming majority—97 percent—work in the executive branch, which includes 14 cabinet departments and more than 90 agencies. Two out of three federal workers have white-collar jobs. Systems analysts and computer scientists form the largest occupational group among those with white-collar jobs. Although most federal departments and agencies are headquartered in Washington, DC, only 14 percent of federal employees work in or near the nation's capital.

Federal Civil Service   About 90 percent of federal government employees fall under the jurisdiction of civil service, or competitive service, laws. The remaining 10 percent, or excepted service, are mostly top-level governments jobs filled by appointment.

Individuals seeking employment with the federal government generally must take a written, oral, or performance examination related to their occupational field. If they pass the examination, their names are

---

Top-Dollar Jobs in Public and Community Services

These are high-paying jobs described in this volume. The figures represent typical salaries or earnings for experienced workers.

$125,000–$750,000	City Manager Lawyer
$45,000–$70,000	Criminologist FBI Special Agent School Administrator Teacher, College

placed on a waiting list according to their scores. When a vacancy occurs within an agency, the hiring agent may select any of the three highest-rated people on the list. For many jobs, however, the hiring agent simply evaluates applicants on the basis of their education, training, and experience in the occupation.

The civil service system comprises a number of pay plans, depending on the nature of the work. For example, the General Pay Schedule covers most white-collar employees, while the Federal Wage System covers most blue-collar employees. Each plan consists of a series of pay grades, or levels, and a range of salary steps within each grade. Workers enter the civil service system at the starting grade for their occupation. Their work is regularly evaluated, and if it is satisfactory, they advance to the next step.

Armed Services

The military currently has about 1.8 million people on its payroll. Defending the nation in times of conflict and deterring aggression are the missions of the armed services, which includes the Army (land-based), the Air Force (air and space), the Navy (sea), the Marines (a branch of the Navy that defends against land invasions), and the Coast Guard (which enforces federal maritime laws, recovers distressed vessels and aircraft, and prevents smuggling). The Coast Guard, which is generally part of the Department of Transportation, becomes part of the Navy in wartime.

Job opportunities in the armed services are varied. Military personnel perform a wide range of functions, some of which are not usually thought of as military in nature. These include operating a hospital, programming computers, maintaining equipment, and running an office. There are more than 2,000 basic and advanced military occupations for enlisted personnel and about 1,600 for officers. Although approximately 25 percent of these occupational specialties are specific to the military, the other 75 percent have civilian counterparts. Job training is perhaps the most attractive benefit for those who enter the armed services.

State and Local Government

More than 4 million people work in state government, and an additional 11 million men and women are employed at the local levels— township, city, and county.

More than 4 million people work in state government, and an additional 11 million men and women are employed at the local levels—township, city, and county. State governments hire more workers in managerial, administrative support, and professional occupations than do local governments. Local governments, however, employ more workers in service occupations, such as fire fighters, police officers, and sanitation workers.

Working for state and local governments is much like working for the federal government. The majority of state and local employees work under a merit system and advance according to set procedures and schedules if they work competently. Unlike federal employees, however, most state and local employees have the right to negotiate their wages through collective bargaining.

Challenges Facing State and Local Governments   City and state governments face many challenges that call for creative leadership and management of new and ongoing issues. As a result of the federal deficit, many programs are being turned over to the states to operate. Often states must pick up much of the expense. Because many states also have financial difficulty, it remains to be seen how many of these programs will continue to operate.

Another challenge facing city and state governments is urban sprawl and the decline of inner cities. As people and industry continue to move farther away from city centers, local governments must build new roads and highways, provide water and sewer systems, and supply police and fire protection for new neighborhoods. At the same time, dwindling tax bases in cities makes it difficult to fund programs to combat crime, poverty, and homelessness.

Education

Approximately 4.6 million jobs exist for teachers in the United States today, including all levels of education from kindergarten to colleges and universities, as well as special education. Other jobs in education include clerical and administrative workers, school librarians, counselors, and health-related specialists.

Elementary and Secondary Education   Nearly 3.3 million teachers are currently employed at the elementary and secondary levels. More than nine out of ten jobs are in the public school systems.

Concern over the generally poor performance of American students on standardized achievement tests has led to many recommendations for improving public schools. One idea is to introduce competition in the form of choice and charter schools. Under a competitive system, parents choose the school they think is best for their children. Schools that are chosen less frequently are assumed to provide a poorer educational environment. Proponents of this approach believe that choice forces teachers and administrators to improve their programs.

Charter schools are autonomous public schools. They operate independent of school district and labor union rules and regulations. The premise behind the charter-school movement is that bureaucracy burdens schools and teachers and prevents them from being creative and effective. Eleven states had laws permitting charter schools in 1994, and a dozen more had similar laws in the works.

Concern over the quality of public education has also put a premium on teacher experience. In the past, school districts tended to hire recent

Concern over the generally poor performance of American students on standardized achievement tests has led to many recommendations for improving public schools.

graduates because they were cheaper to employ. Realizing the value of classroom experience, many school districts now strive to retain or hire veteran staff members. School districts are also recognizing the value of experience in the private sector and are welcoming former business-people into the classroom.

Postsecondary Education   There are approximately 812,000 faculty teaching at colleges and universities across the United States, with the majority at public institutions. College and university faculty teach more than 14 million full-time and part-time students and conduct a significant part of the nation's research. Although for many years "typical" college students were in their late teens or early 20s, that is no longer the case. Nearly one-third of the students on college campuses today are over the age of 30. Many adults are returning to college for new careers or for retraining.

Vocational and Adult Education   About 540,000 other opportunities for teachers exist at the vocational and adult education levels. Students in vocational schools train for a variety of occupations that do not require a college degree, such as welder, machinist, mechanic, cosmetologist, and word processor. Adult education programs, which are usually run by local school districts, offer courses as diverse as reading, writing, mathematics, cooking, aerobics, investing, and dog training.

Social Work

About 484,000 jobs exist in the broad field of social work, nearly 40 percent of them in the public sector. A career in social work, or human services, involves helping people cope with a wide range of problems. Social workers can help people through direct counseling or by referring clients to other specialists. They work in child welfare and family services programs, mental health facilities, schools, hospitals, community organizations, and corporations.

Traditionally social workers help the poor, disabled, and disadvantaged obtain food, shelter, and clothing. In addition, they may work in the mental health field, where they provide such services as crisis intervention, social rehabilitation, and life skills training. Medical social workers help patients and their families cope with catastrophic illness. School social workers counsel troubled children and help to integrate disabled children into the general school population. Many businesses employ social workers to manage employee assistance programs, such as counseling workers whose job performance is affected by emotional problems or substance abuse.

Law

A lawyer is both an adviser and an advocate. As an adviser, a lawyer counsels clients regarding their legal rights and obligations. As an advocate, a lawyer presents arguments to support his or her client in court. Of the more than 626,000 lawyers in the country today, about 20 percent are in government positions. The majority of these are at the local level. In the federal government, most jobs for lawyers are in the Departments of Justice, Treasury, and Defense. For some administrative and managerial jobs in law, legal training is an asset but not a requirement.

The legal profession, both public and private, faces increasing demands to handle litigation more quickly and cheaply and to discourage so-called "frivolous" product-liability and personal-damage lawsuits. One result of this movement is that large law firms are lowering the salaries of their lawyers and hiring fewer lawyers. At the same time, there has been a huge increase in the number of paralegals, or legal assistants. Paralegals, currently numbering 95,000 and growing, help law firms lower their expenses by doing research, preparing documents, and performing other legal work previously done by high-priced lawyers.

Protective Services

Workers in the field of protective services seek to safeguard people and property in a community. These workers include approximately 700,000 police officers, detectives, and special agents; more than 300,000 fire fighters; and about 280,000 corrections officers. While most police officers and fire fighters are employed by local governments, the majority of corrections officers are employed at state correctional institutions—prisons, prison camps, and reformatories. In the past the job of cor-

rections officer consisted of enforcing the rules of the correctional institution. More and more, however, corrections officers are assisting with inmates' rehabilitation by serving as informal counselors and by reinforcing remedial training.

Trends in the Public Sector

At a time when the need for public services is increasing, the resources to provide these services are decreasing. Committed public servants at all levels of government are searching for ways to provide services economically and efficiently. Teamwork is becoming more common as personnel from different agencies collaborate on problem solving.

Privatization and Competition

Privatization is one way in which governments attempt to save taxpayers money and deliver quality services. In the United States privatization means contracting with for-profit businesses to deliver publicly funded services. A city sanitation department, for example, might replace its refuse collectors with a private company that guarantees more economical and efficient trash removal. As might be expected, public-sector employees object to pivatization that leads to job loss.

Governments have always used privatization to obtain services or products that they themselves were unable to supply. For instance, the federal government hires private contractors to make weapons and build highways. Local school boards contract out cafeteria and busing services. During the 1980s and early 1990s, however, governments began privatizing services, such as wastewater treatment plants and correctional facilities, that were traditionally managed by public-sector employees. Privatization has even extended to public schools. School boards in Maryland and Massachusetts recently turned poorly performing public schools over to private education companies.

The premise behind privatization is that business is more efficient than government. However, private companies that have a monopoly on a service or that operate without adequate government supervision can also be inefficient. Consequently, government policy is now shifting from privatization to managed competition. Under this system, more than one company must be available for bidding on a public-service contract. Managed competition also allows public-sector workers to bid for contracts against private companies. Competition provides public employees added incentive to perform their jobs well. For example, when the city of Indianapolis put the job of filling potholes up for bidding, employees of the public works department figured out how they could do the job more economically than private companies.

Government policy is now shifting from privatization to managed competition. Under this system, more than one company must be available for bidding on a public-service contract.

Electronic Technology

The public sector lags behind the private sector in adopting Information Age technology. Even so, government at all levels is attempting to use new electronic media to better deliver public services.

Industry Snapshots

Government

The government employs more workers—18.8 million—than any other business in the United States. Between 1992 and 2005, government employment will grow at the state and local levels but decline at the federal level as program responsibilities shift away from the national government. Population growth in the nation's cities and suburbs will also contribute to more jobs in state and local government.

Military

The decreased threat from Eastern European countries and the former Soviet Union has led all U.S. military forces, except the Coast Guard, to undergo planned reduction through 1997. Nevertheless, job openings should be plentiful for all branches of the armed services through 2005. The reason is that the number of people in the prime age group for recruiting has decreased. As military jobs become more technical and complex, standards for new recruits will continue to rise.

Education

Education employment is expected to rise from 9.7 million workers in 1992 to 12.5 million workers in 2005. This increase will result from population growth among children in kindergarten, elementary school, and high school—as well as growth in the number of older, foreign, and part-time students at the postsecondary level. Demand for special education teachers will be great due to legislation focusing on the needs of individuals with disabilities.

Social Work

The medical and social needs of an aging population and growing numbers of individuals and families in crisis will require more social services. In particular, more school social workers will be needed to respond to the adjustment problems of immigrants, children from backgrounds of poverty and abuse, and mentally and physically disabled children. More medical social workers will be needed to facilitate the trend toward early discharge from hospitals.

Corrections

The number of corrections officers has grown by 80 percent since 1985. Thousands of job openings will continue to be generated each year. A surge in drug-related crime and a shift toward mandatory sentencing have boosted the nation's prison population and led to the overwhelming demand for corrections officers.

Law

Demand for lawyers will continue as the population grows and as middle-income groups increase their use of legal services. Jobs in the public sector are expected to increase, as the government now provides more legal and related services to the poor and elderly. Despite the number of job openings, competition for employment will be intense due to the large numbers of law students graduating each year.

Electronic Pathways to Government   Federal, state, and local governments are using computer bulletin boards to provide quick, convenient access to information and to facilitate communication. From the comfort of their homes, citizens with a computer and modem can obtain the latest U.S. census statistics, read summaries of bills in the state legislature, send electronic mail (e-mail) to the mayor, access the card catalog at the local library, or find out the cost of a driver's license.

In some parts of the country, governments have installed interactive kiosks in shopping malls, supermarkets, and other central locations. The kiosks, which resemble ATM banking machines, inform users about where to go and whom to contact about city services. They also list employment opportunities and explain unemployment benefits. Some kiosks dispense marriage licenses and other government forms.

Saving Time and Money   The public sector is taking advantage of new technology to cut expenses and speed up services. For example, many local government departments now use electronic-pen scanners to read information on monthly bills. The speed and accuracy of this technology allow clerks to spend more time on other tasks.

On the federal level, the Social Security Administration now issues Social Security cards in five days (instead of six weeks), with the use of automated equipment. A new computer system will soon allow direct bank deposit of all Social Security payments, eliminating costly paper checks. The U.S. Postal Service handles more than 50 percent of all mail at least partly by automation. Whereas sorting mail by hand costs $40 per 1,000 letters, automated processing costs only $4. It is predicted that increased automation will eliminate more than 40,000 postal jobs by the year 2005.

Customer Service

A growing trend in the public sector is to regard recipients of community services as customers. A customer service attitude emphasizes courtesy, efficiency, and know-how.

One-Stop Shopping   The customer service approach is making the biggest impression in the delivery of human services, especially services to the poor, elderly, and disabled. The human services system tends to be fragmented and confusing. Clients must shuttle from agency to agency—often miles apart—and submit to repetitive questions. After all that, they may still receive only incomplete assistance. Responding to clients' frustration, government officials in many areas have installed "one-stop shopping." Services such as Medicaid, employment counseling, and welfare benefits are grouped together in an accessible location.

Plastic for Paper   Electronic benefit systems are another way in which government is improving delivery of human services. With this innovation, social service agencies issue welfare recipients a plastic card, similar to a bank debit card, to pay for food or to obtain cash. The plastic cards are safer, more convenient, and more efficient than paper checks and food stamp coupons.

Government Marketing

Governments collect income taxes, property taxes, sales taxes, and many other fees and surcharges to raise money to fund public services. In addition, many localities are now turning to so-called government marketing to help pay the bills.

Government marketing takes several forms. A government unit might operate a store or a mail-order catalog that sells merchandise to the public. The Los Angeles County coroner's office, for example, grosses $20,000 a month through sales of key chains, mugs, towels, and other merchandise.

Another form of government marketing is selling advertising space on public property such as trash barrels and bicycle racks at city parks. While public transit departments have long sold advertising space on

A growing trend in the public sector is to regard recipients of community services as customers.

buses, they now offer advertisers the entire vehicle—from headlights to taillights and from roof to road—for their "body-wrap" ads. Advertisers might also donate uniforms, cars and vans, and other equipment to local governments—all of which bear the company's name and logo.

Some government units sell their services for profits. For example, fire departments might hire out their fire fighters as ambulance drivers, or the park service might open a for-profit campground on public land. The U.S. Department of Energy recently signed a contract with factories along the Mexican border to consult on pollution control.

Other Avenues to Public and Community Services

In addition to government, nonprofit agencies employ workers who serve the public. Corporations also hire people to serve as liaisons with the community. Volunteer opportunities in community service abound.

Nonprofit Agencies

Approximately 65,000 private, nonprofit service organizations exist in the United States. They operate prenatal clinics, food banks, shelters for battered women and the homeless, hospices for people with AIDS, counseling centers for troubled youth, and much more. Federal, state, and local governments contract extensively with nonprofit agencies to provide key social services. Religious and fraternal organizations also sponsor many social service agencies.

Corporations

Many large corporations have community service divisions. These offices direct corporate philanthropy—that is, corporate donations to events and projects in the surrounding community. Community service divisions, especially in banks and other financial institutions, may also look for ways to invest money and other corporate resources in the community. These efforts are driven by a desire to build good public relations and the realization that a healthy community is good for business.

A growing trend is for corporations to work together with community organizations to revive neighborhoods, fix schools, and curb violence.

A growing trend is for corporations to work together with community organizations to revive neighborhoods, fix schools, and curb violence. A good example is the Atlanta Project, launched by former President Jimmy Carter in 1992. This program divides the city of Atlanta into 20 clusters and assigns a corporation to each cluster. Residents of the cluster and corporate employees work together to try to solve problems related to housing, education, health, and public safety.

Volunteer Organizations

Nonprofit agencies, religious groups, and other community organizations offer opportunities for volunteers to get involved in public service. For example, volunteers are needed to construct low-income housing, clean up polluted areas, patrol neighborhoods, and deliver meals to the homebound. While volunteers usually receive no pay for their work, they can learn skills that may be useful for a future career.

Summer Jobs in Public and Community Services

Government

Summer jobs and internships are available at all levels of government. Workers needed include clerical, administrative, and technical staff.

The federal government employs summer staff in positions such as congressional aide and legislative assistant. At the state level, jobs are available in state capitals as well as regional offices. Summer jobs in local government include workers in a county courthouse or town recreation center. Contact:
- local and county government offices
- governor's office and state agencies
- senators and members of Congress
- federal agencies

Sources of Information

Government Job Finder
Daniel Lauber, ed.
Planning/Communications
7215 Oak Avenue
River Forest, IL 60305-1935

Washington Information Directory
Congressional Quarterly, Inc.
1414 Twenty-second Street, NW
Washington, DC 20037

Social Services

Summer workers are needed in day care centers and senior centers.

Institutions for dependent and disabled children need child care workers, as do children's hospitals.

Youth organizations need day camp counselors, recreation helpers, and aides to run summer programs. Contact:
- state department of education
- child care institutions
- public and private day care centers
- social service agencies

Sources of Information

National Association for the Education of
Young Children

1509 Sixteenth Street, NW
Washington, DC 20036

National Association of Social Workers/NASW
Press
750 First Street, NE, Suite 700
Washington, DC 20002

Public Services

Summer positions are available for aides in public and university libraries.

Aides and fund raisers are needed for public-interest groups.

Municipal projects may require summer help, such as highway maintenance workers. Refuse workers and fire fighters are needed to replace vacationing staff. Contact:
- local libraries
- local government agencies
- private maintenance, construction, and sanitation contractors
- public-interest groups

See individual job profiles for Sources of Information.

Law

Law firms often hire summer office workers including receptionists, typists, word processors, and researchers.

Law students can find jobs as summer associates. They may participate in summer training programs available at some firms. Contact:
- law firms
- legal aid associations
- company legal departments

Sources of Information

Martindale Hubbell Law Directory
Martindale Hubbell, Inc.
121 Chanlon Road
New Providence, NJ 07974

American Bar Association
750 North Lake Shore Drive
Chicago, IL 60611

Government programs such as Volunteers in Service to America (VISTA) and Job Corps also offer volunteer opportunities. Some government programs provide financial assistance, health care, or other benefits. AmeriCorps, a national service program established in 1993, repays community service with grants for college tuition.

Public and Community Services—And You

Many changes are occurring in public and community services. What will not change, though, is the reason people seek careers in this area. These careers present opportunities to individuals who want to make a difference in the quality of people's lives. Public and community service jobs offer a chance to be part of a network of people performing tasks that provide their community with the services it requires.

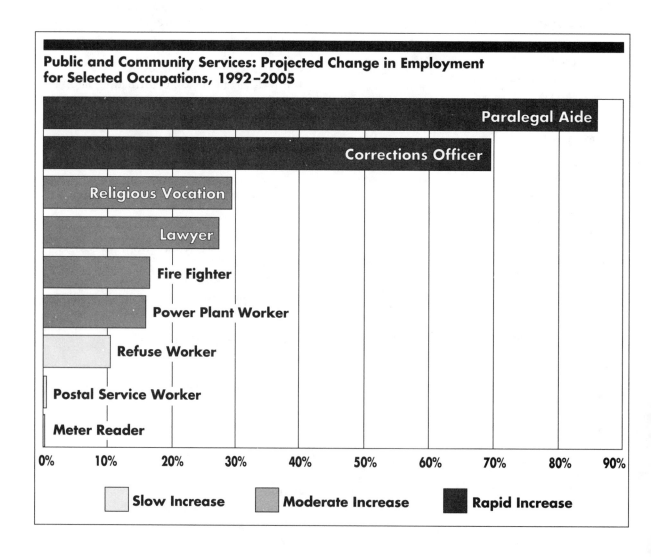

Public and Community Services: Projected Change in Employment for Selected Occupations, 1992–2005

Paralegal Aide

Corrections Officer

Religious Vocation

Lawyer

Fire Fighter

Power Plant Worker

Refuse Worker

Postal Service Worker

Meter Reader

0%   10%   20%   30%   40%   50%   60%   70%   80%   90%

Slow Increase   Moderate Increase   Rapid Increase

Getting into Public and Community Services

G ood jobs rarely, if ever, just fall out of the sky. As anybody who has ever been in the job market knows, getting the "right" job takes planning, perseverance, and patience. There are, however, a number of things you can do to make the process easier and more rewarding. This is true whether you are looking for your first job, reentering the labor market, trying to get a new job, or planning a mid-career change.

This essay is designed to serve as your guide to the process of finding a job in the field of public and community services. It starts off with the basics—helping you define your career objectives. Then it takes you through a number of steps that will help you work out a strategy to achieve these goals.

"Evaluating Yourself" will help you take a close look at your interests, skills, and values so that you can make suitable and satisfying career choices.

Evaluating Yourself

Most people enjoy doing a job well. Quite apart from any praise from employers or fellow workers, there's an inner satisfaction in knowing that you've taken on a challenge and then succeeded in accomplishing something worthwhile. If you are unhappy or dissatisfied in your job and you are just trying to do enough to get by, you may have a job for which you are not suited. It is also frustrating to do work that is not challenging because you are overqualified for it.

Making a Self-Inventory Chart

Before you make any career decisions, give some thought to your areas of interest and to what you do well. One very useful way of going about this is to compile a brief history of yourself in a self-inventory chart. Such a chart will be helpful when you are deciding what jobs you want to consider. It will also save time when you are writing cover letters and resumes, filling in applications, and preparing for job interviews.

Begin your self-inventory chart by listing all the jobs you have ever had, including summer employment, part-time jobs, volunteer work, and any freelance or short-term assignments you have done. Include the dates of employment, the names and addresses of supervisors, and what you earned. Then add a similar list of your hobbies and other activities, including any special experiences you may have had, such as travel. Next, do the same for your education, listing your schools, major courses of study, grades, any special honors or awards, any courses you particularly enjoyed, and any extracurricular activities in which you were involved.

In determining what you do well and what you enjoy doing, you may find a career pattern beginning to develop. If, however, the picture still lacks detail or focus, try making a list of aptitudes, and then rate yourself *above average, average,* or *below average* for each one. Some of the qualities you might include in your list are administrative, analytic,

artistic, clerical, creative, language, leadership, managerial, sales, social, and verbal abilities. You might also rate your willingness to accept responsibility and your ability to get along with people.

Work Characteristics Checklist

Do you want a job in which you can:
- be challenged mentally?
- work with people?
- work with machines?
- work independently?
- work on a team?
- follow clear instructions?
- earn a lot of money?
- have a chance for quick promotion?
- have good benefits?
- travel in your work?
- work close to home?
- work regular hours?
- have a flexible schedule?
- be challenged by deadlines?
- have a variety of tasks?
- have supervisory power?
- be a decision maker?
- do detailed work?

Compiling a Work Characteristics Checklist
Another way of deciding what kind of work to do is to compile a work characteristics checklist. Go through the questions in the left margin, and then make a list of those work characteristics that are most important to you.

It would be a big mistake to reject a job because it does not meet all your requirements. You have to consider which job characteristics are most important. If the characteristics of a job match most of your preferences, you should give the position serious consideration.

Consulting Counselors
It's important to evaluate yourself and your career options realistically. An experienced career counselor can be of great help in this process. Counselors can give you a series of vocational interest and aptitude tests, and they can review them with you, interpreting and explaining the results.

Vocational testing and counseling can be found in guidance and counseling departments of high schools, vocational schools, and colleges. Some local offices of the state employment services affiliated with the federal employment service offer free counseling.

Consultants and career counseling firms are located in most major cities. The reputation of these services should be checked. A list of counseling services in your area is available from The American Counseling Association, 5999 Stevenson Avenue, Alexandria, VA 22304. Send a stamped, self-addressed envelope.

As a rule, counselors will not tell you what to do. They will talk over your options and help you search for conclusions. However, they will leave the final decision up to you. Remember, it's your decision, it's your job, and it's your life.

"Evaluating Jobs" will help you examine the requirements of different jobs to see what positions might best suit your skills and experience.

Evaluating Jobs
After you have taken a good look at what you do well and what you enjoy doing, the next step is to see how different jobs measure up to your abilities and interests. First make a note of all the jobs in this volume that interest you. Then examine the education and training required for these jobs. Decide whether you qualify and, if not, whether it's worth making an effort to get the extra qualifications. If possible, talk with someone who has such a job. Firsthand information can be invaluable. Also look through the appropriate trade and professional journals listed at the end of this essay, and check the section in this volume called "Further Reading and Resources" for books and audiovisual materials that contain more detailed information about the job. In addition, counselors usually have helpful information on careers in public and community services. For more detailed information, you can

write to the public and professional associations listed at the end of each occupational profile.

Once you have found out all you can about a particular job, compare the features of the job with your work characteristics checklist. See how many characteristics of the job match your work preferences. By following this exercise for all the jobs that appeal to you, you should be able to build up a collection of jobs that match your interests and abilities.

Ways to Find Job Openings

Once you've decided what kind of job suits you, the next step is to look for available positions. Obviously, the more openings you can find, the better your chance of landing a job. Usually, people apply for a number of openings before they are finally accepted.

There are many ways to find out about job openings. This section explores a number of job-hunting techniques and explains how you can follow up on job leads.

"Ways to Find Job Openings" outlines the methods and techniques you can use to find openings for the kind of work you want to do.

Job Finder's Checklist

The following list of job-hunting tips may seem obvious, but getting all the bits and pieces in order beforehand is a great help when you're looking for a job.

Resume. Bring your resume up to date. Assemble a supply of neatly typed copies.

References. Line up your references. Ask permission of the people whose names you would like to use.

Contacts. Put the word out to everyone you know that you are looking for a job.

Job market. Find out where the jobs are. Make a list of possible employers in your field of interest.

Research. A little homework can go a long way. Find out as much as you can about a job—the field, the company—before applying for the job. A well-informed job applicant is a step ahead.

Organization. Keep a file on your job-hunting campaign with names and dates of employers contacted, ads answered, results, and follow-up.

Appearance. Make sure that the clothes you plan to wear to an interview are appropriate and that these clothes are neat and clean. You may need to dress more formally than you would on the job. First impressions can sometimes tip the balance.

Ways to Find Job Openings
Applying in Person
Phone and Letter Campaigns
Help-Wanted Ads
Situation-Wanted Ads
Networking
Placement Services
State Employment Services
Private Employment Agencies
Computer Placement Services
Civil Service
Unions
Temporary Employment

Applying in Person

For some jobs, especially beginning positions, your best method may be to apply directly to the company or companies for which you'd like to work. If you are looking for a position as a meter reader or refuse worker, for example, you might make an appointment to see the person responsible for hiring. This is a good method to use for certain kinds of jobs, but applicants for professional or supervisory jobs generally send a letter and resume to the company first. As a rule, applying in person works best when jobs are plentiful or when a company is expanding.

Applying in person will allow you to sharpen your interviewing techniques and give you a look at different places of employment. In the long run, however, you will probably get better results with other approaches that require more advance planning.

Phone and Letter Campaigns

To conduct a phone campaign, use the Yellow Pages of your telephone directory to build a list of companies for which you might like to work. Take down their phone numbers, call their personnel departments, and find out whether they have any openings. This technique is not useful in all situations, however. If you're calling from out of town, for example, a phone campaign can become very expensive. You may not be able to make a strong impression by phone. You also will not have a written record of your contacts with potential employers.

Letter-writing campaigns can be very effective if the letters are well thought out and carefully prepared. In the area of public and community services, your letters should be typed. Handwritten letters do not convey a businesslike impression. Most employers will regard form letters or photocopies as indications of lack of interest or motivation.

Besides using the Yellow Pages, you can often get good lists of company addresses in your field of interest by reading the trade and professional publications listed at the end of this essay. Many of the periodicals publish directories or directory issues. Other sources you can use to compile lists of companies are the trade unions and professional organizations listed at the end of each occupational profile in this volume. The reference librarian at your local library can also help you find appropriate directories.

Your letters should be addressed to the personnel or human resources department of the company or agency. If possible, send it to a specific person. If you don't know who the right person is, try to find the name of the personnel director through the directories in the library. You can also call on the phone and say, "I'm writing to ask about employment at your company. To whom should I address the letter?" If you can't find a name, use a standard salutation. It's a good idea to enclose a resume (described later in this essay) with the letter to give a concise idea of your qualifications and background.

Keep a list of all the people you've written to, along with the date each letter was mailed, or keep a photocopy of each letter. Then you

can follow up, by either a brief note or a phone call, on all those who do not reply within about three weeks.

Help-Wanted Ads

Many people find out about job openings by reading the help-wanted sections of newspapers, trade journals, and professional magazines. Many employers and employment agencies use help-wanted classifieds to advertise available jobs.

Classified ads have their own telegraphic language. Study the box for some common abbreviations. They are usually decodable by common sense, but if one puzzles you, call the newspaper and ask for a translation. The ads tell you how to contact the employers, and they generally state qualifications required. Some give the salary offered. These ads contain a lot of information in a small space. Read them carefully.

As you find openings of interest to you, follow up on each ad by using the method requested. You may be asked to phone or send a resume. Record the date of your follow-up, and if you don't hear from the employer within two or three weeks, place another call or send a polite note asking whether the job is still open. Don't forget to include your phone number, address, or box number.

Many help-wanted ads are "blind ads." These ads give a box number but no name, phone number, or address. Employers and employment agencies place these "mystery" ads for a number of reasons. One is to avoid having to reply to all the applicants in which they are not interested. In other words, it's quite common to hear nothing after answering a blind ad. So don't be discouraged by the lack of response.

Situation-Wanted Ads

Another way of getting the attention of potential employers is with a situation-wanted ad. This can be placed in the classified section of your local newspaper or of a trade journal in your field of interest. Many personnel offices and employment agencies scan these columns when they're looking for new people. The situation-wanted ad is usually most effective for those who have advanced education, training, or experience, since the ad might highlight just the qualifications an employer is looking for. A situation-wanted ad could also be useful for someone interested in part-time work as a teacher or security guard, for example.

A situation-wanted ad should be brief, clear, and to the point. Its main purpose is to tell just enough to interest the employer in granting an interview. It should tell exactly what kind of job you want, why you qualify, and whether you are available for full-time or part-time work. Use abbreviations as appropriate.

If you are already employed and do not want it known that you are looking for a new position, you can run a blind ad. A blind ad protects your privacy by listing a box number at the publication to which all replies can be sent. They are then forwarded to you. You need not give your name, address, or phone number in the ad.

Reading the Classifieds

HELP WANTED

ACADEMIC AIDE—Local college needs a person to handle a variety of student services incl. academic & social counseling. Good oppty. Degree, similar exp. pfd. Call 000-0000 weekdays 10–4, Sat. 10–12.

CHILD CARE
RESIDENT DIRECTOR

Suburban child care agency needs capable person to assume direction of residential program. Must have MSW & min. 3 yrs. admin. and supervisory bkgd. Salary commensurate w/experience. Good fringe benefits. M4711 Chronicle.

An Equal Oppty. Employer

CORRECTIONS OFFICER
HALFWAY HOUSE

Immediate opening for mature, reliable person to supervise and counsel residents at County Pre-Release Center in City, State. Revolving shift work will require evening and weekend hours. Apply in person.

CUSTODIAN f/p $0/hr. Mon–Fri. 2–8:30, Sun. 8–9:30. Protestant Church. Carlson Agency, Main Street

LEGAL SECY. with top qualifications to work with partner in attractive offices. Good skills essential incl. WP. Salary commensurate with ability. 000-0000.

LIBRARIAN

School year. Small private h.s. Metropolitan area. Bachelor of Library Science req. Knowledge of computerized databases helpful. Write Journal Box T 7431.

SECURITY GUARDS

Immediate openings. Full and part time. Uniform supplied. Must be U.S. citizen, have no criminal convictions, have car and phone. 000-0000.

SOCIAL WORKER—Child welfare agency seeks MSW to supervise foster care program. Competitive salary, excel. benefits. Call/send resume and sal. req. to:
S. Allen
Broadfield Child Care
24 Lincoln Ave.
City, State 00000

Classified Abbreviations

addl.	additional
admin.	administrative, administration
appt.	appointment
avail. immed.	available immediately
avg.	average
bkgd.	background
co.	company
col.	college
dept.	department
excel.	excellent
exp.	experience
ext.	phone extension
fee neg.	fee negotiable (fee can be worked out with employer)
figs.	figures
f/p., f/pd.	fee paid (agency fee paid by employer)
f/t	full time
gd. bnfts.	good benefits
grad.	graduate
hr.	hour
h.s.	high school
incl.	including
info.	information
K	thousand
M	thousand
mgr.	manager
min.	minimum
natl.	national
oppty.	opportunity
pfd.	preferred
p/t	part time
refs.	references
req.	required
sal.	salary
sec., secy.	secretary
skls.	skills
temp.	temporary
trnee.	trainee
typ.	typist, typing
w/	with
wk.	week
WP	word processing
yrs.	years

SITUATION WANTED

DAY CARE WORKER seeks p/t work, 3 days/wk. Experienced, good refs. 000-0000.

PRIVATE DETECTIVE

Available by hour, day, week, job. Confidential background, missing person, matrimonial investigations. Experienced, reasonable.

000-0000.

ELEMENTARY TEACHER wishes to tutor child/children for summer. Any subject. Call 000-0000.

FUND RAISER

4 yrs. exp. direct mail and local campaign planning for natl. organization. Willing to travel, work odd hrs.
M3136 Times.

LEGAL SECRETARY—top skills, 3 yrs. exp. with patent attorney. Computer literate. Avail. August. Box 823, Chronicle.

LIBRARIAN

MLS & 3 yrs. technical & reference exp. seeks p/t library job metropolitan area. 000-0000.

MINISTER
DUTCH REFORMED CHURCH

Wishes to relocate to Midwest. 8 yrs. exp., heavy youth work. Box Z47 Gazette.

SCHOOL CUSTODIAN. Avail. immed., West County area. 6 yrs. school exp. Alex Rudman, 000-0000.

YOUTH WORK

Sociology student wants f/t summer job with youth organization. Urban location preferred. Camp counselor exp.

Call Chuck, 000-0000 after 6 p.m.

TEACHER

Exp. in H.S. art and computer graphics desires job in any related field. 000-0000.

Networking includes talking with friends and acquaintances about jobs in your area of interest.

Networking

A very important source of information about job openings is networking. This means talking with friends and acquaintances about jobs in your area of interest. If you would like to work in law, get in touch with all the people you know who work as lawyers, judges, or paralegal aides, or who have friends or relatives in the field. It makes sense to use all the contacts you have.

There's nothing wrong with telling everyone who will listen that you are looking for a job—family, friends, counselors, and former employers. Get them interested in your efforts, and ask for their help in your search. Don't annoy them; just let them know you're looking. This will multiply your sources of information many times over. Contacts don't have to be high-level administrators to be helpful. Sometimes, through a friend, you can find out about a job vacancy before it is advertised. You shouldn't use a contact's name without permission—you may put your informant on the spot with the employer. Don't assume that your friend will go out on a limb by recommending you, either. Once you have received the inside information, rely on your own ability to get the job.

Placement Services

Most vocational schools, high schools, and colleges have a placement or career service. If you are a student or recent graduate, you should definitely check there for job leads. Many employers look first in technical or trade schools and colleges for qualified applicants for certain jobs. Colleges are visited by recruiters looking for people to fill management trainee and other professional positions. These recruiters usually represent large companies such as law firms, or government agencies. Visit your placement office regularly to check the job listings, and watch for scheduled visits by company recruiters.

State Employment Services

Another source of information about job openings is the local office of the state employment service. There are more than 2,700 such offices in the nation, and many employers automatically list job openings at the local office. Whether you're looking for a job in private industry or with the state, these offices, which are affiliated with the federal employment service, are worth visiting.

State employment service offices are public agencies that do not charge for their services. They can direct you to special programs run

---

Notes on Networking

Let people know you're looking. Touch base with friends, acquaintances, teachers, community leaders, former employers— anyone who might know of job openings in your field.

Read newspapers and professional and trade journals for news of developments in your field and for names of people and companies you might contact.

Join professional or trade associations in your field. Contacts you make at meetings could provide valuable job leads. Association newsletters generally carry useful information about people and developments in the field.

Attend classes or seminars. You will meet other people in your field at job-training classes and professional development seminars.

Participate in local support groups such as Women in Business, Job Seekers, Forty Plus, Homemakers Reentering the Job Market, and alumni associations. You can gain information about people and places to contact.

Be on the lookout. Always be prepared to make the most of any opportunity that comes along. Talk with anyone who can provide useful information about your field.

by the government in conjunction with private industry. These programs, such as the Work Incentive Program for families on welfare, are designed to meet special needs. Some, but not all, of these offices offer vocational aptitude and interest tests and can refer interested people to vocational training centers. The state employment service can be a valuable first stop in your search for work, especially if there are special circumstances in your background. For example, if you did not finish high school, if you have had any difficulties with the law, or if you are living in a difficult home environment, your state employment service office is equipped to help you.

Private Employment Agencies

State employment services, though free, are usually very busy. If you are looking for more personal service and want a qualified employment counselor to help you find a job, you might want to approach a private employment agency.

Private employment agencies will help you get a job if they think they can place you. Most of them get paid only if they're successful in finding you a job, so you need to show them that you are a good prospect. These agencies will help you prepare a resume if you need one, and they will contact employers they think might be interested in you.

Private employment agencies are in the business of bringing together people who are looking for jobs and companies that are looking for workers. For some positions, usually middle- and higher-level jobs, the employment agency's fee is often paid by the employer. In such cases, there is no expense to the job seeker. In other cases, you may be required to pay the fee yourself, usually a percentage of your annual salary. Even if you have to pay a fee, it is a worthwhile investment if it leads to a rewarding career. In addition, the fee is tax deductible.

Some agencies may also ask for a small registration fee whether or not you get a job through them. Some agencies may even demand that you pay even though you find one of the jobs they are trying to fill through your other contacts. So be sure to read and understand the fine print of any contract you're about to sign, and ask for a copy to take home. Since the quality of these agencies varies, you should check to see if an agency is a certified member of a state or national association.

Private employment agencies are usually helping many people at one time. They may not have the time to contact you every time they find a job opening. Therefore, you might phone them at reasonable intervals after you've registered.

Computer Placement Services

The latest development in employment services is computer placement. Computer placement services are basically data banks (computerized information files) to which you send your resume or employment profile. When a company that subscribes to the service has a job to fill, it can call up on its computer a certain combination of qualifications and quickly receive information on the candidate or candidates who fill the bill perfectly. For example, an employer might be looking for a criminologist who has at least five years of experience, a background in sociology and fluency in Spanish and who is willing to relocate. Perhaps in the future everyone will use computer placement services. But for the moment, computer placement is still very limited in scope and number of users.

Civil Service

In your search for work, don't forget that the civil service—federal, state, and local—has many public and community services jobs. Civil service positions in this field include border patrol agents, fire fighters, police officers, and customs workers. The armed services are a major employer of many civilians in public and community services. Don't neglect these avenues for finding jobs. Civil service positions usually require you to take a civil service examination. Books are available to help you prepare for these exams, and your local civil service office can give you information too.

Unions

In certain jobs in public and community services, such as highway maintenance workers, power plant workers, and teachers, unions can be useful as sources of information. If you are a member of a union in your field of interest, you may be able to find out about jobs in the union periodical or from people at the union local.

Temporary Employment

A good way to get a feel for the job market is to work as an "office temp." There are many agencies that specialize in placing people in short-term jobs in public and community services. Legal work, child care, and security guard work are among the types of work most in demand. Temporary employment can increase your job skills, your knowledge of a particular field, and your chances of hearing of permanent positions. And, in some cases, a temporary job can lead directly to a permanent position.

"Presenting Yourself on Paper" describes how you can make your written materials—resume, cover letter, application form—work to best advantage to get you a personal interview.

Presenting Yourself on Paper

The first impression you make on an employer is likely to be on paper. Whether in an application form or a letter, you will want to make as good an impression as possible, so that employers will be interested in giving you a personal interview. Your potential employer is likely to equate a neat and clean appearance with good work habits and a sloppy one with bad work habits.

Writing an Effective Resume

When you write to follow up a lead or to ask about job openings, you can do more than just ask for information. You can send information about yourself. The accepted way of doing this is to send a resume with your inquiry letter.

Resume is derived from the French word, *résumer,* meaning "to summarize." A resume does just that—briefly outlines your education, work experience, and special abilities and skills. A resume may also be called a curriculum vitae, a personal profile, or a personal data sheet. This summary can act as your introduction by mail, as your calling card if you apply in person, and as a convenient reference for yourself when filling out an application form or when being interviewed.

A resume is a useful tool in applying for almost any job in the field of public and community services. It is valuable, even if you use it only to keep a record of where you have worked, for whom, and the dates of employment. A resume is usually required if you are being considered for higher-level professional and executive jobs. Prepare it carefully. It's well worth the trouble.

The idea of a resume is to capture the interest of potential employers so that they will call you for a personal interview. Because employers are busy people, the resume should be as brief and as neat as possible. But you should include as much relevant information about yourself as you can. This is usually presented under at least two headings: "Education" and "Work Experience." The latter is sometimes called "Employment History." Many people add a third section titled "Special Skills," "Related Experience," or "Personal Qualifications."

If you prepare a self-inventory such as the one described earlier, it will be a useful aid in preparing a resume. Go through your inventory, and select the items that show your ability to do the job or jobs in which you are interested. You should plan to highlight these items in your resume. Select only those facts that point out your relevant skills and experiences.

Once you have decided the special points worth mentioning, you can start preparing the resume. At the top, put your name, address, and phone number. After that, it's a question of deciding which items will be most interesting to the employer you plan to contact.

State Your Objective   Some employment counselors advise that you state a job objective or describe briefly the type of position for which you are applying. The job objective usually follows your name and address. Don't be too specific if you plan to use the same resume a number of times. It's better to give a general career goal. Then, in a cover letter, you can be more specific about the position you are seeking in the particular firm you are contacting.

Describe What You've Done   Every interested employer will check your educational background and employment history carefully. It is best to present these sections in order of importance. For instance, if you've held many relevant jobs, you should list your work experience first, followed by your educational background. On the other hand, if you are just out of school with little or no work experience, it's probably best to list your educational background first and then, under employment history, to mention any part-time and summer jobs or volunteer work you've done.

Under educational background, list the schools you have attended in reverse chronological order, starting with your most recent training

and ending with the least recent. Employers want to know at a glance your highest qualifications. For each educational experience, include years attended, name and location of the school, and degree or certificate earned, if any. If you have advanced degrees (college and beyond), it isn't necessary to include high school and elementary school education. Don't forget to highlight any special courses you took or awards you won, if they are relevant to the kind of job you are seeking.

Chronological and Functional Resume   Information about your employment history can be presented in two basic ways. The most common format is the chronological resume. In a chronological resume you summarize your work experience year by year. Begin with your current or most recent employment and then work backward. For each job, list the name and location of the company for which you worked, the years you were employed, and the position or positions you held. The order in which you present these facts will depend on what you are trying to emphasize. If you want to call attention to the type or level of job you held, for example, you should put the job title first. But whichever order you choose, be consistent. Summer employment or part-time work should be identified as such. You need to specify months in the dates of employment only if you held a job for less than a year.

The functional resume, on the other hand, emphasizes *what you can do* rather than *what you have done*. It is useful for people who have large gaps in their work history or who have relevant skills that would not be properly highlighted in a chronological listing of jobs. The functional resume concentrates on your qualifications—anything from teaching experience to organizational skills or managerial experience. Specific jobs may be mentioned, but they are not the primary focus of this type of resume.

It is important to include a brief description of the responsibilities you had in each job. This often reveals more about your abilities than the job title. Remember, too, that you do not have to mention the names of former supervisors or how much you earned. You can discuss these points during the interview or explain them on an application form.

Explain Special Skills   You may wish to include a third section called "Special Skills," "Related Experience," or "Personal Qualifications." This is useful if there are points you wish to highlight that do not apply directly to educational background or work experience. Be sure these points are relevant to the kind of work you are seeking. This section is most effective if you can mention any special recognition, awards, or other evidence of excellence. It is also useful to mention if you are willing to relocate or can work unusual hours.

Have References Available   Employers may also wish to know whom they can contact to find out more about you. At the start of your job search, you should ask three or four people if you may use them as references. If you haven't seen these people for a while, you may want to send them a copy of your resume and let them know what kind of

Mia Cheng
Apartment 8
123 Forest Boulevard
Town, State 12345
(000) 123-4567

Objective   Position as reference librarian in public or university
             library.

Experience

1988 to   School Librarian, Manchester School District, Town, State
1996
           Responsible for administration and program planning for
           library of midsize elementary school. Handled all
           acquisitions, cataloging, and maintenance of library
           materials. Worked with superintendent on annual library
           budget proposal. Organized video, film, and pamphlet
           collections. Supervised library study groups. Provided
           reference services for students and faculty.

1987 to   Cataloger, Hamilton University Library, Town, State
1988
           Responsible for identification, cataloging, and
           crossreferencing of new acquisitions. Recataloged older
           holdings to conform to new system. Entered all data on
           university computer system as well as main library card
           file. Prepared ca
           material. Coordin
           special collection

Education

1988   Master of Library
        School of Library

1985   Bachelor of Arts,
        Major in Modern La

Related Skills and Qualific

           Reading and speaki
           Member, American L

References Available upon

State your name, address, and telephone number first.

State job objective or general career goal in a few words.

List education and work experience in reverse chronological order, with most recent item first.

List your work experience first if it is more important than your educational background.

Keep descriptions of your education and work experience brief.

List special skills and qualifications if they are relevant to the job.

Timothy Rodanski
123 Quince Road
Town, State 12345
(000) 123-5678

Experience

Summer,   Assembly Worker, Nash Manufacturing Company, Inc.,
1996   Town, State

           Responsible for assembly of metal casing for lighting
           equipment. Served as member of inspection team on a
           rotating basis.

Part-   Coach, YMCA, Town, State
time,
1992 to   Supervised training and competition matches of boys'
1995   soccer team. Planned practice sessions for beginners and
           experienced players. Organized competition schedule with
           other teams. Responsible for team safety and security of
           equipment.

1992   Grounds Keeper, Twin Meadows Country Club, Town, State

           Responsible for care of golf course. Duties included
           fertilizing, mowing, trimming lawns, and collecting
           litter. Operated club vehicles and power equipment.
           Planted and tended ornamental flowers and shrubs.

Education

1992   Diploma, Provincetown High School, Town, State

           General business program.
           Captain, soccer and track teams.

References Available upon request.

position you're seeking. Your references should be the kind of people your potential employer will respect, and they should be able to comment favorably on your abilities, personality, and work habits. You should indicate whether these people are personal references or former work supervisors. Avoid using relatives. You can list the names and addresses of your references at the end of your resume or in a cover letter. However, it is more usual to state, "References available upon request." Naturally, you should have their names, addresses, and phone numbers ready if you are asked.

Present Yourself Concisely   Tips for making your resume concise include not using complete sentences and omitting unnecessary words. When appropriate, start a sentence with a verb. There is no need to say "I"—that would be both obvious and repetitive.

Present Yourself Well   Employment counselors often recommend that resumes be kept down to one page because employers won't take the time to read many pages. But if you've held many positions related to your occupation, by all means go on to the second page, but don't include beginning or irrelevant jobs. If you have a lot of work experience, limit the education section to just the essentials.

You should also concentrate on the appearance of your resume. It should be typed on a good grade of 8½″ × 11″ white bond paper. If you can't type, a professional typist can do it for you for a small charge. Be sure that it is neatly typed with adequate margins. The data should be spaced and indented so that each item stands out. This enables a busy executive or personnel director to see at a glance the facts of greatest interest.

You will probably need many copies of your resume during your job search. Each copy should be as neat and as clear as your original. If possible, input your resume on a computer and print copies on a good-quality printer, such as an inkjet or laser printer. You may want to have your resume reproduced professionally. A photo-offset printer can make several hundred excellent copies for a moderate fee. A photocopying machine may be more economical for smaller quantities, though.

These suggestions for writing a resume should not be thought of as hard-and-fast rules. Resumes are sometimes adapted to special situations. People with a variety of work experience often prepare several versions of their resume and use the one that's most appropriate when applying for a particular job.

If this is your first resume, show it to someone else, perhaps a guidance counselor, for constructive advice. Above all, remember this cardinal rule when writing your resume: Be truthful, but emphasize your assets. Show the abilities, skills, and specific interests that qualify you for a particular job. But don't go into your weaknesses or doubts about yourself. Do mention any job-related aptitudes that showed up in previous employment or in school. If you feel you have deficiencies in your training, you don't have to mention them in your resume. Don't make up things about yourself; everything that's in your resume can, and sometimes will, be checked.

Writing Application Letters

Most often you will be sending your resume through the mail. You should always send a cover letter with your resume, whether you are writing to apply for a specific job or just to find out if there are any openings.

A good cover letter should be neat, clear, and brief, with no more than three or four short paragraphs. Since your resume is designed to be used for different job openings, your cover letter should be more specific. Try to get the person who reads it to think of you in terms of a particular job. If at all possible, send the letter to a specific person, either to the personnel director or to the person for whom you would be working. If necessary, call on the phone, and ask to whom you should write.

Start your letter by explaining why you are writing. Say that you are inquiring about possible job openings at the company, or that you are responding to an advertisement in a particular publication, or that someone recommended that you should write (use the person's name if you have received permission to do so).

Let your letter lead into your resume. Use it to call attention to your qualifications. Add information that shows you to be particularly well suited for a specific job. The librarian in the sample letter pointed out that she has worked with automated library equipment and on-line reference systems. She also mentioned that she is familiar with community events run at the library in question. In the second sample letter, the applicant for a letter carrier position mentioned his experience working outdoors and stressed that he has a good driving record.

Completing the Application Form

Use your cover letter to call attention to your qualifications.

Many companies ask job applicants to fill out an application form. This form usually duplicates much of the information on your resume, but it will probably ask some additional questions as well. Give complete answers to all questions except those that are discriminatory. If a question doesn't apply to you, put a dash next to it.

You may be given the application form when you arrive for an interview, or it may be sent in advance to your home. When filling it out, print neatly in ink or, if it is sent to your home, type the information. Follow the instructions carefully. If the form asks you to put down your last name first, do so.

Usually, the most important sections of a form are the education and work histories. As in your resume, many applications will ask for these in reverse chronological order, with the most recent experience first. But unlike your resume, the application may ask for information about your earnings on previous jobs. It may also ask what rate of pay you are seeking on this job.

Be prepared to answer these and other questions that you have not answered in your resume. Look at the sample application form, and make note of the kinds of questions that you are likely to be asked—

123 Quince Road
Town, State 12345
November 5, 1996

Ms. Sarah Leahy
Postmaster
Shelburn Central Post Office
Town, State 12345

Dear Ms. Leahy:

As I mentioned during our telephone conversation this
morning, I am interested in employment as a letter
carrier with the Shelburn Central Post Office.

I am accustomed to outdoor work, since two of my previous
positions have involved this type of work. I have a
valid driver's license and a good driving record. I am
available to work any shift.

I enclose my resume as requested. I would be grateful if
you would send me the application form you mentioned. I
have arranged to take the postal service employee's exam
this month.

Thank you for explaining the application process to me.
I look forward to receiving the material.

              Very truly yours,

              Timothy Rodanski

              Timothy

Enclosure

Apartment 8
123 Forest Boulevard
Town, State 12345
November 3, 1996

Mr. Luis Alvarez
Director of Library Services
Suncrest Township
12 Hillside Avenue
Town, State 12345

Dear Mr. Alvarez:

Elizabeth Sansone, reference librarian at Suncrest Public
Library, mentioned that she will be retiring in June. I
am interested in applying for her position.

I have experience in school and university libraries and
am familiar with the major classification systems. I
have worked extensively with automated catalog equipment
and on-line reference systems. I am familiar with the
county interlibrary loan system and with the community
programs run at Suncrest and other local libraries.

I enclose my resume. Since Ms. Sansone has just
announced her retirement, perhaps you would let me know
how you will be conducting the search for her successor.
I am available at any time for an interview and can be
reached at my home.

              Very truly yours,

              Mia Cheng

              Mia Cheng

Enclosure

1 Always print neatly in blue or black ink. When completing an application form at home, type it.

2 Read the application carefully *before* you start to fill it out. Follow instructions precisely. Use standard abbreviations.

3 If you aren't applying for a specific job, indicate the general kind of work you're willing to do.

4 You don't have to commit to a specific rate of pay. Write "open" or "negotiable" if you are uncertain.

5 If a question doesn't apply to you, write "NA" (for not applicable) or put a dash through the space.

6 Mention a disability only if you *wish* to.

7 Traffic violations and so on do not belong here. Nor do offenses for which you were charged but not convicted.

8 Take notes along to remind you of school names, addresses, and dates.

9 If you're short on "real" employment, mention jobs such as babysitting, lawn mowing, or any occasional work.

10 Under the heading "Reason for Leaving," a simple answer will do. Avoid saying "better pay"—even if it's so.

11 Indicate only relevant activities or honors.

12 Your references should be people who can be objective about you, such as former employers, teachers and community leaders.

APPLICATION FOR EMPLOYMENT

The Law Prohibits Discrimination Because of Age, Sex, Religion, Race, Color and National Origin

(PLEASE PRINT PLAINLY)

PERSONAL

Name _____ Last _____ First _____ Middle Initial _____ Social Security No. _____ Date: _____

Present address _____ No. _____ Street _____ City _____ State _____ Zip _____

How many years have you lived at this address? _____ Telephone No. (_____) Area _____

Previous address _____ No. _____ Street _____ City _____ State _____ Zip _____ How long did you live there? _____

Job applied for _____

How did you learn of this opening? _____ Rate of pay expected $ _____ per _____

Do you want to work ☐ Full time or ☐ Part time? Specify days and hours if part time _____

Have you worked for us before? _____

List any friends or relatives working for us _____ If yes, when? _____

If hired, on what date will you be available to start work? _____

If hired, do you have a reliable means of transportation to get to work? _____

Do you have any physical or emotional disabilities that you wish to discuss? _____

Have you ever been <u>convicted</u> of a crime, excluding misdemeanors and summary offenses?
☐ No ☐ Yes
If yes, describe in full _____

PERSON TO BE _____
Name _____
Address _____

EDUCATION

TYPE OF SCHOOL	NAME AND ADDRESS	How Many Years Attended	Graduated	COURSE OR MAJOR
HIGH SCHOOL			☐ Yes ☐ No	
COLLEGE			☐ Yes ☐ No	
POST GRADUATE			☐ Yes ☐ No	
BUSINESS OR TRADE			☐ Yes ☐ No	
MILITARY OR OTHER			☐ Yes ☐ No	

WORK EXPERIENCE (List in order, last or present employer first. Include part-time and summer work.)

DATES FROM	TO	NAME AND ADDRESS OF EMPLOYER	RATE OF PAY START/FINISH	POSITION HELD	REASON FOR LEAVING

ACTIVITIES AND HONORS (List any academic, extracurricular, civic and other achievement you consider significant.)

PERSONAL REFERENCES

NAME AND OCCUPATION	ADDRESS	PHONE NUMBER
1.		
2.		
3.		

PLEASE READ THE FOLLOWING STATEMENTS CAREFULLY AND SIGN BELOW.
The information that I have provided on this application is accurate to the best of my knowledge and subject to validation. I authorize the schools, persons, current employer and other organizations or employers named in this application to provide any relevant information that may be required to arrive at an employment decision.

Signature of Applicant _____

Date of Signature _____

for example, your Social Security number, the names of previous supervisors, and your work attendance record over the past year or two. If necessary, carry notes on such topics with you to an interview. You have a responsibility to tell prospective employers what they need to know to make an informed decision.

Neatness Counts   Take care to think before you write. Avoid crossing out. An employer's opinion of you may be influenced just by the general appearance of your application. A neat, clearly detailed form may indicate an orderly mind and the ability to think clearly, follow instructions and organize information. An employer who sees a sloppy, carelessly written application form may conclude that you don't really care about the job, are incapable of working in a structured setting, or cannot express yourself carefully.

Know Your Rights   Under federal and some state laws, an employer cannot demand that you answer any questions about race, color, creed, national origin, ancestry, sex, marital status, age (with certain exceptions), number of dependents, property, car ownership (unless needed for the job), or arrest record. Refer to the box on job discrimination in this essay for more information about your rights.

Presenting Yourself in an Interview

> **"Presenting Yourself in an Interview" prepares you for a personal interview, usually an essential step in getting a job.**

An interview is the climax of your job-hunting efforts. On the basis of this meeting, the prospective employer will decide whether or not to hire you, and you'll decide whether or not you want the job.

Prepare in Advance

There are a number of things you can do to prepare for an interview. Give some thought to why you want the job and what you have to offer. Review your resume and any lists you made when you were evaluating yourself, so that you can keep your qualifications firmly in mind.

Try to learn in advance as much as you can about the organization. Check with friends who work there, read company brochures, or devise other information-gathering strategies. Demonstrating some knowledge about the company and what it does will indicate your interest.

Try to anticipate some of the questions the interviewer may ask and think of how you would answer. For example, you may be asked: Will you work overtime when necessary? Will you go to night school to improve your skills? Prepare any questions you may have about the company or the position for which you are applying. The more information you have, the better you can evaluate the firm and the job.

For some occupations, employers may want you to demonstrate your job skills. An applicant for a job as a shorthand reporter, for example, might be given a test to determine speed and accuracy. Prospective legal secretaries might be tested on clerical skills.

On the appointed day, dress neatly and in a style appropriate for an interview. When in doubt, it's safer to dress on the conservative side, wearing a tie rather than a turtleneck or wearing a dress or blouse and skirt rather than jeans and a T-shirt. Be on time. Find out in advance

DO YOU KNOW YOUR RIGHTS?

Job Discrimination—What It Is

Federal and State Law

An employer cannot discriminate against you for any reason other than your ability to do the job. By federal law, an employer cannot discriminate against you because of your race, color, religion, sex, or national origin. The law applies to decisions about hiring, promotion, working conditions, and firing. The law specifically protects workers who are over the age of 40 from discrimination on the basis of age.

The law also protects handicapped workers. Employers must make their workplaces accessible to individuals with disabilities—for example, by making them accessible to wheelchairs or by hiring readers or interpreters for blind or deaf employees.

Federal law offers additional protections to employees who work for the federal government or for employers who contract with the federal government. State law often provides protections also—for instance, by prohibiting discrimination on the basis of marital status, arrest record, political affiliations, or sexual orientation.

Affirmative Action

Affirmative action programs are set up by businesses that want to make a special effort to hire women and members of minority groups. Federal employers and many businesses that have contracts with the federal government are required by law to set up affirmative action programs. Employers with a history of discriminatory practices may also be required to establish affirmative action programs.

Discrimination Against Job Applicants

A job application form or interviewer may ask for information that can be used to discriminate against you illegally. The law prohibits such questions. If you are asked such questions and are turned down for the job, you may be a victim of discrimination. However, under federal law, employers must require you to prove you are an American citizen or have a valid work permit.

Discrimination on the Job

Discrimination on the job is illegal. Being denied a promotion for which you are qualified or being paid less than co-workers are paid for the same job may be forms of illegal discrimination.

Sexual, racial, and religious harassment are forms of discrimination and are prohibited in the workplace. On-the-job harassment includes sexual, racial, or religious jokes or comments. Sexual harassment includes not only requests or demands for sexual favors, but any workplace verbal or physical conduct of a sexual nature.

Job Discrimination—What You Can Do

Contact Federal or State Commissions

If you believe that your employer practices unfair discrimination, you can complain to the state civil rights commission or the federal Equal Employment Opportunity Commission (EEOC). If, after investigating your complaint, the commission finds that there has been unfair discrimination, it will take action against the employer. You may be entitled to the job or promotion you were denied or to reinstatement if you were fired. You may also receive back pay or other financial compensation.

Contact a Private Organization

There are many private organizations that can help you fight job discrimination. For example, the American Civil Liberties Union (ACLU) works to protect all people from infringement on their civil rights. The National Association for the Advancement of Colored People (NAACP), National Organization for Women (NOW), and Native American Rights Fund may negotiate with your employer, sue on your behalf, or start a class action suit—a lawsuit brought on behalf of all individuals in your situation.

What to Do If You Lose Your Job

Being Fired and Being Laid Off
Generally, an employer has the right to fire an employee at any time. In many cases, however, an employer can fire you only if there is good cause, such as your inability to do the job, violation of safety rules, dishonesty, or chronic absenteeism.

Firing an employee because of that employee's race, color, religion, sex, national origin, or age (if the employee is over 40) is illegal. Firing an employee for joining a union or for reporting an employer's violation (called whistle-blowing) is also prohibited. If you believe you have been wrongfully discharged, you should contact the EEOC or the state civil rights commission.

At times, employers may need to let a number of employees go in order to reduce costs. This reduction in staff is called a layoff. Laying off an employee has nothing to do with the employee's job performance. Federal law requires employers who lay off large numbers of employees to give these employees at least two months' notice of the cutback.

Unemployment Compensation
Unemployment insurance is a state-run fund that provides payments to people who lose their jobs through no fault of their own. Not everyone is entitled to unemployment compensation. Those who quit their jobs or who worked only a few months before losing their jobs may not be eligible.

How much money you receive depends on how much you earned at your last job. You may receive unemployment payments for only a limited period of time and only so long as you can prove that you are actively looking for a new position.

Each claim for unemployment compensation is investigated before payments are made.

Should the state unemployment agency decide to deny you compensation, you may ask the agency for instructions on how to appeal that decision.

Other Protections for Employees

Honesty and Drug Testing
Many employers ask job applicants or employees to submit to lie-detector tests or drug tests. Lie-detector tests are permitted in the case of high-security positions, such as police officers. Some states prohibit or restrict the testing of applicants or employees for drug use. Aptitude or personality tests are generally permitted.

Other Federal Laws
The Fair Labor Standards Act prescribes certain minimum wages and rules about working hours and overtime payments. Workers' compensation laws provide payment for injuries that occur in the workplace and wages lost as a result of those injuries.

The Occupational Safety and Health Act sets minimum requirements for workplace safety. Any employee who discovers a workplace hazard should report it to the Occupational Safety and Health Administration (OSHA). The administration will then investigate the claim and may require the employer to correct the problem or pay a fine.

Rights Guaranteed by Contract
Not every employee has a written contract. If you do, however, that contract may grant you additional rights, such as the right to severance pay in the event you are laid off. In addition, employees who are members of a union may have certain rights guaranteed through their union contract.

Make sure you understand any contract before you sign it. Read it thoroughly and ask questions. Checking the details of a contract before signing it may prevent misunderstanding later on.

exactly where the company is located and how to get there. Allow for traffic jams, getting lost, looking for a parking spot, and every other possible delay short of a natural disaster.

Winning the Interview

- **Find out all you can about the job and the employer.**
- **Dress appropriately for the job.**
- **Show good manners. Be on time. Don't smoke or chew gum.**
- **Try to be natural. Show self-confidence, but don't put on airs.**
- **Try to be yourself.**
- **Be brief and to the point.**
- **Be prepared to ask questions.**
- **Leave the subject of salary until the end of the interview.**
- **Follow up. Write a note to express interest in the job.**

Maintain a Balance

When your appointment begins, remember that a good interview is largely a matter of balance. Don't undersell yourself by sitting back silently. Don't oversell yourself by proclaiming the talents the company will have at its disposal if it is lucky enough to hire you. Answer all questions directly and simply, and let the interviewer take the lead.

Give specific answers. Give an example that demonstrates your diligence rather than saying, "I'm reliable and hardworking." Leave it to the interviewer to conclude that from the example.

It's natural to be nervous before and during a job interview. Try as much as possible to relax and be yourself. You may even find yourself enjoying the conversation. Your chances of being hired and being happy once on the job are better if the employer likes you as you are.

Avoid discussing money until the employer brings it up or until you are offered the job. Employers usually know in advance what they are willing to pay. If you are the one to talk about money, you may be running the risk of setting a price that's either too low or too high.

Be prepared to ask questions. After all, part of the purpose of the interview is for you to evaluate the company while you are being evaluated. Be ready with questions about your future with the company. Ask about its training programs and its policy on promotions. But don't force these questions on your interviewer. You will probably be given a fair opportunity to ask them. If not, ask them at the end of the interview.

Don't overstay your welcome. Your interviewer will appreciate your interest in the company, but not if it takes too long to express it. Most businesspeople have busy schedules.

Don't expect a definite answer at the first interview. Usually, the employer will thank you for coming and say that you'll be notified shortly. Most employers want to see all the applicants before they decide. If the position is offered at the time of the interview, it is perfectly acceptable for you to ask for a little time to think about it. If you are told straight out that you are not suitable, it may hurt your pride, but try to be polite. Say, "I'm sorry, but thank you for taking the time to see me." Don't say, "I wouldn't want to work here anyway." After all, the company may have the right job for you next week.

Follow Up the Interview

If the job sounds interesting and you would like to be considered for it, say so as you leave. Follow up the interview immediately with a brief thank-you note to the employer for taking the time to see you and for considering your application.

It's a good idea to make some notes and evaluations of the interview while it is still fresh in your mind. Put down the important facts about

the job—the duties, salary, promotion prospects, and so on. Also evaluate your own performance in the interview; list the things you wish you had said and things you wish you had not said. These notes will help you make a decision later. They will also serve as good guidelines for future interviews.

Finally, don't hesitate to contact your interviewer if you haven't heard from the company after a week or two (unless you were told it would be longer). A brief note or phone call asking when a decision might be reached will do no harm. It will simply confirm your sincere interest in the job. Your call will remind the interviewer about you and could work to your advantage.

Take Charge

The field of public and community services offers many job opportunities. Job hunting is primarily a matter of organizing a well-thought-out campaign. Scan the classified ads, watch for trends in local industry that might be reported in the news, and check with people you know in the field. Take the initiative. Send out well-crafted resumes and letters. Respond to ads. Finally, in an interview, state your qualifications and experience in a straightforward and confident manner.

Trade and Professional Journals

"Trade and Professional Journals" lists publications of particular use to anyone interested in pursuing a career in marketing and distribution.

The following is a list of some of the major journals in public and community services. These journals can keep you up to date with what's happening in all branches of your field of interest. These publications can also lead you to jobs through their own specialized classified advertising sections.

Armed Services

Armed Forces Journal International, 2000 L Street, NW, Suite 520, Washington, DC 20036.

Legal Work

ABA Journal, 750 North Lakeshore Drive, Chicago, IL 60611.
Copyright Law Journal, Box 3897, San Francisco, CA 94119.
Federal Bar News and Journal, 1815 H Street, NW, Suite 408, Washington, DC 20006.
Trial, Association of Trial Lawyers of America, 1050 Thirty-first Street, NW, Washington, DC 20007.

Public, Civil, and Social Services

Academe, American Association of University Professors, 1012 Fourteenth Street, NW, Suite 500, Washington, DC 20005.
Administration in Social Work, 10 Alice Street, Binghamton, NY 13904.
American City and County, 6151 Powers Ferry Road, NW, Atlanta, GA 30339.
American Libraries, 50 East Huron Street, Chicago, IL 60611.

American Psychological Association Directory, American Psychological Association, 750 First Street, NE, Washington, DC 20002.

American School Board Journal, 1680 Duke Street, Alexandria, VA 22314.

American Sociological Review, 1722 N Street, NW, Washington, DC 20036.

APA Monitor, American Psychological Association, 750 First Street, NE, Washington, DC 20002.

APWA News, American Public Welfare Association, 810 First Street, NE, Suite 500, Washington, DC 20002.

Association Management, 1575 Eye Street, NW, Washington, DC 20005.

Catholic Digest, P.O. Box 64090, St. Paul, MN 55164.

Child Welfare, Transaction Periodicals Consortium, Department 3092, Rutgers University, Dept. 2000, New Brunswick, NJ 08903.

Christian Century, 407 South Dearborn Street, Chicago, IL 60605.

Chronicle of Higher Education, 1255 Twenty-third Street, NW, Suite 700, Washington, DC 20037.

Community College Journal, One Dupont Circle, NW, Suite 410, Washington, DC 20036.

Corrections Today, American Correctional Association, 8025 Laurel Lakes Court, Laurel, MD 20707.

Environmental Science and Technology, 1155 Sixteenth Street, NW, Washington, DC 20036.

Guidepost, American Personnel and Guidance Association, 5999 Stevenson Avenue, Alexandria, VA 22304.

Journal of Career Planning and Employment, 62 Highland Avenue, Bethlehem, PA 18017.

Journal of Jewish Communal Service, 3084 State Highway 27, Suite 9, Kendall Park, NJ 08824.

Law Library Journal, 53 West Jackson Boulevard, Chicago, IL 60604.

Library Journal, 245 W. 17th Street, New York, NY 10011.

NEA Today, 1201 Sixteenth Street, NW, Washington, DC 20036.

Personnel Journal, P.O. Box 2440, Costa Mesa, CA 92628.

Postal Record, 100 Indiana Avenue, NW, Washington, DC 20001.

Public Administration Review, American Society for Public Administration, 1120 G Street, NW, Suite 700, Washington, DC 20005.

Public Works, 200 South Broad Street, Ridgewood, NJ 07451.

Science and Children, National Science Teachers Association, 1840 Wilson Boulevard, Arlington, VA 22201.

Social Service Jobs, Ten Angelica Drive, Framingham, MA 01701.

Social Service Review, 5720 S. Woodlawn Avenue, Chicago, IL 60637.

Special Libraries, 1700 18th Street, NW, Washington, DC 20009.

Vocational Education Journal, American Vocational Association, 1410 King Street, Alexandria, VA 22314.

Wilson Library Bulletin, 950 University Avenue, Bronx, NY 10452.

Jobs Requiring No Specialized Training

Armed Services Career

Definition and Nature of the Work

The armed services offer jobs in the United States and abroad that are comparable to hundreds of civilian jobs. The Army, Navy, Air Force, Marine Corps, and Coast Guard train people for jobs such as postal clerk, helicopter repairer, court reporter, and dental hygienist in addition to the strictly military jobs, such as those in weapons crews or in the infantry. Some people spend their entire career in the armed services. Others enlist in the military for 3 to 6 years, become well trained in their field, and return to civilian life with valuable experience and military training. Still others stay in the armed services for 20 years, retire from the military with a pension, and return to a civilian job.

In the field of administration enlisted personnel assist in office duties. They type correspondence, compose letters, process orders, work on budgets, and so on. Experienced enlisted personnel and officers have more complex and more responsible duties, such as supervising other personnel.

Those who choose a field such as Maneuver Combat Arms learn to operate and maintain weapons, vehicles, and other equipment. Beginners may first be trained for jobs such as rifleman or ammunition handler. With experience and ability, enlisted personnel may be assigned more difficult positions, such as armor reconnaissance specialist.

In the field of medicine beginning military personnel help care for patients, serve meals, treat minor cuts and wounds, and transport patients within a medical center. Those who had training prior to enlistment, such as registered nurses, are assigned similar jobs in the military. Those who have no previous training may learn jobs such as X-ray technician and physical therapy specialist.

There are many more fields of opportunity, but they are too numerous to mention here. In every field, however, enlistees receive classroom and field training throughout their military careers and are encouraged to advance to the limit of their capabilities.

Education and Training Requirements

Military service is now entirely voluntary, although in an emergency Congress can reactivate the draft. You must be at least 17 years of age to enlist in any branch of the military. Enlistment requirements vary from branch to branch of the service. Air Force personnel must enter active duty before their 28th birthday, but in general, you must be no older than age 35 to enlist. Some jobs are open only to those who have completed high school. You will be given aptitude tests before you enlist. You may enter any field for which you qualify and for which the service has need. If you are interested only in a specific training program, you can enlist for that program and occupation. If you do not qualify for that job, you are free to change your mind about enlisting.

You can enlist for 3 or more years of active duty. If you wish to enlist instead for 6 years of reserve duty, at least 4 months of that time must be spent on active duty. You also may be qualified to apply for Officer Candidate School (OCS) training. College students can join the Reserve Officers Training Corps (ROTC) and begin training while in school. Under this program you receive $150 a month while in school. After you graduate and are commissioned, you must serve on active duty for 2 years. Full-tuition scholarships are also available.

Another way to join the military is to enter one of the service academies, such as the Air Force Academy in Colorado Springs, CO, the Coast Guard Academy in New London, CT, the Army's Military Academy in West Point, NY, or the Naval Academy in Annapolis, MD. Your tuition and expenses are paid, and you receive an allowance while you attend these schools. You must serve on active duty for 5 years after you graduate.

Armed services enlistees are given classroom training as well as on-the-job training. You may participate in off-duty programs ranging from correspondence courses to courses taken at military bases or local civilian schools. You also may be eligible to participate in a transition program offered to personnel 6 months before they resign from the armed services. This program provides counseling, placement, training, and education services to service personnel who have no civilian skills, have been disabled in combat, or have not earned their high school diplomas.

Getting the Job

Each branch of the military service has its own recruiting operation. For information about the branch in which you are interested, you should see the local recruiter. Recruiters have many publications that will describe career opportunities and military life. Your school placement office and state employment office may also have some of these brochures.

Advancement Possibilities and Employment Outlook

There are many possibilities for advancement in the armed services. Those who work hard and show leadership abilities are given additional training to prepare them for advanced positions. Almost all who enlist are rapidly promoted to higher pay grades.

About 1.8 million people are employed in the armed services. Although certain fields may be nearly filled, there are many opportunities for anyone who wants to enter military service. The armed services offer a wider variety of careers than any other employer. They have developed attractive training and education programs. As a result, a growing number of people are deciding that they want a career in the military.

Working Conditions

Persons who are considering a career in the armed services should remember that the primary goal of the military is to train professional soldiers. Enlisted personnel and officers should have a strong desire to serve their country in peace and war. They must be willing to accept the discipline that is necessary to maintain a strong military force. Military personnel must be able to work well with others and obey orders from superiors without question.

Armed services personnel who have noncombat jobs work under conditions similar to those who hold comparable civilian jobs. They generally work a 40-hour week and often have weekends off. Those in combat zones may have jobs that require great courage and physical stamina. When in direct combat, they may work around the clock with very little sleep and no time off. Living quarters for military personnel vary from barracks at training camps and trenches in war zones to comfortable apartments at military bases.

Earnings and Benefits
Salaries for armed services personnel vary according to length of service, type of job, and level of performance. The average annual salary, including allowances, for all armed services personnel is $28,000.

Although military salaries are somewhat lower than those received by civilians doing similar jobs, armed services personnel receive many other benefits that make their total compensation equal to that received by civilians. They receive free meals and living quarters when they live on the military base. If they do not live on the base, they receive an allowance for food and lodging. They receive special pay for hazardous duty, a uniform allowance, free medical and dental care, and 30 days of vacation each year. Other benefits include reduced prices for entertainment and travel and for items purchased at military institutions. Military personnel are eligible for low-cost life insurance, retire-

ment pensions of half pay after 20 years and three-fourths pay after 30 years, and many educational and career training benefits.

Where to Go for More Information

United States Air Force Recruiting Office
4620 Wisconsin Avenue, NW
Washington, DC 20016
(202) 764-0342

United States Army Recruiting Office
3837 Pennsylvania Avenue, SE
Washington, DC 20020
(202) 433-4654

United States Coast Guard Recruiting Office
5950 Richmond Highway
Alexandria, VA 22303
(703) 960-5923

United States Marine Corps Recruiting Office
#2 Navy Annex
Washington, DC 20380-1775
(703) 614-8497

United States Navy Recruiting Station
4620 Wisconsin Avenue, NW
Washington, DC 20016
(202) 764-2526

Border Patrol Agent

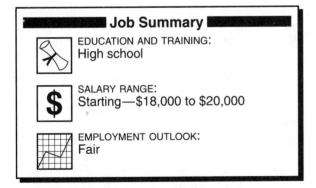

Job Summary

EDUCATION AND TRAINING:
High school

SALARY RANGE:
Starting—$18,000 to $20,000

EMPLOYMENT OUTLOOK:
Fair

Definition and Nature of the Work
Border Patrol agents work at ports of entry and at border crossings. They are federal law enforcement workers who make sure that laws are observed when people or goods cross the United States border. One of their tasks is to check the identification papers of people entering the United States. Agents try to prevent smuggling and the entrance of illegal aliens into this country. To carry out their job properly, they must know all the laws concerning entry into the country.

Border Patrol agents conduct investigations when necessary and speak for the federal government at hearings. They are also responsible for arresting aliens who live in this country illegally. They make suggestions to the courts about immigration matters, including applications for citizenship.

Education and Training Requirements
Border Patrol agents should have a high school diploma and must be in good physical condition. Participation in high school sports and physical education classes is helpful. Agents must pass written and oral civil service tests for the job. Furthermore, they must be fluent in Spanish. Those who do not know the language are given a year to learn it. Agents undergo a 14-week training program to learn the duties of the job.

Getting the Job
You can contact your local Federal Information Center to learn about job openings.

Advancement Possibilities and Employment Outlook

New agents may be promoted after a 1-year probationary period. They may be promoted again at the end of their third year of service. Other promotions are possible, including those to supervisory positions. Some agents are eventually transferred to other jobs dealing with immigration and naturalization.

Each year between 100 and 200 openings occur. The number of openings depends largely on government funding for the patrol. Since the number of people entering the country illegally is increasing, the need for Border Patrol agents is expected to remain constant.

Working Conditions

Border Patrol agents often work outside along international borders. Their job involves working with people. Like all law enforcement personnel, agents must be responsible and able to act quickly. The work can be dangerous. Agents work 40 hours a week and have occasional overtime work. Since borders and ports of entry are open at all times, Border Patrol agents usually work in shifts.

Earnings and Benefits

Earnings depend on the agents' years of service. Border Patrol agents start at about $18,000 to $20,000 a year. Experienced agents earn from about $23,000 to about $28,000 a year. Agents receive paid vacations, health and life insurance, pensions, and other benefits given to federal employees.

Where to Go for More Information

National Immigration Law Center
1102 South Crenshaw, Suite 101
Los Angeles, CA 90019
(213) 487-2531

United States Government Federal Information
   Center
Phone number in local directory.

Building Custodian

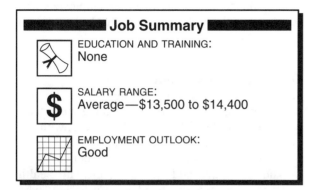

Job Summary

EDUCATION AND TRAINING:
None

SALARY RANGE:
Average—$13,500 to $14,400

EMPLOYMENT OUTLOOK:
Good

Definition and Nature of the Work

Building custodians, or janitors, clean and maintain a variety of buildings ranging from schools to factories. They make minor repairs, such as replacing light bulbs and fixing leaky faucets. Custodians also wash and wax floors, dust, sweep, vacuum carpets, clean bathrooms, and wash windows. They generally do not do work that requires special skills.

In some buildings custodians are responsible for tending furnaces. They kill insects and rodents, if necessary, and collect and discard trash. In northern climates building custodians clear snow from sidewalks. Some custodians mow lawns and do general yard work. A few collect rent and enforce building management rules.

Most companies, hospitals, and schools employ building custodians. These people often work during the day when the buildings are occupied because they must make repairs, such as unclogging drains in public bathrooms, which cannot wait until after the building is empty. Some custodians work only at night when the building is empty because it is easier to clean without disturbing anyone. Many building custodians work for janitorial service firms and clean a number of different buildings.

Custodians use tools such as floor-waxing machines, carpet sweepers, pliers, and screwdrivers. They often use chemicals to wash floors and clean carpets and bathrooms. Custodians work in every state, although the majority work in cities where there are many large buildings.

Education and Training Requirements

No special educational requirements exist. However, high school courses in wood and metal shop that teach how to make simple repairs are very useful in this field. Custodians must be able to do simple arithmetic. Many employers also require good

character references. Building custodians generally learn under the supervision of an experienced custodian. They start by doing cleaning and other basic tasks. As they gain experience, they learn to make repairs and are given more complex duties.

Getting the Job

You can apply directly to schools, apartment buildings, manufacturing plants, and large office buildings. You can also check with janitorial service firms. Another way to find a job is to answer want ads listed in local newspapers. You may be able to find a job through your state employment office. If you would like to work for the state or federal government, you should apply at your local civil service office.

Advancement Possibilities and Employment Outlook

For those who work in a building in which there is only one custodian there is not much chance for advancement. However, experienced building custodians who work in large buildings can advance to the position of building custodian supervisor. Those with administrative ability sometimes start their own cleaning and maintenance services.

The employment outlook for building custodians is good. Almost 2.9 million persons are currently employed as building custodians. New buildings are being constructed every day, and more custodians will be needed to maintain these buildings. The employment growth in this field may be slightly set back by improvements in cleaning equipment and chemical compounds, which will make cleaning easier and faster and thus require fewer workers to do the job.

Working Conditions

Building custodians work during the day or at night, depending on the individual job. They generally work between 40 and 48 hours a week. Most of the work is done indoors, although some work, such as snow removal and ground maintenance, is done outdoors.

Most building custodians have a variety of duties. In addition, they are under relatively little pressure during their workday. However, the work is sometimes tiring because custodians have to move furniture and lift heavy objects. Custodians sometimes work around noisy boilers. At times they work with

dirty and greasy machinery. They may get minor cuts, bruises, and burns while operating machinery or handling chemicals.

Custodians must be able to get along well with others and be courteous to other employees and occupants of the building. They must be honest and trustworthy.

Earnings and Benefits

Many building custodians are members of unions, which set wages by contract. Building custodians earn between $11,000 and $19,400 a year, with the average salary about $13,500 to $14,400 a year. Building custodians generally receive benefits such as paid sick leave and vacations, life and health insurance, and retirement plans. Custodians who work for apartment buildings are often provided with housing at no charge.

Where to Go for More Information

Service Employees International Union
1313 L Street, NW
Washington, DC 20005
(202) 898-3200

Corrections Officer

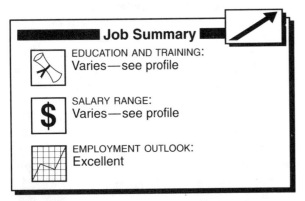

Job Summary

EDUCATION AND TRAINING:
Varies—see profile

SALARY RANGE:
Varies—see profile

EMPLOYMENT OUTLOOK:
Excellent

Definition and Nature of the Work

Corrections officers, or prison guards, are in charge of the daily activities of prisoners. They guard inmates inside and outside the prison. They counsel individuals and groups on prison rules and listen to their complaints and other needs.

Corrections officers inside the prison escort inmates from their cells to the dining room, classroom, hospital, chapel, and work areas. They stand guard over recreational activities. Some corrections officers patrol areas in the building or on the grounds. They check locks, windows, bars, and gates to see that they cannot be used by prisoners to escape. They count the prisoners at set times and report absentees to the central office. They watch for possible disturbances and attempted escapes. Correc-

tions officers also check prisoners for any forbidden articles they may have in their possession.

Other corrections officers work as sentries. They are posted on the grounds or inside the prison in order to watch for suspicious actions. They look for anyone who breaks the prison rules. Anything they judge to be dangerous to the security of the prison is reported to their supervisors.

Other corrections officers escort inmates outside the prison boundaries. They guard prisoners who have jobs in the community as they go to and from their work. Sometimes they escort inmates on court-ordered trips. They bring back escapees and those who have violated parole. Corrections officers may watch over people who have been arrested and those who are waiting to go to trial.

Corrections officers are trained in the use of guns, handcuffs, and other restraint equipment. Most work in state and county correctional institutions. Some work in federal prisons.

Education and Training Requirements

A high school education is required or preferred for jobs in state and county institutions. Most states require a written examination that tests reading and the ability to follow directions. Other states give a civil service examination. A few states request a psychological examination as well. All corrections officer applicants must undergo a rigorous physical examination.

Corrections officers must be United States citizens. Age requirements vary from state to state, although most states require that applicants be at least 18 to 21 years old.

High school courses in government and communications will help you to enter the field. Many 2-year colleges now offer an associate degree in correctional science. Courses offered in such programs include crime and delinquency, administration of justice, the court system, psychology, and sociology.

All newly appointed officers go through a training period lasting 1 to 6 months, depending on the size of the prison. This training may be given in the state department of correction or in the prison itself. Trainees take courses in the principles, practices, terminology, and rules of modern correctional methods. Personal defense, physical restraint of prisoners, and the use of guns are also studied. Many prisons require that officers practice their riflery skills at regular intervals.

Getting the Job

You can apply to any of the state or county correctional institutions in which you wish to work. Your state employment service may list job openings for corrections officers. In some areas you can apply through your local and state civil service commissions. There are more jobs in state prisons than in federal prisons. If you would like a federal job, apply to take the necessary civil service test.

Advancement Possibilities and Employment Outlook

Promotional opportunities for most corrections officers are good. With additional experience, education, and training, qualified officers may advance to a higher rank and salary. Advancement in larger prisons is from corrections officer to sergeant to lieutenant to corrections captain to deputy keeper. The titles for each rank may be different in each institution.

The employment outlook for corrections officers is excellent through the year 2005. Additional officers will be hired for closer supervision of prisoners in existing correctional institutions. New job

opportunities will also result from expansion and the construction of new prison facilities. In addition, there will be jobs to replace officers who retire or change fields.

Working Conditions

Corrections officers usually work an 8-hour day, 5 days a week. They may take turns working the day and night shifts. They are on call for emergencies and may work weekends and holidays. All officers wear uniforms. In large prisons they must stand inspection before their daily work begins.

When officers are in emergency situations they need to keep calm and act quickly. At times there may be trouble between prisoners. Officers may find themselves in personal danger. Corrections officers need to understand the emotional and other needs of the prisoners in their charge. They must respect the prisoners.

Earnings and Benefits

Pay scales vary from one branch of government to another and from state to state. Corrections officers employed in federal institutions average about $30,000 a year. Federal supervisors may earn up to $53,000 a year. Those working for state government average about $23,200 a year, with state corrections sergeants earning more. Salaries for county and municipal corrections officers are comparable to state salaries. There are fewer supervisory positions available in county facilities than in state or federal prisons.

Often housing is provided for corrections officers. In most prisons officers receive life and health insurance, pension plans, sick leave, and paid holidays and vacations.

Where to Go for More Information

American Correctional Association
8025 Laurel Lakes Court
Laurel, MD 20707
(301) 206-5100

National Council on Crime and Delinquency
685 Market Street, Suite 620
San Francisco, CA 94105
(415) 896-6223

Electric Power Service Worker

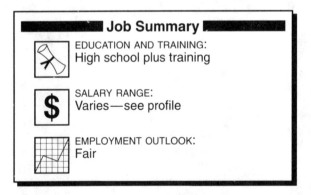

Job Summary

EDUCATION AND TRAINING:
High school plus training

SALARY RANGE:
$ Varies—see profile

EMPLOYMENT OUTLOOK:
Fair

Definition and Nature of the Work

Service workers for electric companies handle matters that relate to customer use. Service workers arrange to have electricity turned on, handle customer complaints, discuss and collect bills, and install, test, and repair electric meters. (A related occupation, meter reading, is discussed elsewhere in this volume.)

The most familiar service worker is the *service representative*. Service representatives work in the offices of the electric company. Some handle customers' questions and complaints on the telephone. Some speak with customers who come into the office. In either case their responsibilities are the same.

Suppose someone just purchased a home. To have electricity supplied, the customer must contact the electric company's service representative. The representative sees that the power is turned on, gets the customer's address for proper billing, and also informs the customer of the different kinds of service available. Service representatives also discuss customers' bills with them to explain how rates are calculated and the reasons for increases.

Electric meter repairers are a skilled group of service workers. They install, test, and repair the meters at the customers' homes, businesses, and factories. Different kinds of meters are used for different kinds of electricity demands. The meters used in factories are different from the ones used in private homes. The service workers must know which kind of meter to use for each kind of customer. Sometimes these workers are specialized *meter installers* or *meter testers*. Installers put in meters, repairers fix them if they are broken, and testers make sure that they operate properly.

In regions that are not heavily populated, the electric power company may appoint one person to perform all customer service jobs. This person is called a *district representative*. These representatives answer questions about service; collect money for bills; install, test, and repair meters; and read the meters at the proper time. If a major repair is necessary, the district representative may contact the central office so that a skilled meter repairer can be sent to the customer.

Education and Training Requirements

Employers generally prefer to hire high school graduates. Although it is not necessary, some service representatives have some college education. Electric meter repairers and installers need a basic knowledge of how electricity works. High school or vocational school courses in electricity and shop are useful.

All training for electric power service workers is done on the job. Meter repairers are trained by experienced repairers. The training period can take up to 4 years. Service representatives and district representatives are also taught by more experienced workers. The amount of time the training takes varies according to the size and location of the power company. Since some electric power companies are owned by municipalities, workers may be required to pass a civil service exam.

Getting the Job

Contact the local electric power company to see whether there are any openings. Sometimes openings are listed in newspaper want ads. Check with the placement office of your high school or technical school. For jobs with municipally owned power companies, contact your municipal civil service commission.

Advancement Possibilities and Employment Outlook

Experienced and diligent service workers have good advancement possibilities with electric power companies. Meter testers and repairers, for example, may advance to working with special, complicated equipment used only by large companies. Service representatives may advance to the position of supervisor.

Most workers advance by demonstrating superior skills on the job. Sometimes advancement is based on seniority alone. Workers with civil service jobs can expect regular advances after a certain period of time. Sometimes an exam must be taken for each step up.

There should be little change in the number of jobs for service workers through the year 2005. Al-

though more power is being used than ever before, increased automation is cutting down on the number of workers needed. Most openings will result when experienced workers retire or leave their jobs for other reasons. Since electric power is always in demand, electric power service workers have very secure jobs.

Working Conditions

Conditions vary with the type and location of the job. Service representatives work in offices, usually with other representatives. Meter repairers, installers, and testers do most of their work at the homes and businesses of the customers. They must drive a company car or truck. District representatives have to do a great deal of driving because they must cover an area by themselves. All service representatives deal directly with the public. They must be tactful and courteous. Almost all electric power service workers work a 40-hour week.

Earnings and Benefits

Earnings vary with the type of job and the company's location. Because they have the most diverse jobs, district representatives generally earn more than other service workers. They average about $25,000 to $35,000 a year. The wages of meter repairers vary according to the workers' experience.

They average about $18,000 to $22,000 a year. Benefits generally include paid holidays and vacations and health insurance.

Where to Go for More Information

Edison Electric Institute
701 Pennsylvania Avenue, NW
Washington, DC 20004-2696
(202) 508-5000

International Brotherhood of Electrical Workers
1125 Fifteenth Street, NW
Washington, DC 20005
(202) 833-7000

Utility Workers Union of America
815 Sixteenth Street, NW, Suite 605
Washington, DC 20006
(202) 347-8105

Electric Power Transmission and Distribution Worker

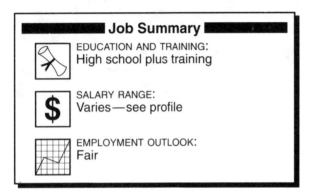

Job Summary

EDUCATION AND TRAINING:
High school plus training

SALARY RANGE:
Varies — see profile

EMPLOYMENT OUTLOOK:
Fair

Definition and Nature of the Work

Electricity is generated in power plants. Once electricity is generated, electric power transmission and distribution workers see that it gets to homes, offices, and factories. One group of workers controls the flow of energy from the generating plant to the customers. Another group of workers takes care of installing and maintaining transmission and distribution equipment such as power lines.

The person in command of electricity flow is the *load dispatcher*. A dispatcher works in the control room of the generating plant, usually with several assistants. The dispatcher makes sure that the amount of electricity produced matches the amount that customers need at any given time. The dispatcher learns how much electricity is required by watching gauges in the control room. When an adjustment in electricity flow is necessary, the dispatcher tells the power plant workers to start or shut down generators. The dispatcher throws switches to route the current to specific areas where there is demand for electricity.

Substation operators work in smaller, regional relay stations. They receive orders from the load dispatcher who works at the generating plant. Substation operators control the flow of electricity for a specific area. Electric power is not generated at substations. Substation operators, however, may have other responsibilities. For example, in small substations there may be only a single worker who is in charge of maintaining the equipment as well as directing the energy flow.

The lines that send electric power from the generating stations to the customers are installed and maintained by *line installers and repairers*. For example, when a new housing development is built, line installers place cables under the ground or on poles to service the new customers. They also set up the connections between the community power lines and individual customers. The job of repairing broken or unsafe lines is done by the same work crews. Some crews are specialized; that is, certain workers may do only installation, while others may specialize in repairing cables.

Line installers and repairers are assisted by ground helpers and cable splicers. *Ground helpers,* or laborers, dig holes in which the poles are placed. They may hold wires and tools for the installers. *Cable splicers* are responsible for making sure that the connections between two different cables are safe. Poor insulation can result in a serious fire. Cable splicers spend much of their time repairing old connections. They must know the proper way to wire connections and the most efficient way of using cable. Some splicers also inspect cables to make sure that they are in good condition.

Troubleshooters are line installers and repairers who have special training. They are in charge of answering emergency calls, and they must be able to choose the safest course of action when a crisis arises. They repair and replace equipment in order to restore service.

Education and Training Requirements

Electric power companies train most of their employees after they are hired. Much of the training is done on the job. Substation operators and load dispatchers train their assistants in the duties of electric power control. Power companies may provide classroom instruction for new workers and for workers seeking advancement. These classes teach the fundamental laws of electricity, safety rules, and how to read blueprints.

A good way to prepare for these jobs is to enroll in a vocational or technical school. You should also take technical courses in high school—mechanical drawing, shop, and any courses related to electricity. Most utility companies prefer to hire high school graduates.

Getting the Job

Job openings are often listed in local newspapers. Check with your school placement office. Contact your local power company to see if it has any openings. Since some power companies are owned by municipalities, you may have to take a civil service test.

Advancement Possibilities and Employment Outlook

Advancement possibilities are good for experienced workers who have shown that they are reliable. Ground helpers may, with experience, move up to become cable splicers or line installers and repairers. It usually takes about 4 years of experience to become a skilled line worker. Assistants at substations may move on to become substation operators. This takes, on the average, from 3 to 7 years. Substation operators with from 7 to 10 years of experience may become load dispatchers.

Only a small increase in the number of job openings is expected through the year 2005. The increasing need for electrical energy will create jobs, but the demand for workers will be offset somewhat by increased mechanization. It is anticipated that only a few thousand new positions will open each year for transmission and distribution workers.

Working Conditions

Working conditions vary greatly depending on the type of job. Load dispatchers and substation operators work inside in comfortable surroundings. They generally work 8 hours a day, 40 hours a week. Weekend and evening work may be required. Since electricity is needed around the clock, a rotation of shifts is normal.

The workers who maintain lines and equipment may have to work in all kinds of weather and during emergencies. Installation workers, however, ordinarily work only during the day. They work 40 hours a week. Troubleshooters and maintenance workers may rotate shifts.

Earnings and Benefits

Electric power transmission and distribution workers' wages vary according to their particular job and the location of the power company. Load dispatchers and other power plant workers earn between $510 and $800 a week. Extra pay is given for overtime. Line installers and cable splicers earn an average of $650 a week. Experienced troubleshooters earn $40,000 or more a year. Benefits generally include medical and accident insurance, life insurance, paid holidays, and vacations. Union workers often receive pension plans.

Where to Go for More Information

Edison Electric Institute
701 Pennsylvania Avenue, NW
Washington, DC 20004-2696
(202) 508-5000

International Brotherhood of Electrical Workers
1125 Fifteenth Street, NW
Washington, DC 20005
(202) 833-7000

Utility Workers Union of America
815 Sixteenth Street, NW, Suite 605
Washington, DC 20006
(202) 347-8105

Federal Government Worker

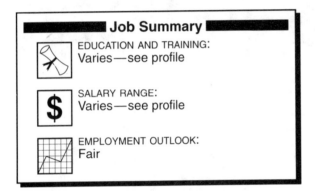

Job Summary

EDUCATION AND TRAINING:
Varies—see profile

SALARY RANGE:
Varies—see profile

EMPLOYMENT OUTLOOK:
Fair

Definition and Nature of the Work

The federal government employs about 3.2 million civilians in the United States and abroad. Almost all of these workers hold jobs that fall under the direction of the Office of Personnel Management. This operating unit oversees the testing procedures for applicants, wage scales for workers, and methods of promoting and firing employees.

Many federal employees hold jobs similar to those existing in private industry. For example, the federal government employs secretaries, lawyers, physicians, biologists, truck drivers, and painters. Other jobs such as postal service worker, government page, internal revenue agent, legislative clerk, and Border Patrol agent are unlike jobs available in private industry.

The Central Intelligence Agency (CIA) employs specialists from many different fields. The CIA gathers information that is used in making foreign policy. Among the agency's personnel are engineers, chemists, and geologists. In addition, there are accountants, linguists, economists, and others. Furthermore, the agency employs clerical and administrative workers.

Federal government workers are employed by all branches of the federal government. Most work for the agencies of the executive branch. For example, they deliver the mail, print money, care for disabled veterans, forecast weather, and catalog and store documents. A smaller number are employed by the legislative and judicial branches of government and work as pages, court stenographers, legislative clerks, and in other jobs.

Opportunities for laborers and skilled workers exist in every branch of the government. The government employs mechanics, maintenance workers, chauffeurs, food service workers, plumbers, truck drivers, and countless other workers of various skills.

About one out of every eight federal government employees works in Washington, DC. The rest work in all 50 states and in foreign countries.

Education and Training Requirements

Educational requirements vary according to the individual job. High school education is sufficient for some jobs. Others require a bachelor's, master's, or doctoral degree. To apply for jobs in the United States the minimum age is 16; for overseas jobs the minimum age is 20.

Most federal government jobs are filled by applicants who have taken competitive exams administered by the Office of Personnel Management. The examinations vary depending on the requirements of the job. Some tests measure the applicants' ability to learn to do the job. Other tests measure the applicants' ability to do the job for which they apply.

Some government agencies use their own testing procedures and merit systems. These include the Federal Bureau of Investigation (FBI), the Foreign Service of the Department of State, the Department of Medicine and Surgery of the Veterans Administration, the Atomic Energy Commission, the Central Intelligence Agency, and the Tennessee Valley Authority.

There are various training programs available to federal government employees. Many federal employees receive some form of on-the-job training. They may receive additional job-related training in their own agencies, in other government agencies, or in facilities outside government. Apprenticeship programs may exist for certain kinds of trade workers. A few work-study programs and summer programs are available for college students.

Getting the Job

All native born and naturalized United States citizens may take the civil service examinations. Announcements for the exams and job openings and application forms may be obtained from your local branch of the Federal Information Center.

Once you have taken an exam you will be quickly notified whether you are eligible for certain gov-

ernment jobs. The names of those who are eligible are placed on a list in descending order of test scores. If an opening occurs in a federal agency, the agency chooses among the top 3 applicants. Those applicants not selected remain on the list for consideration for other vacancies. In addition to taking an exam, you may be required to attend an interview. Some jobs are not filled by examination; in these cases you are rated on the basis of your training and experience.

Advancement Possibilities and Employment Outlook

Federal government workers have many opportunities for advancement. Many jobs are filled by promotions from within agencies. Skilled workers can move up within an agency or be promoted to a job in another agency.

The employment outlook varies greatly depending on the area of employment and the nature of individual jobs. However, little overall growth in the employment of federal workers is expected through the year 2005. Most openings will result from the need to replace workers who retire or transfer to jobs outside government service.

Working Conditions
Federal government workers generally work a 40-hour, 5-day week although at times they may be required to work overtime. Some workers do not have standard work schedules due to the nature of their job. Employees have a great deal of security in their work.

Earnings and Benefits
Over half of all federally employed workers are paid according to a system called the General Schedule. Most other workers are paid according to the Postal Service Schedule or the Federal Wage System. Under the General Schedule system, wages are set by Congress and applied nationwide. Each job is assigned to 1 of 18 grade levels according to the difficulty of the work and the training and experience required. Workers in the lowest grade, GS-1, earn a starting salary of about $12,000 a year. Most high school graduates with no related work experience start at GS-2 with a starting salary of about $13,500 a year. Those with a 2-year associate degree generally start at grade GS-4 with an entrance salary of about $16,700 a year. Those with a bachelor's degree generally start at grade GS-5 or grade GS-7, depending on their academic record. Starting salaries for these positions are about $18,700 and $23,000 a year, respectively. Most applicants with a master's degree or equivalent experience start at GS-11 with a salary of about $34,000 a year. Those in the highest grade, GS-15, have average salaries of about $75,000 to $90,000 a year.

Skilled workers, manual laborers, and service workers are paid under the Federal Wage System at hourly rates. These rates are based on the prevailing rates for similar jobs in private industry and vary according to geographic location.

Federal government workers receive many benefits including paid vacations, holidays, sick leave, low-cost life and health insurance, and retirement plans. In addition, some workers who continue their education in their free time are eligible for reimbursement.

Where to Go for More Information
American Federation of Government Employees
80 F Street, NW
Washington, DC 20001
(202) 737-8700

Federally Employed Women
1400 Eye Street, NW, Suite 425
Washington, DC 20005
(202) 898-0994

National Federation of Federal Employees
1016 Sixteenth Street, NW
Washington, DC 20036
(202) 862-4400

Service Employees International Union
1313 L Street, NW
Washington, DC 20005
(202) 898-3200

United States Government Federal Information
    Center
Phone number in local directory.

Fire Fighter

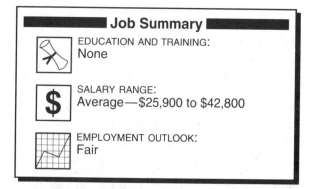

Job Summary
EDUCATION AND TRAINING: None
SALARY RANGE: Average—$25,900 to $42,800
EMPLOYMENT OUTLOOK: Fair

Definition and Nature of the Work
Fire fighters protect life and property from fires. They save lives by rescuing people from fires. They prevent property damage by inspecting buildings for fire hazards and by putting out fires.

Fire fighters are organized in companies under commanding officers. Each person in the fire company has a special task. *Drivers* drive the fire trucks. *Tillers* guide the vehicle attached to the fire truck that carries long ladders. *Hose operators* connect the hoses to fire hydrants. *Pump operators* pump water to make a strong stream of water run through the hoses to put out the blaze. Fire fighters use axes to break down walls or windows so they can enter burning buildings. All fire fighters are trained to give first aid to people who are hurt in fires. Between alarms, fire fighters perform maintenance duties so that their equipment is in working order for the next blaze. Most fire fighters work for the government of their city or community. Some work for private companies. Some fire fighters have another full-time job and fight fires as volunteers.

In large cities fire fighters may work on rescue squads. They go to the scenes of fires in vans that have first aid equipment. They help the injured until ambulances arrive. In addition, rescue squads may be called for injuries and accidents not caused by fire. For example, they are trained to help citizens who have heart attacks.

Fire inspectors and fire science specialists work to prevent fires. *Fire inspectors* usually work for fire departments. They inspect buildings to make sure that safety laws are obeyed. For example, they tour buildings to see that fire escapes are in good condition. They also check automatic fire alarms and sprinkler systems to see that they are working properly.

Fire science specialists work in a number of jobs. Some work for large public buildings owned by the government and private industry. They inspect buildings to see that they are safe from fire. They help plan ways to prevent fires and suggest fire-fighting equipment. Some fire science specialists work for insurance companies. They inspect buildings to set insurance rates. They investigate arson. They work with insurance adjusters to decide the amounts that should be paid to people who suffer injury or loss of property due to fire.

Education and Training Requirements

You may need to pass a civil service examination to get a job as a fire fighter. You can improve your chances of passing the test by completing high school. In addition, you generally must pass a comprehensive physical exam. Working as a fire fighter in a volunteer fire department or in the armed services is useful experience. Newly hired fire fighters receive several weeks of formal training. Some fire departments offer apprenticeship programs that last 3 to 4 years. Experienced fire fighters continue to go on practice drills to maintain their skills at a high level.

Many 2-year colleges and some 4-year colleges offer programs in fire science and fire engineering. Experienced fire fighters sometimes take these courses to prepare for promotion. These courses are also useful for those preparing for jobs as fire science specialists.

Getting the Job

To get a job as a fire fighter you should apply to take the civil service test in your community. You must be at least 18 years old to apply.

Advancement Possibilities and Employment Outlook

Fire fighters are promoted within the department. They advance to higher ranks by passing civil service tests. Supervisors' recommendations are considered when a promotion is made. Advanced ranks include captain, battalion chief, and fire chief. The fire chief has complete responsibility for the entire city or community fire department.

There are currently about 305,000 fire fighters. Some growth should occur in this field as fire departments enlarge or new departments are formed. The outlook is fair, and competition will be keen for jobs in most large cities. Most openings occur when experienced workers retire or leave their jobs for other reasons.

Working Conditions

Fire fighters work under extremely dangerous conditions. Their job requires great physical strength as well as stamina and courage. They are often required to enter burning buildings. They may risk their own lives to save others. Despite the dangers, fire fighters take satisfaction from knowing that they provide a very important public service.

Because fire protection is provided around the clock, fire fighters work in shifts. Hours are irregular. The length of a shift varies from one community to the next. Some fire fighters work an 8-hour day shift or a 14-hour night shift. Others work for 24 hours and then receive equal time off. Fire fighters may be required to live in the fire station for days at a time. They must be able to work as part of a team and follow orders. Many fire fighters belong to labor unions.

Earnings and Benefits

Salaries vary depending on location and years of experience. The average salary for fire fighters is between $25,900 and $42,800 a year. Fire lieutenants and captains may earn $50,000 or more a year.

Fire fighters generally receive paid sick days, vacations, and health insurance. They are usually permitted to retire at half pay when they are 50 years old and have served for 25 years. Fire fighters who are unable to work because of injury on the job may retire at any age.

Where to Go for More Information

International Association of Fire Fighters
1750 New York Avenue, NW, Third Floor
Washington, DC 20006
(202) 737-8484

National Fire Protection Association
One Batterymarch Park
Quincy, MA 02269-9101
(617) 770-3000

Geriatric Aide

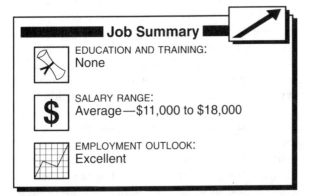

Job Summary

EDUCATION AND TRAINING:
None

SALARY RANGE:
Average—$11,000 to $18,000

EMPLOYMENT OUTLOOK:
Excellent

Definition and Nature of the Work

Geriatric aides offer personal care and assistance to elderly people who no longer have the health, strength, or resources to remain completely self-sufficient. They offer a wide range of services in nursing homes, adult day care centers, specialized recreation programs, health care facilities, and private homes.

Some aides assist medical personnel in caring for patients who are ill, disabled, or medically fragile. Aides' duties might include feeding, dressing, and bathing these individuals as well as monitoring their overall conditions. Other aides are assigned to work in physical therapy, occupational therapy, speech, nutrition, or recreation programs for the elderly. The older adults they serve may range from critically ill patients who need constant medical attention to relatively healthy individuals who require only social activities, transportation, or companionship.

Education and Training Requirements

Many geriatric aide positions have no educational requirements, although a high school diploma is often preferred. Many colleges now offer 2- or 4-year degrees in gerontology for those who plan to

work with the elderly. On-the-job training is often provided, but those who wish to prepare ahead of time might take first aid and cardiopulmonary resuscitation (CPR) training as well as classes in biology, psychology, health care, and sociology.

Getting the Job
College students or graduates might check with the school placement office. Job listings may also appear in newsletters or other publications in the geriatric field. However, you may be able to break into the field by applying directly to nursing homes or public agencies serving the elderly in your area.

Advancement Possibilities and Employment Outlook
Aides who pursue higher education may advance to professional positions in the field, becoming geriatric nurses, therapists, or counselors. Others may obtain additional training and become medical assistants.

The employment outlook is excellent. The older adult population is increasing dramatically, and many of these individuals will require assistance.

Working Conditions
At facilities that offer around-the-clock care, aides are needed at all hours, so night and weekend work is usually required. In addition, aides may be on call for emergencies. The job may be somewhat strenuous if the person being cared for must be lifted or carried. It also may be highly stressful. Because many older individuals are failing mentally or physically, crises may occur frequently. Patience, sensitivity, and good judgment are essential.

Earnings and Benefits
Salaries range from about $11,000 to $18,000 a year, depending on experience and geographic location. Experienced workers can earn up to $24,000 a year. Most of these jobs offer benefit packages that include health insurance, pension plans, and holiday and vacation pay. Opportunities for overtime pay are available frequently.

Where to Go for More Information
National Council on the Aging
409 Third Street, SW, Third Floor
Washington, DC 20024
(202) 479-1200

Highway Maintenance Worker

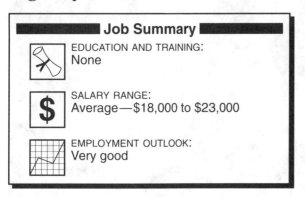

Job Summary

EDUCATION AND TRAINING:
None

SALARY RANGE:
Average—$18,000 to $23,000

EMPLOYMENT OUTLOOK:
Very good

A pneumatic drill, or jackhammer, is used to prepare the eroded spot for repair. Asphalt is then dumped from the truck into the hole. Crew members spread and smooth the asphalt. When it snows, maintenance workers drive trucks and tractors with snowplows and blowers to clear the roads. During the fall and spring they use trucks that blow away leaves that have cluttered street gutters and surface drains. They remove trees that have been damaged in a storm and have fallen across the road. They sometimes cut down and clear away overhanging branches that block drivers' views of stoplights and other road directions.

Definition and Nature of the Work

Highway maintenance workers keep highways and roads in safe condition. They work on state, county, and local highways. They work in large cities, small towns, and rural areas. Their specific tasks vary with the location of the roads they maintain.

Highway maintenance workers repair guardrails and snow fences that are placed along the roadsides. They erect and repair highway markers such as stop signs and signs that direct travelers to major routes. They paint dividing lines between traffic lanes. When the pavement has potholes caused by snow, rain, or heavy traffic, the maintenance crew travels by truck to the place that needs attention.

Education and Training Requirements

Those with a high school education are preferred for the job. Workers may need a doctor's certificate of health to get the job. Workers who drive maintenance trucks must have a driver's license. Those who work in large cities or on state highways must take a civil service examination. This examination tests the workers' ability to read, write, and speak to make sure that they can follow and give directions. Many small towns and cities do not give a written test for the job. Beginners work with more experienced people who train on the job.

Some highway maintenance workers take courses to acquire special skills. Some communities pay the tuition for these courses. For instance, workers who cut and clear away trees may take a course in tree climbing and cutting.

Getting the Job

The best way to get a job as a highway maintenance worker is to apply to the administrator of the borough, town, or county where you wish to work. If you want to work on state turnpikes or highways, you should apply through your state highway commission. If a civil service test is given for the job, apply to take the test. Job openings may also be listed with the state employment office.

Advancement Possibilities and Employment Outlook

Highway maintenance workers can advance from the first grade of laborer to senior maintenance worker to other supervisory positions. Some workers go on to become highway inspectors. These levels of job advancement are common to most departments, whether the department is under civil service or not.

The employment outlook for highway maintenance workers is very good. An increase in the number of new roads built throughout the country is expected to create many jobs for highway maintenance workers. Whenever the amount of traffic increases in states, counties, cities, or towns, more highway maintenance workers are needed. Job openings will also occur when workers retire or change fields.

Working Conditions

Highway maintenance workers need to have good health and physical stamina. They work outdoors in snow, sleet, rain, and summer heat. They use heavy equipment and often must lift fallen trees. Heavy snowfalls and rains often require them to work at night to clear the roads for early morning commuters. They work as part of a team and can enjoy the companionship of other workers.

Earnings and Benefits

Highway maintenance workers are paid through tax monies. Their earnings depend on the size and wealth of the community, county, or state in which they work. Highway maintenance workers often earn about $18,000 to $23,000 a year. Some highway inspectors earn about $30,000 a year. In large cities and for certain specialized types of work, the rate of pay is higher.

All highway maintenance workers receive good health benefits, workers' compensation, Social Security, and paid vacations and holidays. Many highway maintenance workers belong to unions.

Where to Go for More Information

American Federation of State, County and Municipal
    Employees
1625 L Street, NW
Washington, DC 20036
(202) 452-4800

International Brotherhood of Teamsters, AFL-CIO
25 Louisiana Avenue, NW
Washington, DC 20001-2198
(202) 624-6800

Meter Reader

Job Summary

EDUCATION AND TRAINING:
None

SALARY RANGE:
Average—$19,500 to $23,000

EMPLOYMENT OUTLOOK:
Poor

Definition and Nature of the Work

Meter readers check meters that register the amount of water, gas, and electricity used in private homes, apartments, and businesses. They record their readings so that utility companies can charge their customers the correct amount. Meter readers work for city or privately owned utility companies.

Most meter readers are assigned to specific territories and service a number of regular customers. After covering their daily routes they return to their offices, where they update their readings and make

Advancement Possibilities and Employment Outlook

Advancement for meter readers depends largely on their own initiative. Competent readers who attend public education schools or take night classes in personnel relations and mechanical or electrical subjects may be able to advance to supervisory positions. Those in civil service jobs may need to pass another test for promotion. There are also jobs in field and customer services that involve starting and discontinuing service, computing and collecting bills, and investigating customer complaints.

The number of jobs for meter readers will decline. Sophisticated meters are being developed that automatically report readings over telephone lines. Some openings may appear, however, when employees retire or change fields.

Working Conditions

Meter readers work outdoors in all kinds of weather. They generally wear company uniforms and carry a customer route book, a flashlight, and a hook for lifting the lids of meter boxes. Since they deal with the public, it is important for them to be polite and courteous.

Earnings and Benefits

Wages for meter readers vary according to the type of job they have and the area of the country in which they work. A meter reader earns about $19,500 to $23,000 a year. Experienced meter readers may earn up to $26,700 a year. Large cities generally pay higher wages than rural areas or small towns. Supervisory workers generally earn substantially higher salaries.

Benefits that workers receive usually include paid holidays, vacation and sick leave, medical and life insurance, and pension plans. Many meter readers belong to unions.

out reports. Often they discover unusual conditions such as abnormal consumption of gas, water, or electricity; leaks in service lines; or broken or defective meters. Occasionally they find that someone has tampered with a meter to avoid or reduce payment for services. All such circumstances are reported to supervisors for investigation and correction.

Education and Training Requirements

Most utility companies require meter readers to have a high school education or its equivalent. To qualify for a position with a municipal utility company, you may need to pass a civil service test.

After a few weeks of on-the-job training, you will qualify as a meter reader. This training includes following the routes of experienced readers and learning how they record the amounts of gas, electricity, and water that have been consumed.

The ability to handle money, some knowledge of mathematics and electricity, and good vision and hearing are essential.

Getting the Job

The best way to get a job as a meter reader is to apply directly to utility companies. You can also inquire at the state employment office.

Where to Go for More Information

International Brotherhood of Electrical Workers
1125 Fifteenth Street, NW
Washington, DC 20005
(202) 833-7000

Utility Workers Union of America
815 Sixteenth Street, NW, Suite 605
Washington, DC 20006
(202) 347-8105

Police Officer

▰▰▰▰ Job Summary ▰▰▰▰

EDUCATION AND TRAINING:
None

SALARY RANGE:
Starting—$18,000 to $22,000
Average—$24,500 to $41,200

EMPLOYMENT OUTLOOK:
Fair

Definition and Nature of the Work

Police officers protect the lives and property of citizens. They work to prevent crimes, catch lawbreakers, and maintain order. In small towns police officers perform many duties. In large cities there is a more definite division of duty. Police officers may work as patrol officers on foot or in a squad car. They may be assigned to traffic control or crime prevention, or they may work as detectives who investigate crimes. Officers who work inside the police department may be assigned to work in the crime laboratory, with police records, or in the communications department. Filing reports of incidents is an important part of every officer's job. Officers who are involved in criminal cases testify at court trials and hearings.

Police officers are supervised by senior officers. The chain of command is modeled after that of the armed services. In large cities sergeants, lieutenants, and captains direct the work of squads or companies of officers. Ranking officers generally report to police chiefs or commissioners. In small towns the chief of police may be the only ranking officer.

Education and Training Requirements

There are no specific educational requirements for this position. Many police departments require at least a high school education. A few require some college education. Requirements generally specify that you be at least 21 years of age. In many communities you must meet minimum requirements for height and weight. In addition, you must have good eyesight.

Since most police departments fall under civil service regulations, you must pass a test for the job. You must also pass a strict physical examination. Police departments check the character and back-ground of applicants. Senior officers screen applicants.

New recruits often go through formal classroom training in a police academy. After graduating they continue to train on the job with experienced officers for 3 to 12 months. In small communities there may be no formal training program. Officers are usually encouraged to continue their education by taking college courses in criminal justice.

Getting the Job

You can apply to take the civil service test for police officer. In many departments, if you have completed high school or are attending college in criminal justice, you can enter police work as a cadet or trainee while you are still in your teens. You may then be appointed to regular police work when you are 21 years old if you meet the necessary requirements.

Advancement Possibilities and Employment Outlook

For each promotion to a higher rank in the police department, officers must take a civil service test. A good work record or special honors help officers

get ahead. Police officers who have investigation abilities may advance to detective. Other positions include sergeant, lieutenant, captain, and inspector.

The employment outlook for police officers is fair. The number of openings will depend on the amount of funding available to police departments. The total number of positions will rise slowly, and there will be openings to replace officers who retire or leave their jobs for other reasons. However, competition for jobs will be keen.

Working Conditions

Police work can be very dangerous. In addition, officers work outdoors in all kinds of weather. But despite the dangers police get a great deal of satisfaction from knowing how important their work is. Officers are guided by the rules of their departments, but they have a good deal of independence. They must make quick decisions while on duty and be tactful and patient with people who are in trouble.

Police protection is provided 24 hours a day. Therefore, police work in shifts. Officers usually rotate shifts. The scheduled workweek is 40 hours. However, officers are on call at all times for emergencies. Officers usually wear uniforms. Most police departments provide uniforms or uniform allowances. Many police officers belong to labor unions.

Earnings and Benefits

Earnings vary depending on location and experience. Recruits may start at about $18,000 to $22,000 a year. Experienced officers may earn $24,500 to $41,200. Those with higher rank earn more. Officers who work overtime receive premium pay or equal time off.

Benefits include paid health and life insurance, sick days, and vacations. Many officers are covered by pension plans that allow them to retire with half pay after 20 or 25 years of service.

Where to Go for More Information

Fraternal Order of Police, Grand Lodge, National
   Headquarters
1410 Donelson Pike, Suite A-17
Nashville, TN 37217
(800) 451-2711

International Association of Chiefs of Police
515 North Washington Street
Alexandria, VA 22314-2357
(703) 836-6767

Postal Service Worker

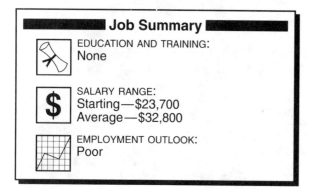

▰ Job Summary ▰

EDUCATION AND TRAINING:
None

SALARY RANGE:
Starting—$23,700
Average—$32,800

EMPLOYMENT OUTLOOK:
Poor

Definition and Nature of the Work

Postal workers direct the mail to the right destination. Their work involves sorting, distributing, and delivering mail; knowing postal rates and regulations; and helping the public with information.

There are more than 578,000 postal workers and many types of jobs. Most jobs fall into one of two categories. *Postal clerks* work indoors and handle the bulk of the mail. *Letter carriers* work most of the time outdoors and deliver mail to the correct address.

In large cities postal clerks may have specialized tasks. *Distribution clerks* unload the mail from trucks and do rough sorting into parcel post, magazines, letters, and foreign mail. They have to memorize distribution "schemes" according to geographic areas. *Window clerks* weigh mail, sell stamps and money orders, and answer questions and complaints. In small towns the postal clerks attend to all of the above duties.

Letter carriers may have residential, business, parcel post, or rural routes. They arrive at the post office early in the morning to sort the mail for their routes. They know the names of persons and companies on their routes. They handle insurance receipts and registered and COD mail, and they make records for the post office. They may deliver the mail on foot with a shoulder bag or small cart, or they may use a small truck. Rural letter carriers cover their routes by car.

Overseeing the work of letter carriers is a supervisor. Another supervisor directs the postal clerks.

These supervisors are usually employed at large post offices where there is a large staff. *Postmasters* manage post offices and have complete responsibility for them.

Education and Training Requirements

All postal workers must be citizens of the United States, have a high school education or its equivalent, and be at least 18 years of age. They are required to take an examination that tests their reading accuracy and speed and their ability to follow instructions. Letter carriers and postal clerks must also be able to carry a 35-pound shoulder bag and lift 70-pound mailbags. Many jobs require a driver's license and passing a road test.

On-the-job training is given to all postal workers. Postal clerks and letter carriers usually train as substitutes until vacancies occur in their office or department. Beginning clerks learn many postal regulations and practice sorting for speed and accuracy. In large towns they are taught how to run a sorting machine. Letter carriers work inside the post office for a while to understand postal procedures.

Getting the Job

You can ask your local post office for a job application blank and the times and places of the examinations. After you take the test, your name is put on a list. The appointment is made from the 3 highest scores. The remaining names of applicants are kept for future selection.

Advancement Possibilities and Employment Outlook

Job advancement in the postal service varies with the size of the post office. There are more opportunities in large offices that employ supervisors. Postal workers with seniority may receive a preferred assignment, such as working the day shift. Whenever there is an opening, a request for a preferred assignment is made by a written bid. The job is then given to the qualified bidder with the longest service.

The usual path for advancement for postal clerks is from top-level clerk to supervisor to postmaster. Postal clerks and letter carriers are first graded as substitutes. The time they serve at this level depends on the size of the community, although efforts are being made to reduce the waiting period for everyone. Supervisors' and postmasters' jobs

require experience, education, and passing an examination.

The employment outlook is poor. Although there are thousands of openings each year to replace workers who retire or transfer, there are many applicants for each position. Also, automation is eliminating many jobs. For this reason employment in the postal service will decline somewhat through the year 2005.

Working Conditions

There are many modern post office buildings, and a major effort is being made to replace or modernize older buildings. Most jobs require strenuous lifting and moving of mail. Letter carriers need good health and physical stamina to work outside in all kinds of weather. Postal clerks sometimes have periods of pressure when large mail loads need to be dispatched quickly. They often work in groups or teams and enjoy the friendship and cooperation of their fellow clerks. Everyone in the postal service enjoys steady work because the ups and downs of business cycles do not affect their jobs. Many postal workers belong to labor unions.

Earnings and Benefits

Salaries and benefits vary with the worker's experience and the location of the post office. Letter carriers and postal clerks currently earn $23,700 to start and average $32,800 a year. Postal workers receive time and a half for overtime and premium pay on holidays. Benefits include pension plans and health and life insurance. Paid vacations range from 13 days the first 3 years to 26 days after 15 years of service. Paid sick leave can be accumulated over several years.

Where to Go for More Information

American Postal Workers Union
1300 L Street, NW
Washington, DC 20005
(202) 842-4200

National Association of Letter Carriers
100 Indiana Avenue, NW
Washington, DC 20001
(202) 393-4695

National Rural Letter Carriers' Association
1630 Duke Street
Alexandria, VA 22314
(703) 684-5545

Power Plant Worker

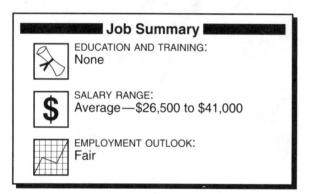

Job Summary

EDUCATION AND TRAINING:
None

SALARY RANGE:
Average—$26,500 to $41,000

EMPLOYMENT OUTLOOK:
Fair

Definition and Nature of the Work

Power plants produce electricity by drawing energy from various natural resources. Some plants burn oil or coal to create steam. Others make use of the power of falling water to turn turbines and generate power. Still others draw on radioactive ores like uranium to produce nuclear power. Power plant workers' jobs vary somewhat from plant to plant depending on the type of fuel used and the age of the equipment. Nuclear power plants have their own specialized technology and require several specialized workers. However, some jobs in nuclear power plants are very much like jobs in conventional plants. For instance, nuclear reactor operators do a job similar to that of boiler operators.

Some jobs that are central to the operation of most power plants are boiler operator, turbine operator, and switchboard operator. *Boiler operators* run the boilers that burn coal or oil to heat water until it becomes steam. The pressure of the steam turns the turbines that generate electricity. Boiler operators see that the right mixture of fuel and air gets into the boiler. The pressure must be high enough to turn the turbines but not so high that the boiler will explode. Boiler operators read gauges, meters, and thermometers to get the information they need to regulate the boiler. In large power plants workers sometimes operate more than one boiler.

Turbine operators also watch pressure gauges and thermometers. Their equipment tells them how fast the turbines are spinning and at what temperature they are operating. Turbine operators record readings from the gauges and thermometers and check to see that the turbines are working properly as they spin to turn the electrical generators. Turbine operators shut down the turbines when less electricity is needed and start them again when the need increases. Turbine operators often have helpers and junior operators working with them.

Switchboard operators regulate the amount of electricity that flows out of the power plant onto the power lines. They also control the voltage of the electricity and check to see that it is maintained at the proper level. The switchboard operator usually sits at a desk facing a wall filled with meters and dials. These show how much electricity is being produced and where it is going. Operators use remote control switches to run generators and distribute electricity. They take orders over the telephone from load dispatchers who monitor the needs of customers in the system. The switchboard operators in turn tell turbine operators when to start up or shut down the turbines.

In some modern plants *control room operators* do the work of boiler, turbine, and switchboard operators. All the necessary meters, dials, and gauges are centralized so that one operator can run the generator and distribute electricity using remote control switches. Control room operators work with several assistants. Whether a plant is new or old, the operators are supervised by the *watch engineer,* who sees that each worker does what is necessary to keep the electricity flowing. The watch engineer reports to the *plant superintendent,* who takes final responsibility for all work done in the plant and is the chief supervisor of all the workers.

There are power plants located throughout the country. Most plants are located in population centers where energy needs are highest.

Education and Training Requirements

Many employers prefer applicants with a high school education. You can prepare for power plant jobs by taking algebra, science, and shop courses in high school. Most operators learn their skills by working in power plants as clean-up workers, helpers, and then junior or assistant operators.

Many workers spend a long time as assistant operators before being promoted to operator. Four to 8 years of on-the-job training are usually required before a worker is considered fully qualified

as a boiler, turbine, or switchboard operator. Some states require operators of power plant machinery to be licensed.

Getting the Job

Apply directly to power plants. These jobs are rarely advertised in newspapers because there are usually more applicants than there are jobs. You would therefore be wise to apply to several plants.

Advancement Possibilities and Employment Outlook

A boiler operator or turbine operator may be promoted to assistant switchboard operator and then to switchboard operator. Switchboard operators usually must have 5 to 10 years of experience before becoming watch engineers.

Little change in the employment of power plant workers is expected through the year 2005. Although production of electricity is expected to increase, the larger and more automated equipment that is used in power plants generally will require fewer operators.

Working Conditions

During a typical day power plant workers come into contact with other workers. There is usually plenty of light and fresh air in power plants, but the equipment is often noisy. Most power plants are clean and safe. However, there is much controversy over whether workers in nuclear power plants are endangered by radiation leaks.

Boiler and turbine operators spend most of their time on their feet. Switchboard operators can usually sit down as they work. All operators can expect to work on some holidays and weekends. Since there is a demand for electricity 24 hours a day, operators must take turns working night shifts. When they work weekends and evenings, plant operators usually receive extra pay. Eight-hour days and 40-hour weeks are standard. Operators may be required to work overtime in an emergency. Many operators belong to labor unions.

Earnings and Benefits
Salaries for operators depend on where they work and what jobs they do. Power plant operators earn, on average, wages ranging from $26,500 to $41,000

a year, depending on the position and level of seniority. Workers usually receive higher wages for night shifts. Benefits generally include paid vacations and holidays, health insurance, and pension plans.

Where to Go for More Information

Edison Electric Institute
701 Pennsylvania Avenue, NW
Washington, DC 20004-2696
(202) 508-5000

International Brotherhood of Electrical Workers
1125 Fifteenth Street, NW
Washington, DC 20005
(202) 833-7000

National Association of Power Engineers
One Springfield Street
Chicopee, MA 01013
(413) 592-6273

Refuse Worker

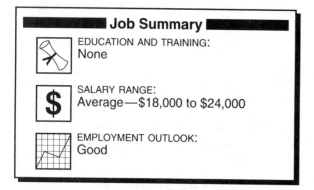

■ Job Summary ■

EDUCATION AND TRAINING:
None

SALARY RANGE:
Average—$18,000 to $24,000

EMPLOYMENT OUTLOOK:
Good

Definition and Nature of the Work
Refuse workers clear cities and towns of waste materials. They remove refuse from industrial plants, institutions, businesses, and private homes, and they oversee the final disposal of waste material.

Generally refuse workers are employed in either of two categories. *Refuse collectors* collect garbage and other waste material and deliver it by truck to a disposal area. Crews of refuse collectors dump waste material from trash containers into the truck. The truck driver starts a device that raises the refuse bin attached to the rear of the truck. This refuse bin dumps the waste material into an opening in the truck body. The driver then brings the refuse to the disposal area.

Refuse workers who work at the disposal area are called incinerator operators and landfill operators. *Incinerator operators* control the equipment

that burns the refuse and garbage. They direct other workers who feed the refuse into a furnace. Incinerator operators turn a valve to admit liquid or gaseous fuel, or they signal workers to shovel coal into the furnace. They light the fire and see that the furnace is kept at the right temperature to burn the refuse. They supervise the ash removal from grates. They may turn a valve or water line to sprinkle and settle ashes. They also may supervise the maintenance of equipment. *Landfill operators* use equipment that dumps refuse into landfills where the waste material is pressed down and covered with earth.

Refuse workers may work directly for cities or towns. However, many cities and towns contract for this work with a privately owned disposal service. Private disposal services may have many trucks and crews that operate in a number of different municipalities. Incinerator and landfill operators may work for a single municipality or for a centrally located waste disposal area that provides service to several cities and towns.

Education and Training Requirements
Those who have a high school or vocational school education are preferred. You may qualify for the job by passing a civil service examination or other oral or written test. Since refuse workers must be

strong, a doctor's certificate of health is required. Truck drivers must have a driver's license. Beginners are trained on the job. They work with more experienced workers who teach them the necessary skills.

Getting the Job
The best way to apply for work as a refuse worker is through your city or town administrator located at your town or city hall. Or you can apply directly to a private disposal service. You can also apply to take a civil service test or you can contact the state public utility commission.

Advancement Possibilities and Employment Outlook
Refuse collectors usually start as laborers. Later they may become truck drivers or supervisors, usually after passing a written test or civil service examination. Most incinerator and landfill operators are under civil service and must take a civil service examination for advancement. Laborers in incinerator plants may be promoted to truck drivers, heavy equipment operators, or incinerator opera-

tors by taking civil service examinations for each advancement.

The employment outlook for refuse workers is good. Jobs become available when workers retire or leave the job for other reasons. Whenever the population of a town or city increases, there are more job openings. The increasing emphasis on recycling refuse may create new jobs for refuse workers.

Working Conditions
Refuse workers should enjoy physical labor and working outdoors. They lift heavy containers, drive trucks, and operate heavy equipment. They work a 40-hour week, but sometimes overtime work is required. They work as part of a team and enjoy the companionship of their fellow workers. Refuse workers enjoy steady employment and security in their jobs.

Earnings and Benefits
The earnings of refuse workers vary greatly depending on geographic location and the specific task that is performed. Many refuse workers earn an

average salary of $18,000 to $24,000 a year. Some refuse truck drivers receive salaries of about $28,000 or more a year. In general, wages for refuse workers tend to be higher in large cities than in small municipalities. Most refuse workers are members of labor unions. Differences in union scales also greatly affect earning levels of refuse workers.

The benefits that are available to most refuse workers include paid holidays and vacations, medical and hospital insurance, workers' compensation, and pension plans.

Where to Go for More Information

American Federation of State, County and Municipal
    Employees
1625 L Street, NW
Washington, DC 20036
(202) 452-4800

International Brotherhood of Teamsters, AFL-CIO
25 Louisiana Avenue, NW
Washington, DC 20001-2198
(202) 624-6800

Security Guard

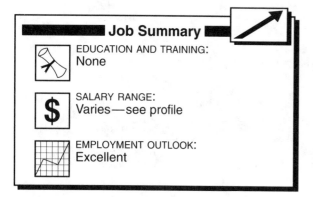

Job Summary

EDUCATION AND TRAINING:
None

SALARY RANGE:
Varies—see profile

EMPLOYMENT OUTLOOK:
Excellent

Definition and Nature of the Work

Security guards protect people and property. They keep buildings and their contents safe from robberies, fires, and other damage. Sometimes they give directions or information to visitors who enter the building. Guards work in public buildings such as banks, museums, and government offices. Many work in retail establishments. Others work in factories and offices. They are employed by the companies they protect, by building management, and by private security agencies that provide protective services for clients.

The duties of security guards vary according to the size of the building they guard, the number of guards who share the work, and the kind of security system used. In large security systems guards generally work under security directors. In small establishments guards may work alone. Most security guards patrol buildings and grounds on foot. Those who cover a large area may use a car or motor scooter. They may work with trained dogs who alert them to intruders. Guards check windows, lights, and doors for clues to suspicious activities. They make sure that fire extinguishers, sprinkler systems, and alarm systems are in working order. In some security systems guards report to a central station at regular intervals on their rounds of duty. If a guard fails to report, the central office sends investigators to find out if there is a disturbance. Guards summon police and fire departments when necessary. Guards who work in buildings in which there are many robberies may carry guns.

Some security guards work at loading platforms in warehouses, factories, railroads, and ports. They prevent thieves from stealing material or equipment that is being prepared for shipment. Security guards also protect people carrying jewels or large sums of money. Some guards work with up-to-date electronic alarm systems. They monitor panels of dials and closed-circuit television screens in a central station. If any unusual activities show up on the panel, they send a runner to investigate.

Guards may have other duties as well. They may answer the telephone at night or run the elevator. Some guards request people who enter and leave the building to sign in and out in a register. They stop people they do not know and question them about their reasons for entering the building. They also check the packages of those entering and leaving to prevent theft.

Education and Training Requirements

Employers generally prefer high school graduates. Previous training in police or military police work is useful. Many employers train guards on the job. Others provide several weeks of formal classroom training in alarm systems operations, first aid, and emergency procedures.

Getting the Job

You can apply directly to businesses and protective agencies for which you wish to work. If you apply for a job in a government agency, you must pass a

civil service test. Jobs are sometimes listed with private employment agencies, in newspaper want ads, and at state employment offices. Large department stores require extra guards during holiday rush periods. Part-time or temporary work can help you to get a permanent guard job.

Most employers require that guards be bonded, or insured. Bonding companies investigate the background and character of security guards. Bonding companies protect employers against dishonest and unreliable workers.

Advancement Possibilities and Employment Outlook

With experience, guards can advance to supervisory positions. Security guards who work in government agencies have the best opportunities for advancement. These guards are promoted by civil service tests. In small companies advancement may be limited.

The employment outlook is generally expected to be excellent. Jobs will be created as industrial plants and stores expand. Openings will also occur as experienced guards retire or change jobs. Some jobs may be eliminated by automation, however.

Working Conditions

Security guards are on their feet most of the time as they patrol their places of work. Most guard work is done at night. In small companies guards may be needed only for an 8-hour shift during the night. In large institutions and companies guards may be needed to cover a full 24-hour day, 7 days a week. Guards generally rotate shifts. The work may be dangerous. Many guards wear uniforms. Some employers provide uniforms or a uniform allowance. Many guards belong to labor unions.

Earnings and Benefits

Earnings vary depending on experience, location, and duties. Wages of guards in private industry range from about $15,300 to $27,700 a year. Federally employed guards earn average salaries that range from $14,600 to $21,700 a year. Benefits generally include paid vacations, holidays, health insurance, and pension plans. Government guards receive the same benefits as do other workers in government service.

Where to Go for More Information

American Federation of State, County and Municipal
   Employees
1625 L Street, NW
Washington, DC 20036
(202) 452-4800

International Association of Security Services
P.O. Box 8202
Northfield, IL 60093
(312) 973-7712

International Union of Security Officers
2404 Merced Street
San Leandro, CA 94577
(510) 895-9905

State Police Officer

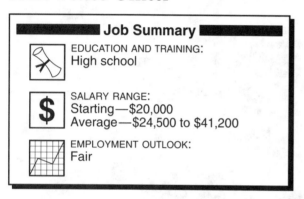

Job Summary

EDUCATION AND TRAINING:
High school

SALARY RANGE:
Starting—$20,000
Average—$24,500 to $41,200

EMPLOYMENT OUTLOOK:
Fair

Definition and Nature of the Work

State police officers, or troopers, patrol and enforce laws on highways. Troopers issue traffic tickets, investigate highway accidents, administer first aid, direct traffic, call emergency services, and make out reports. They also help motorists by radioing for automobile mechanics and by giving directions and tourist information. Sometimes they check the weight of commercial vehicles and give the public information about highway safety.

In areas that do not have regular police forces, troopers often investigate crimes. They frequently assist city or county police with their cases. However, most of their work is restricted to highway matters.

Like members of city police forces, state troopers often specialize in certain areas of work. They conduct fingerprint classification, pilot police aircraft, and do chemical and microscopic analyses of pieces of evidence for cases they are investigating. Others work in special units such as the mounted police or canine corps.

Education and Training Requirements

Most states require you to have a high school education. In high school you should take courses in

English, social science, government, chemistry, and physics. A course in driver education is also useful. State police officers sometimes continue their education while on the job. Many 2- and 4-year colleges now offer courses in criminology and police science.

All states provide recruits with a formal training program that generally lasts for several months. During this time you will learn about state laws, procedures for accident investigation, and traffic control. You will also be taught how to use a gun, administer first aid, and handle a car at very high speeds.

Getting the Job

To apply, you must be a United States citizen and, in most states, at least 21 years old. In some states you must pass a civil service examination. There may also be certain physical and personal requirements. Good eyesight, honesty, and a sense of responsibility are essential. You can go directly to the nearest state police headquarters, or you can apply to take a civil service test. You will be selected on the basis of your score on the civil service exam, a personal interview with an officer, and an investigation of your character.

In some states you can become a cadet when you graduate from high school. You will receive a salary as you attend classes to learn about police work. If you do a good job performing nonenforcement duties, you may become a trooper at age 21.

Advancement Possibilities and Employment Outlook

New recruits are required to serve a probationary period lasting from 6 months to 3 years. After this period they become eligible for promotion. In most states they must pass an examination to qualify for each advancement in rank. The ranks are, from lowest to highest, private, corporal, sergeant, first sergeant, lieutenant, and captain. Most troopers begin as privates. If state police officers show administrative ability, they may become a commissioner or director.

The number of job openings for state police officers is expected to grow more slowly than in the past due to tight budgets in most states. Some openings will occur to replace experienced officers who retire or leave their jobs for other reasons. Stiff competition is expected in many states.

Working Conditions

State troopers work irregular hours since police protection is provided 24 hours a day. Generally troopers take turns working on three 8-hour shifts. Sometimes they must work weekends and holidays. In an emergency situation troopers must be ready to offer their services.

State troopers spend most of their time driving police cars and are exposed to all types of weather. Like other police officers, they are often exposed to dangerous situations and may have to risk their lives in the line of duty.

Work as a state trooper can be very rewarding. Troopers help many people by aiding stranded motorists and preventing accidents. At all times they must be tactful, patient, and alert.

Earnings and Benefits

Salaries vary from state to state. Beginning salaries for state police officers average $20,000 a year. The annual salaries of experienced state police officers average about $24,500 to $41,200, although some officers earn more. Earnings increase with advancement to higher ranks. Salaries of state police sergeants average about $32,000 a year, while those of state police lieutenants average $37,000 a year.

Most states provide officers with uniforms or an allowance for their purchase. Benefits usually include paid vacations, sick leave, health and life insurance, and pension plans.

Where to Go for More Information

Fraternal Order of Police, Grand Lodge, National
    Headquarters
1410 Donelson Pike, Suite A-17
Nashville, TN 37217
(800) 451-2711

International Association of Chiefs of Police
515 North Washington Street
Alexandria, VA 22314-2357
(703) 836-6767

Jobs Requiring Some Specialized Training/ Experience

Crime Laboratory Technician

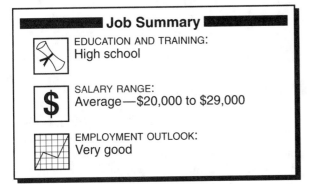

Job Summary

EDUCATION AND TRAINING:
High school

SALARY RANGE:
Average—$20,000 to $29,000

EMPLOYMENT OUTLOOK:
Very good

Definition and Nature of the Work

Crime laboratory technicians, also called police science technicians, help to solve crimes. They use scientific laboratory methods to analyze evidence found at the scene of a crime or accident. Their findings may be the deciding factor in the identification of the guilty and the protection of innocent people who are falsely accused of crimes.

Crime lab technicians work in any of a large number of specialties in the crime laboratory. *Ballistics technicians* examine bullets found in the body of a victim or at the scene of a crime. They match the bullets to the gun believed to have been used in the crime. *Chemical and physical analysis technicians* may examine a chip of paint from an automobile or a piece of glass found in a victim's clothes in order to determine facts about a crime or accident. They also examine hair, earth, blood, narcotics, biological tissues and fluids, and poisons. *Documents technicians* analyze handwriting on forged checks. They also examine the handwriting of blackmail notes and anonymous letters as well as the paper on which they are written. *Instruments technicians* match marks found on the victim to the tool believed to have been used by the suspect in the crime. These instruments range from a crowbar to a stone. *Fingerprint technicians* analyze fingerprints, footprints, and tire treads to help identify criminals. *Photography technicians* go to the scene of the crime to take pictures of the victim and the surrounding area where the crime has occurred. *Polygraph technicians* give lie detector tests to suspects and interpret the results.

Crime lab technicians work closely with agents of the Federal Bureau of Investigation (FBI) and with state and local police officers. Sometimes the evidence from the scene of the crime is collected by detectives, crime investigators, or other police officers, who deliver the evidence to the crime laboratory. However, sometimes police science technicians themselves go to the place where the crime or accident has occurred.

The technician uses many kinds of equipment in the crime lab. A microscope may be used to examine a strand of hair or a piece of glass or to match a suspect's shoe to a shoe print. Infrared photography or ultraviolet light may be used to analyze documents and handwriting or stains of blood on clothes. X-ray machines can reveal the contents of packages without opening them, or they can be used to photograph dental work to help identify a victim. Spectrographs enlarge tiny fragments of evidence ranging from metal to a speck of earth.

The work of crime lab technicians is supervised by crime scientists or professional criminologists. Police science technicians may work in local police

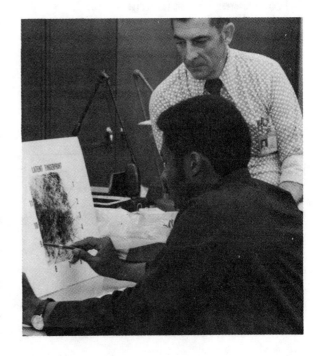

departments or in state, regional, or federal agencies that have crime laboratories. They are civilians with scientific training who aid in law enforcement.

Education and Training Requirements

A strong background in science is very important for the work of crime lab technicians. High school courses that help prepare you for this kind of work include mathematics, biology, chemistry, and physics. Many crime laboratories now require an associate degree in crime technology from a 2-year college. The program of study includes courses in scientific crime detection. More advanced criminology courses can be taken either in 2-year colleges or in 4-year colleges and universities. These courses include investigative photography, fingerprint science, criminal investigation and evidence, criminal law, and court procedures.

Getting the Job

If you want to become a crime lab technician, you can apply directly to any police department that has a crime laboratory. In addition, your college placement office should be helpful. Your state employment office may list job openings. You can also apply to take a civil service test. In addition to passing a test, you may be required to have an interview with the crime scientist who will be your supervisor.

Advancement Possibilities and Employment Outlook

There are several ranks for crime lab technicians that are set by the civil service. To advance from one rank to another, crime lab technicians may need to take a civil service examination. These examinations require advanced knowledge in a technical specialty. For this reason crime lab technicians should study the newest techniques in their field. They can advance through several ranks to a supervisory position.

The employment outlook for crime lab technicians is very good. Their work is recognized as basic to the solution of crimes. Currently there are more jobs available than there are people qualified to fill them.

Working Conditions

Precision and accuracy are absolutely necessary for scientific investigation. There is satisfaction in preparing scientific evidence for court cases. Sometimes crime lab technicians present evidence in court themselves. They also take satisfaction in knowing that their scientific work brings criminals to justice.

Earnings and Benefits

Salaries of crime lab technicians vary with the employer. Most earn from about $20,000 to $29,000 a year. Salaries increase when technicians advance from one rank to another. Excellent health and life insurance, paid vacations, holidays, and sick leave are provided by all law enforcement agencies that employ crime lab technicians.

Where to Go for More Information

International Association of Chiefs of Police
515 North Washington Street
Alexandria, VA 22314-2357
(703) 836-6767

Day Care Worker

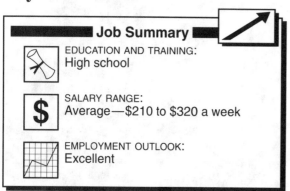

Job Summary

EDUCATION AND TRAINING:
High school

SALARY RANGE:
Average—$210 to $320 a week

EMPLOYMENT OUTLOOK:
Excellent

Definition and Nature of the Work

Workers in day care centers help preschool children up to five years of age in their educational and personal growth. Under a director's supervision, day care workers provide infants with all primary care necessary. For toddlers and older children, they provide both independent and group activities designed to develop the children's self-esteem, encourage curiosity, and offer security and comfort. Workers use a variety of games and exercises to aid in the growth of children's imagination, physical skills, and speech. Day care workers are also concerned with the children's health and nutrition. They may encourage the children to participate in the preparation of breakfast and lunch.

Some day care centers are nonprofit organizations that are operated or subsidized by community or government agencies. Other day care centers are privately owned operations. There are also companies that run day care centers for the children of their employees. In some day care centers, the children's parents are trained to assist staff members.

Education and Training Requirements

The minimum requirement for day care workers is a high school education. Some centers require some form of on-the-job training. Many workers find it useful to enroll in formal education programs that include courses in education, nutrition, home economics, psychology, English, history, biology, and speech. Many 2-year colleges have programs that lead to an associate degree in preschool or early childhood education.

If you are interested in going on to an administrative position in day care, you will need a bachelor's degree. Some centers require teaching certification for higher level positions.

Getting the Job

The best way to find a job in the field is to apply directly to day care centers. Your state department of education can tell you where state-run centers are located. Job openings are often listed in the newspaper. If you have taken college courses or have a bachelor's degree, your school's placement office can help you.

Advancement Possibilities and Employment Outlook

Day care workers usually start as staff assistants. After a period of training they may be given the responsibility of caring for their own group of children. After extensive experience working in day care centers, it is possible to move up to a position of supervisor. Those workers with college degrees in early childhood development or in related fields may start at positions of more responsibility.

The job outlook for day care workers is expected to be excellent through the year 2005. Because more parents are now working outside the home, there is an increasing need for day care workers to look after their children.

Working Conditions

Many day care centers are open 12 hours each day. Their staff members generally work 8-hour shifts. Usually a worker is in charge of a group of from 6 to 12 children. Some centers are in modern buildings specially designed for day care. Others are in remodeled homes or older buildings. Some are on the premises of the factories or businesses that provide care for the children of their employees.

Day care workers must enjoy being with children and must know how to make them feel secure. Day care workers must be able to share ideas and develop programs with other workers on the staff.

Earnings and Benefits

There is a wide range in earnings for day care workers. Wages and benefits vary according to the type of center. Location and the credentials of the workers also affect wages. Generally the salaries are not very high at the centers run as nonprofit organizations. The earnings of day care workers average about $210 to $320 a week.

Where to Go for More Information

National Association for the Education of Young
    Children
1509 Sixteenth Street, NW
Washington, DC 20036-1426
(202) 232-8777

National Child Care Association
1029 Railroad Street
Conyers, GA 30207-5275
(800) 543-7161

Detective

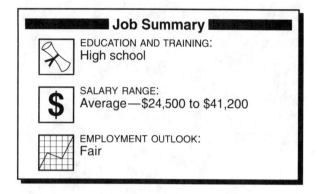

Job Summary

EDUCATION AND TRAINING:
High school

SALARY RANGE:
Average—$24,500 to $41,200

EMPLOYMENT OUTLOOK:
Fair

Definition and Nature of the Work

There are over 250,000 detectives in the United States today. Many work for police departments. Other detectives are employed by business and industry. Detectives investigate, prevent, and solve crimes against people and property.

Police detectives work for police departments and investigate criminals' actions, gather facts for cases, observe suspects, and assist in the arrest of criminals. They develop sources of information to help them solve murders, robberies, narcotics crimes, and other illegal actions.

Many police detectives wear ordinary clothes in order to play an undercover role. They are called *plainclothes detectives*. They often go to places that a suspect is known to frequent, familiarizing themselves with the suspect's habits and actions. For example, a detective assigned to a gambling case might spend a great deal of time at the suspect's favorite bar, posing as another gambler and trying to learn as much as possible about the case. The detective might also have an informer in the neighborhood who provides information on the suspect. Having gathered enough information to make an arrest, the detective can make the arrest with the help of police reinforcements.

Private investigators work for private detective agencies. Most are former police officers, although some are trained by the private agencies themselves. Many lawyers hire private detectives to gather information for court trials. Parents often hire them to locate missing children. Sometimes private detectives work as *bodyguards* for people who are in personal danger. They also are hired by companies to investigate fraud and the passing of bad checks. Many insurance companies hire private detectives to investigate insurance claims. Private detectives gather information from police sources, interview

witnesses, and observe suspects. They have no power to make arrests.

Detectives are also employed by private companies as security guards, house detectives, store detectives, and bouncers. *Store detectives* guard against customer shoplifting and employee theft and make sure that no disturbances are created. *Bouncers* work in restaurants, nightclubs, bowling centers, and other places of entertainment to make sure that order is maintained and bills are paid. *House detectives,* or hotel detectives, insure that hotel guests are not disturbed and evict troublemakers.

Detectives use modern techniques and tools, including computers and elaborate communications systems, to prevent and solve crimes ranging from shoplifting to mass murder.

Education and Training Requirements

A high school education is required for both police and private detectives. While in high school you should take college preparatory subjects such as English, science, math, and social science. It is also helpful to take a foreign language, journalism, and typing. In addition, you should take physical education courses to keep physically fit. If possible you should continue your education at a college where you can major in police science and take courses in criminology and law.

If you want to work on a police force, you will begin as a police officer. Applicants for positions as police officers usually must be at least 21 years old, meet certain height and weight requirements, and be in good physical condition. After you have demonstrated that you have the skills necessary for detective work, you may be assigned to detective duty on a probationary basis. Some police departments require that you pass an exam.

Most police detectives are trained for 6 weeks to several months, depending on the program. If you successfully complete the training program, you will probably be assigned to detective work permanently. During your career you may be required to take refresher courses periodically to update your skills and techniques.

Since many private detectives are former police detectives, their education and training requirements are similar to those of police detectives. Private detectives also learn skills on the job from experienced private detectives. Private agencies may or may not have formal training programs. Private detectives may have to meet licensing requirements before they are eligible to be employed in some states.

Getting the Job

You can apply directly to police departments and private detective agencies in your area. For a job as a private detective apply to hotels, restaurants, manufacturing firms, and department stores. Law firms also use the services of private detectives.

Advancement Possibilities and Employment Outlook

Skilled and experienced police detectives can advance to chief of detectives or chief of police. Private detectives can advance to senior positions in detective agencies or become supervisors of security or detective staffs in private companies. Good detectives can start their own detective agencies.

The employment outlook for detectives is fair. Those who want to work on police forces should keep in mind that they first may have to work as uniformed police officers for several years. Some openings will occur because of growth of police forces, but most openings appear as police detectives retire or change fields.

On the other hand, many more opportunities for private detectives should develop. Companies, hotels, and restaurants increasingly use private detectives to protect their own and their customers' property.

Working Conditions

A detective's job may be exciting and dangerous or routine and safe, depending on the types of assignments. A police detective working on a narcotics smuggling case may be exposed to the threat of physical violence or death. On the other hand, a private detective working as a security guard may only check employee identification cards and handle routine complaints. The work of most detectives falls between these two extremes.

Detectives often work irregular hours, including nights and weekends. Although they may have to work more than 40 hours a week on certain cases, they are generally given time off to compensate for their overtime.

Detectives usually find their work interesting because of the variety of cases on which they work. Although they are exposed to danger at times, they are trained in self-defense. At times they may find

the work discouraging if they cannot solve cases or if they spend a great deal of time pursuing false leads.

Earnings and Benefits

Salaries for detectives vary widely and depend on the location and responsibilities of the job and the detective's experience. Police detectives earn between $24,500 to $41,200 a year. Detectives in supervisory positions may earn $45,000 a year. Generally private detectives make considerably less than police detectives with comparable experience. However, talented private detectives who run their own agencies may earn considerably more.

Detectives may receive benefits such as paid sick leave and vacations, life and health insurance, and retirement pensions. Detectives who have their own agencies must provide their own benefits.

Where to Go for More Information

International Association of Chiefs of Police
515 North Washington Street
Alexandria, VA 22314-2357
(703) 836-6767

Institutional Child Care Worker

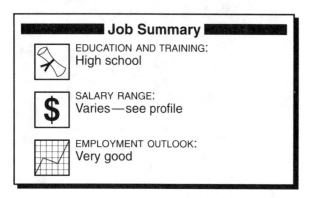

Definition and Nature of the Work

There are hundreds of thousands of children in institutions and many reasons for their being there. Sometimes children need a setting other than their own homes in order to overcome emotional problems they may have developed with their own families. Abandoned children and those whose parents are unable to give them proper care may be placed in institutions by courts or social service agencies. Most of these children are placed in institutions until a good foster home can be provided. Children with physical and mental disabilities may also be institutionalized.

Institutional child care workers help these children by giving them care and guidance in their educational and leisure activities and helping them to overcome handicaps.

Children who live in institutions are usually from six to 18 years old. Generally child care workers are in charge of a cottage with from five to 15 children of the same age. Sometimes a husband and wife team acts as house parents. House parents in both public and charitable institutions live in the cottages with the children. The workers give the children some of the affection ordinarily provided by actual parents. They teach the children to care for their living quarters and see that they are well fed and clothed and in good health. In addition, child care workers follow the program for each child in their unit as it has been planned by medical doctors, psychologists, and other specialists. Child care workers help to rehabilitate children both physically and emotionally.

Some institutional child care workers help mentally retarded children. Child care workers teach them to get along better with other people by living and learning in a group. Some of these children are trained for a job and return to live with their families. Many children with cerebral palsy, epilepsy,

and sight and hearing difficulties also need institutional aid. They undergo various forms of therapy that help them deal with their particular disabilities.

Government agencies and private charities operate institutions for children. Child care workers work in homes for dependent and neglected children, in state schools for the mentally retarded, and in training schools for juvenile delinquents. They work in children's hospitals and in the pediatric units of general hospitals.

Education and Training Requirements

A high school education is the minimum requirement for child care workers. Your grades are not as important as your interest in children, in further education, and in child care training. Many 2-year junior and community colleges offer programs leading to an associate degree. Courses include group work, child and adolescent development, the techniques of child care, and problems faced by children in institutions. Students are supervised in field work in several different types of institutions where they work directly with children. In addition, courses are given in English, social science, science, health, and physical education.

Some state and voluntary institutions send their child care workers to a 2-year college for further training. Sometimes child care workers work part time in the institution while attending college at no cost. Some public agencies give 2 years off with pay for this training. Many institutions also have special seminars and workshops that help workers to learn how to care for institutionalized children.

Getting the Job

Your state mental health department can refer you to institutions seeking child care workers. You can write or visit these institutions to find out the beginning requirements for child care work. If you are a graduate of a 2-year college program, your college placement office can help you find a position. The field work you have done at different kinds of institutions while you were in college will give you personal contacts for job applications. These contacts will also help you decide in which kind of institution you would prefer to work. Volunteer work with children and summer camp jobs are assets for beginning child care workers.

Advancement Possibilities and Employment Outlook

Experienced child care workers who are graduates of a 2-year college program may become supervisors of several child care units. Some child care workers earn a bachelor's degree in psychology or social work in order to advance in the field. A few colleges are developing 4-year programs in the child care field for people who wish to become institution administrators.

The employment outlook for institutional child care workers is very good. There is a continuing demand by institutions for qualified child care workers. Both men and women are needed as house parents and for other child care duties.

Working Conditions

Child care workers usually work 40 hours a week and serve an 8-hour shift a day. In small rural communities they may have a longer workweek and take turns at different 8-hour shifts in the 24-hour day. However, they may be on call 24 hours a day in case of emergencies.

Child care workers must enjoy children and have warm personalities. They need a great deal of patience and an understanding of the problems that institutionalized children have to face. In addition, they must be familiar with the deprived cultural and economic conditions from which many of the children come.

Earnings and Benefits

There is a great variation in the salaries of child care workers, depending on the location of the work and the worker's experience and education. Some child care workers earn from about $12,000 to $20,000 a year. Untrained child care workers may receive less. Generally public institutions pay higher salaries than charitable institutions. Nearly all institutions offer pension plans, health insurance, paid vacations, holidays, and sick leave.

Where to Go for More Information

American Federation of Teachers
555 New Jersey Avenue, NW
Washington, DC 20001
(202) 879-4400

American Speech-Language-Hearing Association
10801 Rockville Pike
Rockville, MD 20852
(301) 897-5700

Council for Exceptional Children
1920 Association Drive
Reston, VA 22091
(703) 620-3660

National Industries for the Blind
524 Hamburg Turnpike, CN 969
Wayne, NJ 07474-0969
(201) 595-9200

Institutional Housekeeper

Job Summary

EDUCATION AND TRAINING:
Varies — see profile

$ SALARY RANGE:
Average — $210 to $375 a week

EMPLOYMENT OUTLOOK:
Good

Definition and Nature of the Work

Institutional housekeepers take care of public residential and service areas. These include the interiors of hotels, hospitals, school dormitories, and government residences, such as embassies. The size of the institution determines the number of workers on the housekeeping staff and the range of duties that an individual housekeeper will perform. Members of a hotel's housekeeping staff may be required only to clean and straighten up guest rooms. Embassy housekeepers may do everything from serving at a banquet to walking dogs.

Institutional housekeepers clean floors, windows, and furniture; make beds and change linens; wash dishes; and take care of indoor plants. Head housekeepers coordinate cleaners, maintenance staff, kitchen workers, and doorkeepers. They may also order linen and cleaning supplies and act as the liaison between management and housekeeping staff.

Education and Training Requirements

While some employers prefer housekeepers to have a high school education, experience and a sense of responsibility are more important than formal qualifications. Institutional housekeepers may supervise a large housekeeping staff, many of whom may not speak English. So foreign language skills and the ability to deal with people will prove useful.

Some vocational schools and community colleges offer training programs in housekeeping. These courses may help in promotion to head housekeeper positions.

Getting the Job

In larger cities employment agencies specialize in finding jobs for domestic and institutional housekeepers. You can register with one of these agencies or apply directly to hotels and hospitals in your area. Also check newspaper ads for these positions.

Advancement Possibilities and Employment Outlook

Housekeepers usually advance by getting a raise in salary. They can also take jobs in institutions that offer better working conditions. Housekeepers can become head housekeepers who supervise other workers. Some housekeepers start their own firms that provide domestic and institutional housekeeping services.

The employment outlook is good through the year 2005. Housekeeping has always been an area with high turnover of personnel, and jobs are always plentiful.

Working Conditions

Some of the work housekeepers do is physically demanding. They may have to lift and carry heavy objects during cleaning. They may spend long hours

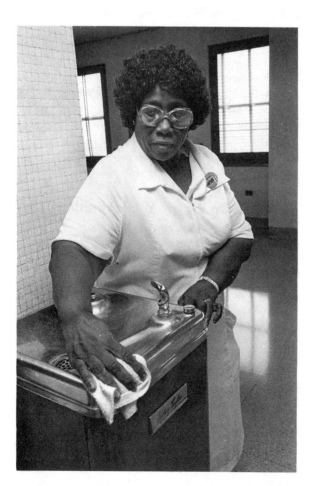

standing. Working hours vary. Institutional house-keepers often begin working before breakfast and finish after the rooms and halls are clean and tidy. Others work later shifts, and may even have accommodations provided.

Earnings and Benefits

Housekeepers earn $210 to $375 a week. The average annual salary for a housekeeper who supervises a large staff is $26,000. There is, however, a wide range of salaries for this job. Most institutional housekeepers receive limited health insurance, retirement plans, and vacation benefits.

Where to Go for More Information

Service Employees International Union
1313 L Street, NW
Washington, DC 20005
(202) 898-3200

Legal Assistant, Corporate

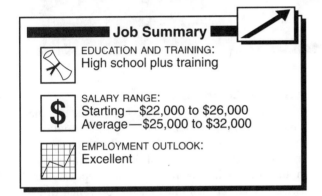

Job Summary

EDUCATION AND TRAINING:
High school plus training

SALARY RANGE:
Starting—$22,000 to $26,000
Average—$25,000 to $32,000

EMPLOYMENT OUTLOOK:
Excellent

Definition and Nature of the Work

The growing complexity of laws governing private industry has made legal services increasingly costly for businesses. Rather than rely entirely on the services of attorneys, many businesses use corporate legal assistants to handle the legal tasks that do not require a lawyer's expertise. Corporate legal assistants, also called corporate paralegal aides or legal technicians, work for banks, insurance companies, manufacturers, and many other types of businesses.

Corporate legal assistants work under the supervision of a corporate attorney to research background material, write reports, and help prepare financial statements and tax returns. Their work may involve them in the preparation of employee contracts, labor and management negotiations, stock option plans, contracts, and mortgages. Other tasks include indexing and summarizing documents and drafting organization documents such as calendars and agendas of board meetings.

The legal profession's use of computers and other technological equipment has grown immensely. Legal assistants are emerging as the trained operators of the computer terminals. Litigation assistants working on a large antitrust case, for example, must handle thousands of documents. Computer storage systems can make the storage and retrieval of documents much more manageable than by conventional methods. Legal assistants can analyze and code the documents and depositions and search and retrieve data from the computer.

Education and Training Requirements

Many businesses require that their corporate legal assistants have specialized training in business law, legal procedures, and terminology. There are many formal paralegal training programs, ranging from 2-year programs to 4-year and postgraduate programs. The 2-year associate degree programs generally require that students have a high school diploma. The 4-year programs often require that the student have a high school diploma and receive a passing score on an entrance examination. To enter paralegal programs offered by law schools, a bachelor's degree and high scores on standardized legal aptitude tests are usually required. Legal assistants who plan to work in business should, in addition, try to take courses in business law, personnel management, finance, or other subjects related to their future work. Legal assistants may take special courses in on-line data base searching. These research data bases facilitate thorough and fast legal research. A trained paralegal can check legal citations and retrieve information. Companies that design legal research computers also employ paralegals as market analysts, sales representatives, and systems programmers.

The National Association of Legal Assistants began sponsoring a certification exam in 1976.

Getting the Job

The placement offices of business schools and legal training programs often post recruiting bulletins and job vacancy announcements for corporate legal assistants. Paralegal associations maintain job banks or referral services and can provide a listing of firms in which jobs are available. Classified ads in newspapers and private and state employment agencies may offer job leads. Another way to find work is to apply directly to those companies that hire corporate legal assistants.

Advancement Possibilities and Employment Outlook

Since law is an increasingly important element in modern business practice, corporate legal assistants often find that their skills form a good base for administrative positions of increased responsibility. Some corporate legal assistants use their specialized knowledge as the foundation for more advanced training at law school.

The employment outlook for corporate legal assistants is excellent through the year 2005. Corporate legal assistants may find work in insurance companies, estate and trust departments of large banks, and real estate companies. Because of increasing costs of legal services, these workers will be in high demand to perform the auxiliary tasks associated with corporate legal matters. The growth of prepaid legal plans will also increase the number of jobs available.

Working Conditions

People employed as corporate legal assistants may have to handle confidential business information in the course of their work, so an ability to use discretion is important. Most of their work takes place in an office or in law libraries, but corporate legal assistants sometimes must travel to branch offices and other locations. Overtime work beyond the standard 35- or 40-hour workweek may occasionally be required.

Earnings and Benefits

Entry-level salaries range from $22,000 to $26,000 a year, leading up to a salary of $25,000 to $32,000 a year for experienced corporate legal assistants. Benefits generally include paid holidays and vacations, health and life insurance, and pension plans.

Where to Go for More Information

American Bar Association
750 North Lake Shore Drive
Chicago, IL 60611
(312) 988-5000

National Association of Legal Assistants
1516 South Boston Avenue, Suite 200
Tulsa, OK 74119-4013
(918) 587-6828

National Association of Paralegal Personnel
P.O. Box 8202
Northfield, IL 60093
(312) 973-7712

Paralegal Aide

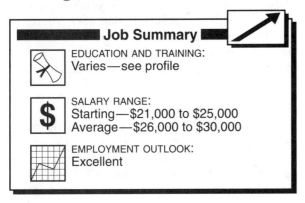

Definition and Nature of the Work

Paralegal aides assist lawyers in the details of legal research. They perform their work under the supervision of a lawyer or a senior paralegal. Their work differs from that of legal secretaries, who focus primarily on the clerical functions in a law office, such as typing, filing, and receiving clients. Paralegal aides research public documents, records, and law books for materials that the lawyers will use in preparing their cases. They may prepare probate inventories (investigations of the validity of wills) and inheritance and income tax returns, or they may contact clients for information the lawyers need for specific legal cases. Paralegal aides also analyze and follow procedural problems that arise in different kinds of law cases. For example, many cases are settled out of court by the opposing attorneys. Paralegal aides may research a particular case to see whether it is to their client's advantage to settle out of court or go before a judge. Computerized legal research is another area where a paralegal aide may play an essential role. Paralegals now receive specialized training in searching online data bases so they can operate computer-assisted legal research systems.

Private law firms are the largest employers of paralegal aides. These workers are also employed by judges and various government agencies. The duties of those workers will vary.

Education and Training Requirements

Paralegal aides must have some knowledge of law, legal procedures, and legal terminology, and they must be able to apply this knowledge to their work. There are several hundred paralegal training programs nationwide. Most of the programs are completed in 2 years and require a high school diploma for admission. Other training programs are given by 4-year colleges, universities, and law schools. For admission to a paralegal training program offered by a law school, a college degree and high scores on an entrance examination are usually required. The length of time for training may vary from a few months for a special course to 4 years or more. Courses include law office management, accounting, insurance, and torts. The American Bar Association approves those legal aide training programs that meet stringent quality criteria.

Paralegal aides who begin as legal secretaries can pick up valuable legal experience. They may take legal courses while working as legal secretaries in order to move up to the position of paralegal aide.

Getting the Job

You should register with your school placement office where lawyers and law firms send their requests for paralegal aides. Or you may apply directly to a law firm or lawyer for any staff openings that may occur. Paralegal associations maintain job banks and can provide listings of private and public employers. If you are interested in a government position, you can apply to take the necessary civil service test.

Advancement Possibilities and Employment Outlook

Individual law firms usually set their own standards for salary increases corresponding to the paralegal aide's experience and responsibilities. Moving from a small law firm to a larger one may provide better advancement possibilities. In a large law firm a paralegal aide may progress from researching minor legal matters to handling tasks of great responsibility.

Experienced paralegal aides may advance to positions with supervisory responsibility over other legal assistants. Some paralegal aides advance by entering law school and becoming attorneys.

The employment outlook for paralegal aides is excellent through the year 2005. The demand for legal services continues to grow rapidly. Well-trained paralegal aides are needed to perform many tasks that will ease the work loads of lawyers. In addition to private law firms, consumer organizations, government agencies, and the court system also employ paralegal aides. The best opportunities will be for graduates of formal paralegal programs.

Working Conditions

Paralegal aides must be mature and responsible people. Their work requires intelligence and analytical ability. Those individuals who work in the legal field must exercise discretion and confidentiality. A keen interest in the law is necessary. Paralegal aides enjoy working with clients and take a special interest in many of the cases. They may attend formal meetings with clients and be present at court proceedings.

Most paralegal aides work full time, although those who are training to be lawyers may work only part time. Full-time paralegal aide work consists of 8-hour days, 5 days a week. However, sometimes an important case requires special attention, and paralegal aides may have to work overtime.

Earnings and Benefits

Earnings for paralegal aides vary depending on the size of the employer, with larger firms generally paying higher salaries. Beginning salaries for paralegal aides average from $21,000 to $25,000 a year. Experienced paralegal aides often earn $26,000 to $30,000 or more a year. The average annual salary for paralegal aides working for the federal government is $37,600.

Many employers provide benefits that include paid vacations and holidays, life and health insurance, and pension plans.

Where to Go for More Information

American Bar Association
750 North Lake Shore Drive
Chicago, IL 60611
(312) 988-5000

National Association of Legal Assistants
1516 South Boston Avenue, Suite 200
Tulsa, OK 74119-4013
(918) 587-6828

National Association of Paralegal Personnel
P.O. Box 8202
Northfield, IL 60093
(312) 973-7712

Shorthand Reporter

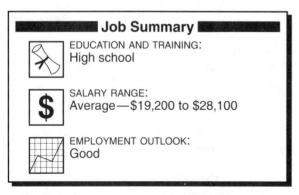

▚▚▚▚ Job Summary ▚▚▚▚

EDUCATION AND TRAINING:
High school

SALARY RANGE:
Average—$19,200 to $28,100

EMPLOYMENT OUTLOOK:
Good

Definition and Nature of the Work

Shorthand reporters are specialized stenographers who record all the words that are spoken during a legal or business proceeding. They record by writing in shorthand, which is the use of symbols or abbreviations. Some shorthand reporters use stenotype machines. When they use stenotype machines, they strike one or more of the machine's 21 keys at a time and their notes come out on a pad or roll of paper. After they have recorded what has been said, they transcribe (translate into words) their notes into reports.

About one-half of all shorthand reporters are *court reporters*. They work for courts at all levels, ranging from local traffic courts to the United States Supreme Court. They sit at a table near the witness, taking down every word either by hand or by machine. Since their records are official, speed and accuracy are essential. During a trial they are often asked to read aloud from their notes. After the trial the reporter dictates the notes into a dictating machine for later transcription.

Hearing reporters perform similar tasks for government agencies. A hearing is similar to a trial. The parties are often represented by lawyers who plead the case and question witnesses. *Legislative reporters* work for the federal or state legislatures, taking down the debates and speeches of the legislators.

General, or *freelance, reporters* are either in business for themselves or work for an agency of shorthand reporters. They are hired on a fee basis to cover arbitration hearings, trade association meetings, and the meetings of boards of directors and stockholders. Courts and government agencies often hire general reporters on a temporary basis. Recording depositions (pretrial examinations) is a major part of the general reporter's work.

Education and Training Requirements

A high school diploma or its equivalent is required to become a shorthand reporter. The major qualification for this type of work is exceptional stenographic skills. Most shorthand reporting jobs require at least 160 words of dictation a minute. Good typing is also important. To achieve these skills, most shorthand reporters attend a 2-year training program.

Most business and secretarial schools offer programs in shorthand reporting. A training program generally includes courses in shorthand, typing, transcribing, medical terminology, legal and Latin words and phrases, business law, English grammar and punctuation, editing, court procedure, and economics. Shorthand reporters are usually trained to use the stenotype machine rather than manual shorthand.

Getting the Job

If you are a competent shorthand reporter, you will have no trouble getting a job after you complete your training program. Your school's placement office will help you. You may find good opportunities while working for a freelance reporter who has already built up a large clientele.

The National Shorthand Reporters Association can furnish you with information about agencies and firms that need reporters. This service is free to members and nonmembers.

You can apply to take a federal civil service examination if you wish to work for one of the federal agencies. You also need to take an examination if you wish to work for state courts or agencies. Also check with your state employment service for help finding a job. Many states require that you take a shorthand speed test for certification.

Advancement Possibilities and Employment Outlook

Under civil service regulations shorthand reporters must accumulate experience and take another examination to advance. Those who wish to transfer from federal or state agencies to federal courts must meet the standards set by the courts.

The outlook for shorthand reporters is good. There will be a steady demand for qualified shorthand reporters through the year 2005 as business and government expansion increases the number of hearings, trials, and conferences that must be recorded. There may be some competition for entry-level positions due to advances in transcribing testimony. Government budget constraints may slow growth in demand somewhat.

Working Conditions

Good shorthand reporters can usually choose the type of work and the part of the country in which they would like to work. There are opportunities in all parts of the country and in foreign countries as well.

In large cities court reporters are generally employed by one court. In smaller, less populated areas where one judge serves many courts, the reporter travels the circuit. The court reporter's work is varied since there are so many different types of cases, ranging from a civil case, such as an automobile accident, to a criminal case, such as a murder trial.

Good organization, careful attention to detail, accuracy, speed, a sense of responsibility, and an even disposition are all extremely important. A reporter must be able to record all types of speech no matter how many distractions there are.

Sometimes there is a lull between assignments when the work becomes routine. The reporter must be patient and flexible enough to adjust to both the slow and demanding paces.

Earnings and Benefits

Earnings vary widely according to the location and nature of the work. Court reporters earn an average of $19,200 to $28,100 a year. Some reporters with many years of experience can earn up to $50,000 a year. By working hard, freelance reporters can earn more than other types of reporters. However, since they are not permanently on staff, they are not eligible for employee-sponsored benefits such as insurance and pension plans. All federally employed shorthand reporters receive paid holidays and vacations, health insurance, and pension plans.

Where to Go for More Information

National Court Reporters Association
8224 Old Courthouse Road
Vienna, VA 22182-3808
(703) 556-6272

Teacher's Aide

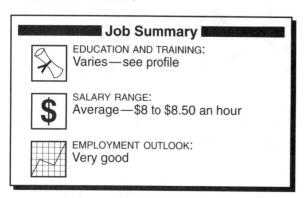

Job Summary

EDUCATION AND TRAINING:
Varies—see profile

SALARY RANGE:
Average—$8 to $8.50 an hour

EMPLOYMENT OUTLOOK:
Very good

Definition and Nature of the Work

Teacher's aides assist certified teachers in schools. All teacher's aides work under the guidance and supervision of the classroom teacher or school administrator to whom they are assigned. Their assistance enables teachers to devote more time to teaching.

Noninstructional teacher's aides act as general assistants for teachers. Their duties vary with their qualifications and the needs of the school in which they work. Noninstructional teacher's aides do many of the simple housekeeping tasks that need to be done in every classroom. They put the classroom in order after each class session. They pass out and put away supplies such as paper, pencils, and textbooks, and they prepare bulletin boards. Teacher's aides also help with clerical tasks. They take attendance, keep the roll book, and keep health records up to date. They do typing and filing in the school office and help students to fill out library cards. They act as monitors who supervise children in study halls and during test periods. They supervise students on the playground and to and from the school bus.

Technical aides are in charge of audiovisual equipment such as television sets, film projectors, tape recorders, and phonographs. They set up the equipment and operate it during the lesson.

Many schools that employ teacher's aides provide 1- or 2-week preservice training courses. This training helps the aides to understand the tasks they will perform in the school and to become familiar with the educational policies of the school. Pretraining programs include information on understanding children at different age levels and the learning process. In addition, most schools provide training while the teacher's aides are working. In-service training sessions may be workshops or conferences with teachers and other aides that are held throughout the school year. During these meetings problems that arise in the classroom are discussed. For example, teacher's aides may be taught how to handle disciplinary problems.

Instructional teacher's aides help teach the classes. Those who play the piano aid in music instruction. Aides who can draw help in art classes. Teacher's aides who have some college training may take charge of the classroom while the teacher works with smaller groups, or they may work with individual students who have been absent or need special help. Sometimes instructional teacher's aides correct papers or tests by using the correction key supplied by the teacher. In many schools they help to teach reading, math, spelling, and social studies.

Teacher's aides may be employed in preschool classrooms, in elementary schools, or in junior and senior high schools. Generally they are concentrated in the early grades.

Education and Training Requirements

Teacher's aides have a wide range of educational backgrounds. The education that is required varies in each school district depending on the duties to be performed, the grade level at which the teacher's aide assists, and the type of school district. A high school diploma is often needed, and some schools require that aides have some college background. Generally more training is required for more responsible jobs.

Newly hired teacher's aides usually are given some form of on-the-job training to prepare them for their duties. Some 2-year community colleges offer a teacher's aide program leading to an associate degree. These programs include courses in educational psychology and the history of education as well as courses in the materials and methods of teaching English, biology, math, art, and music. Some states have instituted certification procedures for teacher's aides.

Getting the Job

The best way to apply for a position as a teacher's aide is through the administration office of the school district in which you wish to work. Sometimes job openings for teacher's aides are listed with the state employment office or in local newspapers. Applicants are interviewed by either the classroom teacher or a school administrator. Usually the tasks you will be expected to perform are clearly defined for you in a job specification sheet.

Advancement Possibilities and Employment Outlook

Advancement in the form of higher earnings and more responsibility usually comes with increased experience. Advancement possibilities for teacher's aides who further their education also are very good.

A number of teacher's aides advance by taking college courses leading to a bachelor's degree. Aides are then eligible to become fully certified professional teachers. Teachers acquire certification by

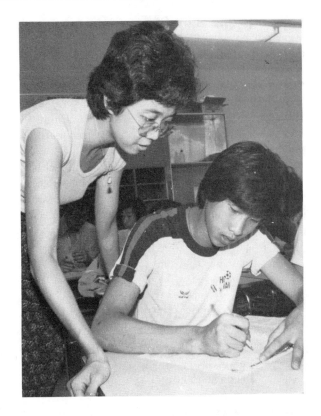

passing a special examination that is given to all people seeking to teach in their state.

Projected growth in elementary school enrollments should increase the demand for teacher's aides, especially in the southern and western states. Since turnover is relatively high among teacher's aides, many openings will occur to replace aides who leave their jobs. However, the job outlook is heavily dependent on the economy and the funds available for hiring. When school districts or local school boards have the necessary funds available, they can hire more teacher's aides. Some school districts receive government grants to finance teacher's aides' positions.

Working Conditions

Teacher's aides work the full school day, 5 days a week. The school year generally runs from September to June. Some teacher's aides assist teachers during the summer or find other jobs. Aides must enjoy working with children or young people, and they must be able to work with supervising teachers, school administrators, and parents. They have to be willing to follow the directions of supervisors. Many teacher's aides find their work rewarding because they have the satisfaction of helping all kinds of children progress in their education.

Earnings and Benefits

Salaries vary depending on the location of the work and the qualifications and experience of the teacher's aide. The wages for teacher's aides whose duties include some instructional tasks average about $8.50 an hour. The earnings for teacher's aides involved in nonteaching activities average about $8 an hour. Some aides with experience may earn as much as $16,000 a year.

Benefits are not always provided for teacher's aides. In school districts where they are available, benefits generally include paid holidays and vacations, medical and hospital insurance, and pension plans.

Where to Go for More Information

American Counseling Association
5999 Stevenson Avenue
Alexandria, VA 22304
(703) 823-9800

American Federation of Teachers
555 New Jersey Avenue, NW
Washington, DC 20001
(202) 879-4400

National Education Association of the U.S.
1201 Sixteenth Street, NW
Washington, DC 20036-3290
(202) 833-4000

Youth Organization Worker

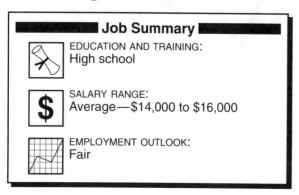

Job Summary
EDUCATION AND TRAINING: High school
SALARY RANGE: Average—$14,000 to $16,000
EMPLOYMENT OUTLOOK: Fair

Definition and Nature of the Work

The YMCA down the street, the Boy Scout troop that meets in the church basement, and the teen center just opened in the civic center are all managed by youth organization workers. These workers are employed by many different organizations, from the Police Athletic League to the 4-H Club, but they all share the goal of helping young people enjoy themselves and grow to become responsible adults.

Youth organization workers are employed full time or part time, as salaried employees or as volunteers. In large organizations, such as Hillel or the Girl Scouts of America, both full-time and part-time workers are employed. Full-time workers manage the organization on a daily basis. Executive directors raise funds, develop new programs, balance budgets, plan for new buildings, and supervise other workers. Activities and program directors plan specific programs for youths and organize other workers to help run these programs.

Education and Training Requirements

You need at least a high school education for most youth organization jobs. Most full-time activities and program directors have an associate degree or a bachelor's degree. Almost all executive directors have a bachelor's degree.

While in high school you should take courses in English, math, science, and social studies. In college you should take courses in sociology, child psychology, recreation, public speaking, art, music, and physical education. Many youth organization workers earn a degree in recreation with a special emphasis in youth work.

During the summers you can gain valuable experience by working as a volunteer for any youth agency. You might work as a day camp counselor, a municipal recreation helper, or an aide in a church youth fellowship organization.

Getting the Job

You can apply directly to any youth agency for a job as a youth organization worker. Your school placement office may also be able to help you find a job. You can also apply to the national or regional headquarters of organizations such as the Boy Scouts of America or the YMCA.

Advancement Possibilities and Employment Outlook

The possibilities for advancement in youth organization work are good. Most workers begin their career as an assistant to a program or recreation director. With experience they are promoted to program or recreation director. Those who have the skill and training that are required may be promoted to executive director of a youth agency.

There is a great need for youth organization workers. However, most youth organizations are funded through private grants and charitable donations. Opportunities in the field depend on available funds. Currently grants and donations have declined due to changes in the tax law.

Working Conditions

Working conditions for youth organization workers vary. Some work a 5-day, 40-hour week. Others work mainly at night and on weekends. Workers generally spend a good deal of time outdoors, although youth organization executives may work indoors most of the time.

Youth organization workers generally must be in good physical condition, since much of the work involves supervising recreation programs for youngsters. They must be patient, kind, and fun-loving. Above all, youth organization workers must enjoy working with youngsters.

Earnings and Benefits

Salaries for youth organization workers vary widely and depend on the location and duties of the job and the experience of the worker. Many youth organization workers with a college degree earn average salaries of about $14,000 to $16,000 a year. Supervisors may earn about $17,000 to $22,000 or more a year. Part-time workers and those without a college degree can expect to earn less.

Youth organization workers generally receive benefits such as paid sick leave and vacations, life and health insurance, and retirement pensions.

Where to Go for More Information

American Alliance for Health, Physical Education, Recreation and Dance
1900 Association Drive
Reston, VA 22091
(703) 476-3400

National Community Education Association
3929 Old Lee Highway, Suite 91-A
Alexandria, VA 22030-2401
(703) 359-8973

Jobs Requiring Advanced Training/ Experience

Adult Education Worker

Job Summary

EDUCATION AND TRAINING:
College

SALARY RANGE:
Average—$18,700 to $38,800

EMPLOYMENT OUTLOOK:
Very good

Definition and Nature of the Work

Adult education workers administer and teach in programs set up for community members who are over 18 years of age. Adult education workers teach evening and night classes. Many of these teachers work for the evening division of public high schools. Others work for community colleges, private and religious organizations, and community groups.

The aim of the program and range of subjects vary from one school to another. However, most schools offer adult basic education and continuing education. Basic education courses are intended for people who are too old to qualify for regular high school attendance. Teachers provide instruction in reading, writing, arithmetic, and, in some schools, English as a second language. These courses lead to a general equivalency diploma (GED), which is comparable to a high school diploma.

Continuing education, on the other hand, is generally intended for people who have completed their basic education. Continuing education courses teach specific skills that range from typing to flower arranging. Courses in literature, history, and Bible interpretation may also be offered. The courses offered depend on the needs of the community.

Education and Training Requirements

Requirements vary by state and employer. Basic education workers who teach in public high schools may need teacher certification. Some basic education teachers need only a bachelor's degree. Administrators may need teaching experience and advanced degrees such as a master's or a doctoral degree in community education and administration.

Many continuing education programs, however, need workers with specific skills rather than those with academic degrees. A program that needs someone to teach ceramics is more likely to hire an experienced potter than a teacher with college training and little experience with ceramics.

Getting the Job

If you have a specific skill you would like to teach, write your local director of community schools or school board and propose a course. If you are interested in teaching basic education, you can write to the school board and ask about openings. Applications can be sent directly to the superintendent of schools. Teaching positions for private courses often become known by word of mouth. Openings are sometimes listed in local newspapers or with the state employment service.

Advancement Possibilities and Employment Outlook

Generally continuing education teachers begin by working part time. They may decide to pursue teaching on a full-time basis or become program administrators. Advancement to other kinds of teaching positions may require further education and perhaps certification in some cases. Basic education workers can also use their experience to become administrators. However, there are few administrative jobs.

The job outlook is very good. Many schools that want to put their facilities to best use are starting evening classes. Growth in the field is likely to continue through the year 2005.

Working Conditions

Many adult education personnel work part time. They generally teach 1 or 2 courses a week. Most people teach in addition to holding a full-time job. They usually teach in the evening because both students and teachers generally work during the day.

Sessions usually last from 1 to 3 hours and courses meet from 1 to 5 times a week. The size of their classes ranges from 3 to 60 students. Teachers may lecture or hold discussions or workshops. Classes are most often held in public high schools, community colleges, or at the facilities of community organizations. Some are conducted in prisons and private homes.

Earnings and Benefits

Workers are often paid by the hour and their wage varies with each school, state, or private sponsor. Adult education workers often earn about $18,700 to $38,800 a year. Adult education workers who work part time receive about $300 a week. In some programs teachers receive a flat fee per course. There are generally few, if any, benefits for part-time workers.

Where to Go for More Information

American Counseling Association
5999 Stevenson Avenue
Alexandria, VA 22304
(703) 823-9800

National Community Education Association
3929 Old Lee Highway, Suite 91-A
Fairfax, VA 22030-2401
(703) 359-8973

National Education Association of the U.S.
1201 Sixteenth Street, NW
Washington, DC 20036-3290
(202) 833-4000

City Manager

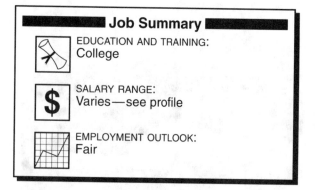

Job Summary

EDUCATION AND TRAINING:
College

SALARY RANGE:
Varies—see profile

EMPLOYMENT OUTLOOK:
Fair

Definition and Nature of the Work

City managers are professional administrators who bring sound managerial practices to government. They work to make city governments operate with the same efficiency with which businesses are run. Managers keep their cities running smoothly from day to day despite legislative or political upsets that may occur. City managers are appointed by city councils or mayors to carry out the policies of elected officials. City managers must take direction from the elected representatives of their cities. Most managers report to the city council; others report to the mayor. While managers may make proposals to the mayor or council, they are not authorized to take action on their own. Furthermore, they do not take sides publicly in political disputes. Most city managers are employed by the government of small and medium-sized cities—generally those with populations of 10,000 to 500,000 people.

City managers direct the various services provided by the city and administer government functions. They are in charge of preparing budgets, hiring administrative officers, and keeping records. They supervise department heads such as tax collectors, police commissioners, and the chiefs of fire protection, traffic, and sanitation. Managers may spend a great deal of their time proposing ways to cut or control the costs of services. Since many cities employ great numbers of unionized teachers, police

officers, fire fighters, and refuse workers, city managers may be heavily involved in labor relations and contract negotiations. City managers often meet with business and community groups to explain city policies and hear citizens' demands.

Because they deal with a broad range of problems, city managers must be familiar with many aspects of government and public works. However, they may call in consultants to advise on specific problems such as urban renewal. City managers try to improve efficiency by using new methods and procedures. For example, the city council directs the city manager to cut costs in the tax collection system. After reviewing the system and considering alternatives, the city manager decides to replace the existing method of billing taxes with a data processing system that uses computers. Then the city manager hires a consulting firm of computer experts to direct the change from one system to another. Before putting the plan into action, however, the manager must present it to the city council for approval.

Most city managers have assistant city managers and administrative assistants on their staff. In a small city there may be only a city manager and one administrative assistant. In a large city the manager may have an assistant city manager for each of several important departments such as transportation and education.

Education and Training Requirements

You must have a college education to become a city manager. College courses in economics, sociology, statistics, urban planning, political science, finance, and management may prove useful. However, most city councils and mayors prefer to hire those who have a master's degree in public administration. Some graduate programs in the field require internships that last from 6 to 12 months in addition to other academic requirements. Internships give students a chance to work in city governments as assistants to city managers, enabling them to get practical knowledge in the field as well as work experience that may help them find jobs.

Recent graduates generally expand their skills by working as administrative assistants or assistant city managers. They are given more responsibility as they gain more experience.

Getting the Job

Internship jobs sometimes lead to permanent jobs after graduation. Your college placement office may be able to help you find a job in city management. Professional organizations and journals may list job openings for city managers. You may also apply directly to the manager of a city in which you would like to work.

Advancement Possibilities and Employment Outlook

City managers can take jobs in larger cities in which the management problems are more complex and the work is more challenging. Others go into related fields. For example, some become teachers in colleges and universities.

There are about 11,000 city managers in this country. Many more are employed as assistants. As more cities employ city managers, qualified people will be needed in greater numbers to fill new positions. However, an increase in the number of qualified applicants available will create stiff competition for the available jobs through the year 2005. Those with a master's degree will have the best opportunities.

Working Conditions

City managers work long hours to serve the needs of their cities. They work under pressure to carry out the policies and programs of their governments. They are also in a position to feel pressure from civic groups and labor unions. Managers must be available when crises develop. City managers spend most of their time in the office. Their work involves a great deal of contact with the public and with others in government. Sometimes they travel to attend meetings and conferences.

Earnings and Benefits

Salaries vary depending on the size of the city and the amount of responsibility a manager has. Most assistant city managers earn salaries ranging from about $25,000 to $35,000 a year. Most city managers earn between about $35,000 and $60,000 a year. Annual salaries for managers of cities with more than 1 million inhabitants range up to $127,000. Benefits include paid holidays and vacations, health insurance, and pension plans.

Where to Go for More Information

International City/County Management Association
777 North Capitol Street, NE, Suite 500
Washington, DC 20002-4201
(202) 289-4262

United States Conference of Mayors
1620 Eye Street, NW
Washington, DC 20006
(202) 293-7330

College Student Personnel Worker

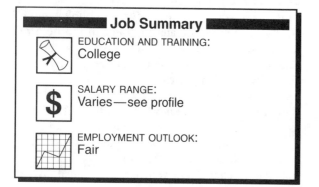

Job Summary

EDUCATION AND TRAINING:
College

SALARY RANGE:
Varies—see profile

EMPLOYMENT OUTLOOK:
Fair

Definition and Nature of the Work

Modern colleges and universities are such large and complex institutions that they require staffs of trained workers to coordinate activities. College student personnel workers are go-betweens who reconcile the needs of the students with the requirements of the administration. College student personnel workers are active in every phase of college life. They carry out administrative policies in the day-to-day operation of the school and keep the administration informed of the effect its policies have on the students. College student personnel workers also interpret student opinion to decision makers in the college or university.

Deans of students coordinate the administrative staff and assist college presidents in planning college policy. Deans evaluate both academic and nonacademic student programs. *College admissions officers* interview applicants and read their application forms and essays to decide whether the college will admit them. Admissions officers judge prospective students in terms of the needs of the individual college. Furthermore, they try to determine whether the school will meet the needs of the student. *Registrars* keep records of all student grades and transcripts. This is primarily an office job, so registrars must be familiar with record-keeping methods, budgeting, and other office procedures.

College placement counselors help to place students and alumni in jobs; they also help students determine career goals and the education required to meet those goals. Placement counselors administer occupational interest tests and interview students. They set up exhibits and interviews when corporation representatives visit the campus to recruit students. *Financial aid officers* help students obtain scholarships and government loans. *Student counselors* offer counseling services to students who are experiencing emotional difficulties because of academic or other problems. *Foreign student advisers* work with international students by helping them adjust to the college both socially and academically. *Student center staff members* help students to plan programs and activities. Some student centers house dining facilities and bookstores in addition to recreational facilities. In such cases staff members are responsible for the maintenance of these facilities.

Education and Training Requirements

College student personnel workers generally have at least a bachelor's degree. College and graduate school courses in administration, educational psychology, and student personnel work can prove extremely helpful. Workers with little or no experience usually start as assistants. People with graduate training in counseling or psychology generally work in the various counseling jobs. Higher administrative jobs often require a doctoral degree as well as several years of experience in higher education.

Getting the Job

Your college or graduate school placement office may have information on college student personnel positions. Your own college may have openings on its staff. Private employment agencies and newspaper want ads sometimes list these openings.

Advancement Possibilities and Employment Outlook

In large universities there are generally several members in a department or office such as the registrar's office. With experience, an assistant may become head of the department. Further education and experience can qualify workers for top-level posts such as dean of students or college president. College administrators sometimes go on to government posts in departments of education.

The job outlook for college student personnel workers is fair. Some new jobs will become available each year; there will also be replacement positions as workers retire or leave the field. How-

ever, staff reductions are expected overall due to tightened budgets and declining enrollments in many 4-year institutions. Competition among job seekers will be keen.

Working Conditions

Each college student personnel job is somewhat different. However, all the jobs involve contact with students, so workers should enjoy working with people. Some staff members combine their administrative duties with teaching. Most college student personnel workers work at least 40 hours a week. Top-level positions require many extra hours for consultations, meetings, and attendance at college functions.

Earnings and Benefits

Salaries vary with the individual institution and the specific job. Annual salaries of college student personnel workers range from about $24,000 to $41,500 for student counselors to about $47,500 for admissions officers and registrars. Benefits include sabbatical leave in some schools, paid vacations, and health and retirement plans.

Where to Go for More Information

American Counseling Association
5999 Stevenson Avenue
Alexandria, VA 22304
(703) 823-9800

National Association for Women in Education
1325 Eighteenth Street, NW, Suite 210
Washington, DC 20036-6511
(202) 659-9330

National Association of College Admission
 Counselors
1631 Prince Street
Alexandria, VA 22314
(703) 836-2222

Criminologist

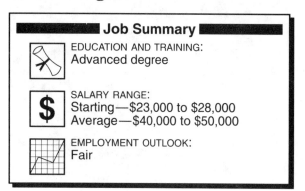

Job Summary

EDUCATION AND TRAINING:
Advanced degree

SALARY RANGE:
Starting—$23,000 to $28,000
Average—$40,000 to $50,000

EMPLOYMENT OUTLOOK:
Fair

Definition and Nature of the Work

Criminologists study criminal laws, the social and psychological conditions that cause crime, the criminals themselves, and methods of rehabilitation. One branch of criminology, called criminalistics, develops ways to detect and solve crime. All criminologists work toward the same ends: to insure that criminal laws are just and practical, to protect society, and to help criminals reenter society as useful citizens.

Criminologists use several procedures to study crime and develop practical methods to prevent criminal actions and to control and treat criminals. They study data about crimes, arrests, and convictions in order to determine the social background from which most criminals come. Are most criminals poor? Why do some members of a social class commit crimes? By understanding the role that social background plays in crime, criminologists can study ways to change social conditions so that crime can be diminished.

Some criminologists study the criminals themselves. Criminals' personal histories may reveal incidents that influenced them. Because of their knowledge of case histories, criminologists are able to suggest ways to help individuals before they turn to crime.

Other criminologists study the history and theories of crime and the nature of the criminal justice system. Criminologists investigate what effects being arrested or convicted have on people. One aim of these investigations is to try to find ways to prevent

someone who is sent to prison for a minor crime from being influenced by hardened criminals. Criminologists may point out that certain punishments do not prevent crime.

Criminologists interested in crime detection develop scientific methods to study clues. Lie-detector tests and fingerprinting are advances made by crime researchers. When a crime is committed, these and other techniques are used by crime laboratory technicians to identify the criminal.

Criminologists work in a variety of places. They are employed by colleges or universities in teaching and research. Some are administrators of large social agencies or prisons. Some plan and direct juvenile and adult crime-prevention projects. A few criminologists put their theoretical knowledge to practical use as police commissioners.

Education and Training Requirements

You will need a master's or a doctoral degree in subjects related to criminology. Some of these graduate courses include abnormal psychology, community studies, criminal law, the analysis of court cases to understand crime and justice, juvenile delinquency, police science, and statistics.

Getting the Job

Nearly all public and private agencies, universities, and colleges list their job openings with college or university placement services. You can also apply directly to the agencies or colleges that hire people in this field. Other good sources for job openings are professional organizations.

Advancement Possibilities and Employment Outlook

Advancement in the field of criminology depends on education and experience. A doctoral degree is generally required for a top position as a professor, director of a research department, administrator of a large social agency or special crime-prevention project, or police commissioner.

There are comparatively few positions for criminologists. The number of new jobs in the field will depend on the amount of public funding for crime-prevention projects and agencies.

Working Conditions

Criminologists in social agencies generally work in offices. Those who are involved in casework may do counseling or interview criminals. Those in the field of criminalistics work in laboratories. Administrators, such as police commissioners, may be in the public eye. Because of the public's concern about crime, administrators may be under a great deal of pressure. Criminologists must keep abreast of new developments in their field. They generally work many more than 40 hours a week.

Earnings and Benefits

Salaries of criminologists vary according to the responsibilities of the job and the size of the population served. Both training and experience affect criminologists' earnings. Beginning criminologists earn about $23,000 to $28,000 a year. Those with experience can earn from about $40,000 to $50,000 a year. Police commissioners, prison administrators, and others who administer public or private agencies or crime-prevention projects earn higher salaries. Those who work as consultants on special projects are paid on a fee basis. Pension plans, health insurance, and paid holidays and vacations are generally available.

Where to Go for More Information

American Sociological Association
1722 N Street, NW
Washington, DC 20036
(202) 833-3410

National Council on Crime and Delinquency
685 Market Street, Suite 620
San Francisco, CA 94105
(415) 896-6223

Customs Worker

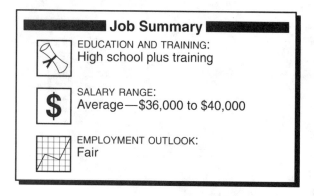

Job Summary

EDUCATION AND TRAINING:
High school plus training

SALARY RANGE:
Average—$36,000 to $40,000

EMPLOYMENT OUTLOOK:
Fair

Definition and Nature of the Work

Customs workers enforce the laws governing the import and export of goods. Most of these laws are designed to protect citizens' health and to raise revenues for the federal government. Some tariff laws protect selected businesses from foreign competition. Occasionally, under congressional order, customs workers enforce boycotts of certain nations' goods for political reasons. Overall, the task of customs workers is to protect the interests of the American people.

There are many categories of customs workers. *Customs inspectors* look for banned or taxable items in tourists' belongings and in the cargo of ships and planes. For example, it is against the law to bring narcotics into the country. Inspectors check to see whether anyone is trying to smuggle in such illegal items. Inspectors have other duties also. Tourists must pay taxes, or duties, if they bring back goods whose value exceeds a certain limit. Inspectors make sure that the tourists declare the true value of goods they are bringing into the country. Then the inspectors collect the tax. If items are being brought into the country illegally, it is the job of customs inspectors to confiscate them.

Customs agents investigate violations of the law. They are highly trained in the field of investigation. In some cases agents and inspectors cooperate on an investigation by combining their powers of observation and action. *Import specialists* perform the paperwork necessary for the processing and issuing of customs documents. They also classify goods. They decide how much duty is owed by interpreting the relevant customs regulations. Since a wide variety of merchandise passes through United States borders and ports of entry, import specialists often become expert in one or two fields of goods, such as antiques or machinery.

Education and Training Requirements

Most customs workers must be at least 21 years old. They must be United States citizens. High school coursework in foreign languages, English, and history may be useful. College-level courses in foreign languages and business are also helpful. Since a majority of customs work involves interpreting and enforcing the law, some knowledge of legal affairs is valuable. All customs workers must have a high school diploma and some further education or experience. Customs inspectors and import specialists generally need either a bachelor's degree or 3 years of experience relating to customs control. They may also be required to pass a civil service examination. Customs agents usually have at least a bachelor's degree or prior law enforcement experience, including several years of experience in criminal investigation.

Getting the Job

Contact your local Federal Information Center for information about customs workers' jobs. State employment offices may have the civil service information on applications and on job openings. Newspapers published near an international border or a port of entry may list openings. Also check the placement office of your school.

Advancement Possibilities and Employment Outlook

Government employees have many opportunities for advancement. Supervisory or management jobs are available to workers who qualify. Years of experience usually qualify workers for high-level office jobs. Many high-level customs officers work their way up through the ranks.

The employment outlook is moderately favorable. The great volume of goods being imported and exported, as well as increased efforts against smuggling, will probably result in a slight increase in the number of job openings through the year 2005.

Working Conditions

Customs personnel usually work in rotating shifts, since ports and borders operate 24 hours a day. Most customs workers have a 40-hour workweek and receive extra pay for overtime. They often work outside in all kinds of weather. Sometimes the job calls for quick thinking and action. Agents should be accurate judges of character and be both alert and observant. Their work may be dangerous. Most jobs are located along United States borders, in airports, and near large cities.

Earnings and Benefits

Customs workers have civil service ratings, so their salaries vary according to their grade and rank. Most import specialists, inspectors, and customs agents earn average salaries of about $36,000 to $40,000 a year. Salaries can increase as responsibilities increase. Workers can expect excellent benefits including paid vacations, sick leave, and health insurance.

Where to Go for More Information

National Customs Brokers and Forwarders
    Association of America
One World Trade Center, Suite 1153
New York, NY 10048
(212) 432-0050

National Treasury Employees Union
901 E Street, NW, Suite 600
Washington, DC 20004
(202) 783-4444

United States Government Federal Information
    Center
Phone number in local directory.

FBI Special Agent

Job Summary

EDUCATION AND TRAINING:
College plus training

SALARY RANGE:
Starting—$30,600
Average—$47,900 to $56,600

EMPLOYMENT OUTLOOK:
Poor

Definition and Nature of the Work

Federal Bureau of Investigation (FBI) special agents investigate violations of United States laws and report their findings to the office of the United States attorney general. They investigate crimes such as kidnapping, extortion, espionage, bank robbery, fraud, and sabotage. To carry out their jobs, they talk to witnesses, observe the activities of their suspects, do research, and participate in raids.

Since their work is strictly investigative, special agents do not express opinions about the guilt or innocence of suspects. These decisions are left to lawyers employed by the federal government. If agents are called on to testify in court, they relay the information they have gathered. Since much of their work is confidential, they are not allowed to discuss it with any outsiders, including members of their families. On some assignments they may have to carry firearms.

Agents work from field offices located in the United States and Puerto Rico and from the national headquarters in Washington, DC. To uncover facts, they use the crime detection laboratory

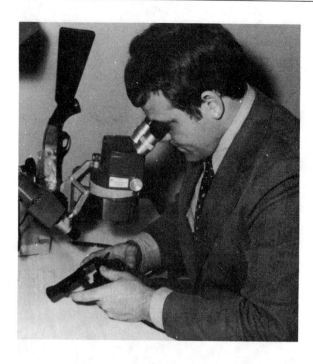

in Washington where experts analyze blood, paint, and fragments that agents find at the scenes of crimes. There is also a fingerprint file that they use.

Some federal crimes such as tax evasion and counterfeiting are investigated by other agencies. However, agents may be called in for assistance. FBI agents also make character and security checks on many employees of the government.

Education and Training Requirements

To become an FBI special agent you must be a graduate of a state-accredited law school or an accredited 4-year accounting school. If you are a graduate accountant, you must have at least 1 year of practical experience in accounting or auditing. You may also be considered for a position as an FBI agent if you have a bachelor's degree in a physical science, or if you have a bachelor's degree and fluency in a foreign language useful to the bureau.

To become an agent you must be a citizen of the United States, between the ages of 23 and 35, and in good physical condition. Excellent eyesight and hearing are essential. Your background and character are investigated thoroughly, and you must pass physical, written, and oral examinations. The written examinations are similar to those required for employment by the federal civil service.

During the first year, which is probationary, agents receive 15 weeks of intensive training in Washington and at the FBI Academy in Quantico, Virginia.

They learn self-defense, FBI rules and methods, fingerprinting, criminal law, and weapons use. When this training course is completed, they are assigned to one of the field offices for the remainder of the year, after which they are given permanent assignments.

Getting the Job

If you are interested in getting a job as an FBI special agent, you should write to the director of the FBI requesting information on vacancies, requirements, and employment applications.

Advancement Possibilities and Employment Outlook

Special agents are eligible for periodic salary increases. After demonstrating ability and proving that they are capable of assuming more responsibilities, agents may be promoted to supervisory or administrative positions.

Openings are limited. The rate of turnover in the FBI is very low. Each year some agents are hired because of expansion, but most people working as agents remain in their positions until retirement.

Working Conditions

FBI special agents must be ready for assignments in all places at all times. They are subject to call 24 hours a day. Since agents generally put in many extra hours, they are compensated with an annual bonus in a fixed amount.

The work can be both exciting and dangerous. Agents work alone or in small groups. Agents who can accept the responsibilities of the job find it a rewarding career. The work is seldom routine.

Earnings and Benefits

Beginning special agents earn about $30,600 a year. Many experienced agents earn $47,900 or more a year. Supervisory agents can earn $56,600 or more a year. Agents may earn an additional 25% a year in overtime pay. Benefits include paid holidays and vacations, medical insurance, and pension plans.

Where to Go for More Information

Federal Bureau of Investigation
10th Street and Pennsylvania Avenue, NW
Washington, DC 20535
(202) 324-3000

Foreign Service Worker

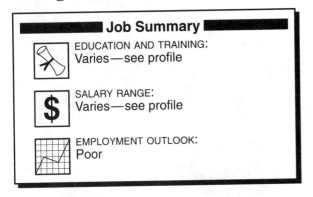

Job Summary

EDUCATION AND TRAINING:
Varies—see profile

SALARY RANGE:
Varies—see profile

EMPLOYMENT OUTLOOK:
Poor

Definition and Nature of the Work

Foreign service workers represent the United States in countries with which we have diplomatic relations. The foreign service, a branch of the United States Department of State, includes officers and reserve officers as well as support staff members and specialists.

Foreign service officers interpret American foreign policy to the government of the foreign, or host, country and help to foster friendly political and trade relations. They make periodic reports to their supervisors in the State Department on political activities, market conditions, public opinion, and all other important matters that affect United States policy. Sometimes foreign service officers help to negotiate treaties and agreements between the United States and foreign governments. Such negotiations are entered into to protect American shipping, economic, and legal interests. Foreign service officers help to insure the welfare of Americans visiting or residing in the foreign country.

Foreign service officers can specialize in one of four areas of service: administrative, consular, commercial-economic, or political. However, most workers are knowledgeable in more than one field.

Officers with administrative duties plan, develop, and direct the operations of their offices. They are in charge of their post's expenses and budget, the acquisition and maintenance of government property, and the supervision of personnel. Consular officers assist Americans with problems they face in foreign countries, issue passports and visas to Americans abroad, and help foreigners who want to visit the United States obtain visas. Commercial-economic officers promote United States business in foreign countries, analyze and report on foreign economic trends, and negotiate commercial and economic agreements. Political officers interpret United States foreign policy to other governments, promote understanding between the United States and foreign countries, and negotiate agreements.

Foreign service reserve officers perform similar tasks on a temporary basis. They work where they are needed most. Reserve officers usually have special skills that the department needs in fields such as agriculture, labor, economics, and finance.

Foreign service staff members provide the support needed to operate State Department offices in other countries. Workers include secretaries, nurses, communications and records assistants, and specialists in budget and fiscal problems.

Education and Training Requirements

Education requirements vary with the level of the job. Foreign service officers must be at least 21 years old and a United States citizen. Applicants must pass a written examination to be eligible for a foreign service appointment. Although there is no formal requirement that the applicant have a college degree, many candidates for foreign service officer positions have a bachelor's as well as a postgraduate degree.

To gain an appointment, candidates do not have to be fluent in a foreign language. After being hired, however, they must develop professional competence in at least 1 foreign language before the end of their initial 4-year probationary period on the job.

Education and training requirements for foreign service support staff members and specialists vary according to the nature of the job. All applicants must be United States citizens and at least 21 years old.

Foreign service secretaries must type 40 words a minute and take dictation at 80 words a minute. They must also have 3 to 5 years of experience in general office clerical, secretarial, or administrative work. Education beyond high school may be substituted for part of the required experience. To work as a communications and records assistant you need a minimum of 18 months of experience in the communications field. You will also be required to pass qualifying tests in typing, clerical, and verbal abilities. Staff members employed as diplomatic couriers, or mail carriers, generally are college graduates who have had military experience. All applicants and their dependents must pass comprehensive medical examinations to qualify for a foreign service appointment.

Getting the Job

You must apply directly to the Department of State. Foreign service officers must take a competitive examination, which consists of written and oral tests. The written test assesses the applicant's general intelligence, problem-solving abilities, writing skills, and knowledge of history, government, geography, commerce, administration, and economics. Candidates who pass the written test take the oral examination before a board of foreign service officers. The oral examination tests verbal ability. Board members ask questions on American culture, history, economics, politics, and foreign affairs. Foreign service reserve officers do not have to take the competitive examination.

Candidates accepted into the foreign service are prepared to serve in a particular geographic area. The training period may last up to 2 years or more, depending on the needs of the service and the officer's qualifications. It forms the initial part of the 4-year probationary appointment that newly hired candidates serve before they become commissioned officers. After several overseas assignments, foreign service officers specialize in one area and, if they wish, may return to school to expand their knowledge and skills.

Staff secretaries may take a 3- to 4-week training course and then be assigned overseas. Others may choose to work in Washington, DC, for 1 year before applying for an overseas assignment.

All applicants for foreign service positions are investigated thoroughly before employment to make sure that they are loyal to the American government.

Advancement Possibilities and Employment Outlook

The opportunities for advancement in foreign service are good. Officers may rise through the ranks of the foreign service. Promotions are based on ratings from superiors. Highly ranked officers may be appointed as ambassadors. Staff workers are also promoted on the basis of their merit ratings. If they meet the necessary requirements they may eventually become officers.

Employment in the foreign service is highly sought after, although the field is comparatively small. Competition for appointment as a foreign service officer is very stiff, with applicants far outnumbering available posts.

Working Conditions

Foreign service workers travel widely and meet many people of different nationalities. Maintaining relations with other countries is highly rewarding work and members of the foreign service take great pride in their accomplishments. However, the work is physically and mentally demanding. Workers are under pressure much of the time. They are not always sent to the countries of their choice, and living conditions in some areas are substandard. Employees are on duty at all times, and work hours are often uncertain.

Earnings and Benefits

Beginning foreign service officers earn between $18,000 and $28,000 a year. Those with special skills can earn $30,000 or more a year. Experienced officers can earn up to about $88,000 a year. Support staff members often start at about $15,500 a year.

Foreign service workers receive benefits such as paid vacation and sick leave, a housing allowance if government housing is not available, and special compensations for certain types of duty.

Where to Go for More Information

American Foreign Service Association
2101 E Street, NW
Washington, DC 20037
(202) 338-4045

Diplomatic and Consular Officers, Retired
1801 F Street, NW
Washington, DC 20006-4497
(202) 682-0500

Fund Raiser

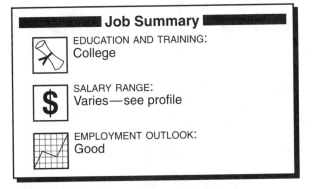

Job Summary

EDUCATION AND TRAINING:
College

SALARY RANGE:
Varies—see profile

EMPLOYMENT OUTLOOK:
Good

Definition and Nature of the Work

Hospitals, charities, colleges, and other nonprofit institutions need a great deal of money to meet operating expenses. There are professional fund raisers to organize fund drives and solicit contributions from corporations and individuals. Politicians running for office often hire fund raisers to solicit contributions from individual voters. Fund raisers develop plans for fund drives, organize volunteers to ask for funds, and monitor the progress of fund drives at every step. They may meet with corporation officers, government officials, and community leaders who wish to help solicit funds or plan fund-raising programs.

Fund raisers begin their work by figuring out how much money the institution or person needs. They

add to this sum an estimate of the expenses of the fund drive itself to determine the goal for the fund-raising campaign. Once the fund-raising goal and budget are set, fund raisers begin to plan the campaign. They must decide on the length of the campaign, slogans and other publicity, how funds will be solicited, and who will do the soliciting. Once the campaign is under way, fund raisers must make sure it goes according to schedule. They regularly analyze the progress of the campaign, review its strong and weak points, determine who was successful in raising funds and who was not, and plan changes in the campaign to make it more successful in the future.

Fund raisers work either on a consulting basis or full time for one institution. Consulting fund raisers work for firms that specialize in offering this service. Usually they are given temporary offices at the institution so that they can meet with management when necessary. Some fund raisers take on several small-scale fund drives at the same time. Politicians generally employ consultants for short periods of time. Colleges and universities, large hospitals, and national charities often employ full-time fund raisers. These professionals plan and supervise major campaigns.

Fund raisers must be able to work well with other people. They have to be able to sell the public on

the worthiness of their cause. They must also have the managerial skill to direct and inspire those who are soliciting funds. In addition, they must have a working knowledge of finance and tax laws so that they can explain to potential contributors the tax advantages of charitable or political contributions.

Education and Training Requirements

Most fund raisers learn their skill by working as volunteers in fund-raising campaigns. However, a formal education is also important, and most fund raisers have graduated from a 4-year college or university.

While in high school you should take college preparatory courses in English, mathematics, social studies, and foreign language. College courses in accounting, business administration, economics, psychology, speech, and statistics are useful. Some colleges offer courses that relate directly to fund raising. In addition, professional societies often hold seminars and workshops in fund-raising techniques.

Getting the Job

You can apply directly to fund-raising consulting firms and to institutions such as hospitals, colleges, and charities for a position as an assistant fund raiser. You might also consider getting a job as a public relations worker, since fund raising is closely re-

lated to public relations. Your college placement office and state and private employment agencies may also be able to help you find a job. Newspaper want ads may list beginning jobs in fund raising.

Advancement Possibilities and Employment Outlook

With experience, workers may become directors of fund-raising programs. Some become the heads of consulting firms or start their own firms. Fund raisers may seek more challenging positions by taking on larger drives with bigger organizations.

The employment outlook for fund raisers is good. There are more than 16,000 professional fund raisers working in the United States. Fund raising is a relatively new and small field. However, qualified fund raisers will continue to be in demand in the future.

Working Conditions

Fund raisers generally work irregular hours including nights and weekends. They travel a great deal, especially when they are working on national campaigns. They must be able to work well with people, from college presidents to volunteer solicitors. They must be able to work well under pressure and remain calm and organized to direct their campaign successfully.

Earnings and Benefits

Salaries for fund raisers vary according to the size of the institution and its location and the fund raiser's experience. Fund raisers working in the Northeast tend to earn higher salaries. Earnings for fund raisers average about $44,000 a year. Those with a great deal of experience may earn $90,000 or more a year.

Fund raisers employed by institutions and consulting firms usually receive paid holidays and vacations, health insurance, and pension plans. Self-employed fund raisers must provide their own coverage.

Where to Go for More Information

American Association of Fund-Raising Counsel
25 West 43rd Street, Suite 820
New York, NY 10036
(212) 354-5799

National Society of Fund Raising Executives
1101 King Street, Suite 700
Alexandria, VA 22314
(703) 684-0410

Government Inspector and Examiner

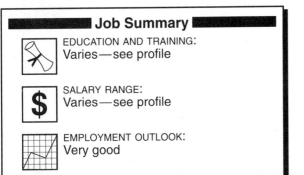

Job Summary

EDUCATION AND TRAINING:
Varies—see profile

SALARY RANGE:
Varies—see profile

EMPLOYMENT OUTLOOK:
Very good

Definition and Nature of the Work

Government inspectors and examiners work for a variety of government agencies. Their duties vary within each agency and for each job. Generally, their job is to enforce the laws and regulations of agencies. Some government inspectors, however, oversee the work of the government agencies themselves; their job is to make sure the agencies are run honestly and efficiently. Inspectors and examiners work on all levels of government—federal, state, county, and municipal.

Many inspectors work on behalf of public health. Some *food and drug inspectors* work for the Department of Health, Education, and Welfare. They inspect food, drugs, and cosmetics to make sure that they are safe and fresh enough for public consumption. They travel to firms that manufacture, warehouse, or sell these products. Because the field is so wide, most inspectors specialize in one aspect of the work. *Meat graders* and *grain inspectors* work for the Department of Agriculture to make certain that food products are safe to eat. They see that meat is handled and labeled according to government regulations. *Agricultural quarantine inspectors* are responsible for keeping potentially contaminated meats and produce away from good foods. Many of these inspectors work at United States ports of entry to make sure that bad foods do not enter the country.

Other inspectors work in the area of safety. For example, *aviation safety officers* investigate plane accidents. They also inspect facilities to see that the laws of the Federal Aviation Administration are followed. *Construction inspectors* see that buildings are erected according to approved blueprints.

A great number of inspectors are in charge of collecting taxes and enforcing tax laws. On the federal level these people work for the Department of the Treasury and the Internal Revenue Service. *Alcohol and tobacco tax inspectors*, for example, check the quantities of liquor and tobacco that are sold and collect the proper amount of tax monies.

Still other inspectors handle claims and examine the use of funds. For example, many agencies, including the Social Security Administration, employ *claim examiners* who see that people receive the correct benefits. There are *budget examiners* in all agencies who help to plan and regulate the agencies' finances.

Education and Training Requirements

Requirements vary considerably. In general, applicants must be United States citizens and at least 18 years of age. To be hired they must pass a civil service examination. For a number of positions a bachelor's degree or specialized coursework is required, although relevant work experience often can be substituted for part of the educational requirements.

Newly hired government inspectors and examiners are usually given on-the-job training under the guidance of an experienced worker. Some employees serve a probationary period before they become permanent employees.

Getting the Job

To become a government inspector you should apply to take the necessary civil service test. Job bulletins for state, county, and municipal governments are usually available from the post office or the state and local civil service commissions. For information about federal jobs contact your local Federal Information Center.

Advancement Possibilities and Employment Outlook

Workers generally advance by moving up the civil service ranks. They usually take a civil service test for each promotion. Inspectors and examiners may become supervisors or heads of their departments.

Employment of most government inspectors and examiners is expected to increase faster than the average through the year 2005. This growth reflects a growing public demand for safer products and a cleaner environment. Many job openings will occur when experienced examiners and inspectors retire or leave their jobs for other reasons.

Working Conditions

Many inspectors and examiners spend time traveling. Their actual working conditions vary with each department. Inspectors and examiners often work overtime or irregular hours. They are either paid extra for overtime or given the same number of hours off. Generally government employees work a 40-hour week.

Earnings and Benefits

Inspectors and examiners earn anywhere between $24,800 and $59,300 a year. The average salary is about $32,800 a year. Workers receive periodic raises. Increases are also granted for merit. Federal government workers receive generous benefits including travel expenses, paid vacations and holidays, sick leave, health and life insurance, and pension plans.

Where to Go for More Information

Food and Drug Administration
5600 Fishers Lane
Rockville, MD 20857
(301) 443-3170

Internal Revenue Service Worker

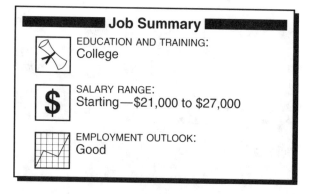

Job Summary

EDUCATION AND TRAINING:
College

SALARY RANGE:
Starting—$21,000 to $27,000

EMPLOYMENT OUTLOOK:
Good

Definition and Nature of the Work

Internal Revenue Service (IRS) workers implement tax collection for the federal government. They work in the national office in Washington, DC, and in regional offices throughout the United States. IRS personnel work in a number of professional positions. *Internal revenue agents* are accountants. They examine the tax returns and accounting records of business and individual taxpayers to determine how much tax money is owed. Agents may question individual taxpayers or go over the accounting books of large enterprises. Several agents may cooperate on complex cases. Agents also advise taxpayers on accounting methods and assist government attorneys involved in tax cases.

Unlike auditors in business, IRS *tax auditors* are not accountants. They are trained as experts in IRS regulations. They examine tax returns in cases where adherence to tax regulations is at issue. Auditors speak with taxpayers in the office. *Internal auditors* are accountants. They audit the operations of the IRS itself. *Revenue officers* collect delinquent, or late, taxes. *Special agents* investigate cases of suspected tax fraud and advise government attorneys of their findings.

Some IRS workers are lawyers. *Tax law specialists* interpret federal tax laws. They prepare publications for taxpayers and IRS workers. Tax law specialists are employed only in Washington, DC. *Estate tax attorneys* interpret laws relating to estate and gift taxes.

Education and Training Requirements

Requirements vary depending on the specific position. However, all professional IRS workers need at least a bachelor's degree. Internal revenue agents, internal auditors, and special agents need a back-

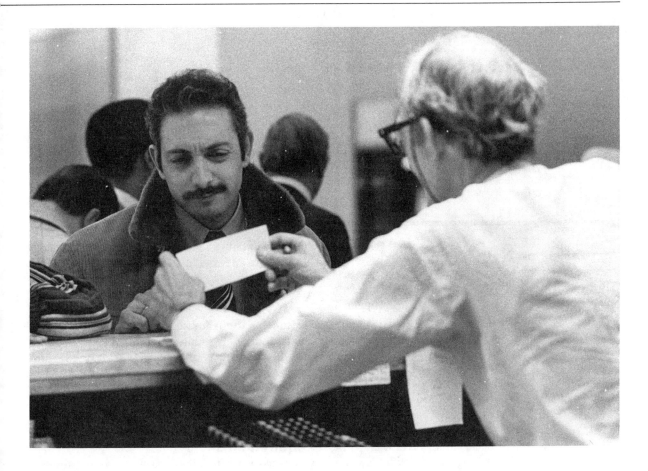

ground in accounting. Business courses are useful for tax auditors. Tax law specialists and estate tax attorneys need law degrees. To learn about the current requirements for specific job titles you should contact the IRS recruitment office in the city in which you want to work. All IRS workers receive both formal and on-the-job training after they are hired.

Getting the Job
You may apply directly to the IRS recruitment office in the city in which you would like to work. In addition, you may need to take the federal civil service examination.

Advancement Possibilities and Employment Outlook
IRS workers can advance with further education and experience. Many go into administrative work. Internal revenue agents with a master's degree in accounting earn higher salaries. They can also go into private tax work. The employment outlook is generally good. Because the volume of tax returns grows larger each year, qualified workers are in demand.

Working Conditions
Internal revenue agents and special agents spend time both in the office and in the field. Meeting a wide variety of people is part of the job. Other IRS personnel work in the office. Tax work demands care, attention, and a responsible attitude. A 40-hour workweek is standard.

Earnings and Benefits
Beginning internal revenue agents earn from about $21,000 to $27,000 a year, depending on their academic record and experience. Experienced agents average about $34,000 to $45,000 a year.

Benefits that IRS workers receive include paid holidays and vacations of from 2 to 5 weeks, health and life insurance, and retirement plans.

Where to Go for More Information
Internal Revenue Service
1111 Constitution Avenue, NW
Washington, DC 20224
(202) 622-5000

Lawyer

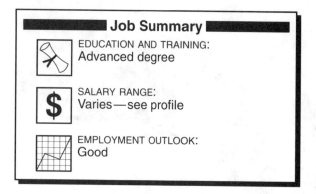

Definition and Nature of the Work

Lawyers are experts in the law and its applications. They can interpret laws, apply laws to specific situations, and draft new laws. Lawyers draw up legal documents, handle out-of-court settlements, and represent their clients in court. They may spend much of their time preparing arguments—both oral arguments to be presented in court and written briefs. Much of their work involves researching precedents, which are earlier interpretations of a law and the history of judicial decisions based on a law. Lawyers are also called attorneys and counsels.

Many lawyers are specialists in certain areas of legal work. Lawyers who practice criminal law defend clients who have been charged with a crime. Criminal lawyers are hired by people facing prosecution. Public defenders are employed by the government to represent people who cannot afford to pay lawyers.

Civil law concerns disputes that do not involve criminal misconduct. Divorce suits and damages suits fall under civil law. Some lawyers handle only certain types of civil cases. Labor law concerns disputes between management and unionized workers. Patent law concerns disputes over the rights to inventions. International law is the system of treaties and informal agreements that govern nations' dealings with one another. Attorneys who practice real estate law handle the details of transactions that involve buying, selling, renting, and developing land and buildings.

Some lawyers practice corporate law. These lawyers advise corporations on their rights, responsibilities, and obligations in business transactions. They may also represent their companies in government investigations and hearings.

In addition to specializing in one branch of law, such as tax law, lawyers might also specialize in the type of work they do. Some lawyers do research and prepare legal documents such as contracts. Others may spend a good deal of time in court.

Most lawyers have private practices. They handle a wide range of legal problems. Some work for law partnerships or firms. Lawyers may also find employment with corporations and with federal, state, and local government agencies. Some lawyers become district attorneys. Others teach law. Lawyers often enter other fields, such as politics, in which a legal background is helpful.

Some lawyers become *judges*. Judges are either elected or appointed to their positions. Judges preside over every court in the nation. During a trial the judge settles disputes over procedure. The judge decides what questions lawyers are permitted to put to witnesses and what evidence is admissible by law. If a jury is present, the judge interprets the law to its members. The judge tells the jury what it is asked to decide, how to evaluate the evidence, and what recommendations for settlement it is permitted to make. Judges also sentence criminals. Judges who preside over courts of appeal confirm or overturn the decisions of judges in the lower courts.

Education and Training Requirements

In order to practice law you must be admitted to the bar, or organization of lawyers, in the state in which you want to practice. In most states admission to the bar requires graduating from law school and passing the bar examination. In some states you are permitted to take the bar examination if you have substituted legal work experience for formal training. If you do not attend law school you must study law on your own to prepare for the bar examination. And in certain states graduates of "preferential" law schools located in the state may be admitted to the bar without taking the examination.

Most lawyers get a college degree and a law school degree. Your college courses should include English, history, political science, economics, and social science. You may want to major in engineering if you hope to be a patent attorney or in accounting if you are planning to be a tax lawyer. Occasionally students are given early admission to law school after 2 or 3 years of college. But most students complete college before going on to complete 3 years of law school. Law school courses include classes in contracts, property law, criminal law, and constitutional law. In the last 2 years of law school students specialize in the areas of law in which they hope to work. Law school graduates may spend several months studying for the bar examination.

Some state bars have cooperative arrangements with other states. These arrangements enable lawyers who are members of one state bar to practice in another state without taking that state's bar exam.

Getting the Job

Your law school placement office can help you find jobs. Many law firms and corporations send representatives to law schools to recruit graduating students. Part-time or summer jobs during law school sometimes lead to permanent jobs after graduation. Students with good grades and those who have worked on the law reviews published by each law school have the best chance to be hired by top law firms. If you are interested in working for the government, arrange to take the necessary civil service test. Many corporations including insurance companies, banks, accounting firms, and manufacturers employ lawyers. Check the want ads of your local newspaper for current openings.

Advancement Possibilities and Employment Outlook

Most beginning lawyers start in salaried positions as associates in law firms or as research assistants or law clerks to experienced lawyers or judges. After several years of experience, lawyers may become partners in their firms or set up their own practices. Some lawyers go into politics or become judges. Some become prosecutors or are elected district attorney.

Currently about 626,000 lawyers are employed nationwide. The demand for lawyers will increase through the year 2005. However, competition for available jobs will be stiff due to the large numbers of people going into law as a career. Lawyers who want to work for law firms will find the best opportunities in big cities, while those who are interested in setting up their own practices will find more opportunities in small towns or suburban areas.

Working Conditions

Lawyers often work long hours when they are doing research and preparing for court cases. Lawyers in private practice can schedule their own work loads. Lawyers who work for law firms are assigned cases and must often work overtime to prepare for court or to draw up legal documents. Lawyers are often involved in civic and community affairs. All lawyers must spend some time keeping up with new laws and court decisions in their areas of interest.

Earnings and Benefits

Many lawyers entering practice earn starting salaries ranging from about $30,000 to over $50,000 a year in some large law firms. Beginning lawyers who are employed by the federal government start at salaries ranging from $27,800 to $33,600 a year depending on their qualifications.

Lawyers who start their own practices right after graduating from law school generally earn very little for the first few years. After they get some experience and build their businesses they can do quite well. The most experienced lawyers can earn anywhere between $134,000 and $1 million a year. They can charge yearly fees, or retainers, with extra charges for court appearances or special work. Sometimes they charge hourly fees or work on a percentage basis when lawsuits or estates are involved.

Associates in law firms work on a salary basis and receive raises as they take on more responsibilities. After some years of experience they may become partners in their firms and receive a percentage of the firm's profits. Lawyers generally receive paid holidays and vacations, health and life insurance, and pension plans. Those in private practice must make their own insurance and retirement arrangements.

Where to Go for More Information

American Bar Association
750 North Lake Shore Drive
Chicago, IL 60611
(312) 988-5000

The Association of Trial Lawyers of America
1050 Thirty-first Street, NW
Washington, DC 20007
(202) 965-3500

National Association of Women Lawyers
American Bar Center
750 North Lake Shore Drive
Chicago, IL 60611
(312) 988-6186

Lawyer, Corporate

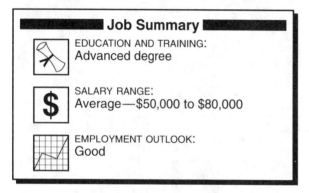

Job Summary

EDUCATION AND TRAINING:
Advanced degree

SALARY RANGE:
Average—$50,000 to $80,000

EMPLOYMENT OUTLOOK:
Good

Definition and Nature of the Work

Corporate lawyers advise their clients or employers on their legal rights and obligations. As advocates they may represent companies in both criminal and civil court cases. Corporate lawyers may work in-house as full-time employees of the company; or they may be self-employed lawyers specializing in company law advising corporate clients.

Whether in-house or outside counsel, corporate lawyers keep the company out of trouble by anticipating and helping to circumvent problems and always keeping clients updated regarding new laws and regulations. They advise on such things as labor relations, employee contracts, tax matters, suits against the corporation, employee injury, patents, and contracts with raw materials suppliers.

The head of a corporation's legal department may be called the general counsel and hold vice presidential status. The counsel is supported by legal staff.

Education and Training Requirements

A high school diploma, a college degree, and 3 years of law school are minimum requirements for work as a corporate lawyer. While all law students take core courses on corporate law, trusts, tax, and insurance law, those interested in a corporate law specialty should also take relevant electives, such as creditors' rights, trade regulations, commercial transactions, and trial advocacy. To practice law you must be admitted to the bar in the state in which you want to practice. In most states admission to the bar requires graduating from law school and passing the bar examination.

Getting the Job

Job experience during law school will prove helpful for job hunting later. Typing briefs, working in the law school library, or searching records as a junior court clerk will give you job contacts and a firsthand view of the legal world. Many corporations send representatives to law schools to recruit graduating students. Check law journals and newspaper ads for corporate law vacancies.

Advancement Possibilities and Employment Outlook

The job outlook for corporate lawyers is good through the year 2005. Corporations are eager to protect themselves from skyrocketing damage suits, so it is worth their while to employ a team of legal advisers to keep them from expensive litigation. Corporate experience may later lead to a lucrative outside practice advising a number of corporate clients.

Working Conditions

Corporate lawyers are usually assigned their own offices with their own secretaries and access to legal research assistants and a legal library. They often work long hours, especially when they are prepar-

ing court cases. Lawyers who are employed by corporations with district branches may travel to various locations to investigate legal problems.

Earnings and Benefits

Average earnings are about $50,000 to $80,000 a year for corporation legal staff. With experience and specialization, this can increase to $100,000 a year for a general counsel. Benefits for corporate employees usually include pensions, vacations, and health insurance.

Where to Go for More Information

American Bar Association
750 North Lake Shore Drive
Chicago, IL 60611
(312) 988-5000

Lawyer, Public Service

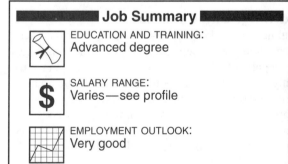

Job Summary

EDUCATION AND TRAINING:
Advanced degree

SALARY RANGE:
Varies—see profile

EMPLOYMENT OUTLOOK:
Very good

Definition and Nature of the Work

Lawyers who work in public service may specialize in several areas such as legal aid, government law, or environmental law. *Legal aid lawyers* offer legal services to people who cannot afford to pay for them. These services include giving legal advice; drawing up legal documents, such as contracts and wills; and representing the client in court proceedings. Legal aid lawyers may also work as legal consultants for public interest organizations, such as the American Civil Liberties Union (ACLU) and the National Association for the Advancement of Colored People (NAACP).

Many lawyers work for state, federal, and local government agencies. *Government lawyers* draft regulations to implement laws, prosecute criminals, or work as judges and magistrates in the courts.

Environmental lawyers assist community groups in preparing injunctions against companies whose activities threaten environmental standards. Environmental lawyers are also consulted on major real

and those who have worked on law reviews published by law schools have the best chance to be hired. A civil service test is required for government jobs.

Advancement Possibilities and Employment Outlook

Most public agency lawyers start as research assistants or law clerks to experienced lawyers or judges. After several years of experience, they may become district attorneys or heads of the legal department in a state or federal agency. They may then move to private law firms and use the valuable expertise and contacts they have gained in the public arena.

In recent years there has been a boom in environmental law, and there are now more than 14,000 lawyers in the field. The boom is expected to continue because of renewed attention to air pollution and landfill problems. Some environmental lawyers work for private law firms and build up the staff and reputation of the environmental department. Others work for the Environmental Protection Agency and such organizations as the Sierra Club and the Natural Resources Defense Council.

estate transactions because buyers and lenders fear inheriting cleanup costs from previous toxic leaks or asbestos in buildings.

Education and Training Requirements

A high school diploma, a college degree, and a good LSAT (Law School Aptitude Test) scores are required for admission to law school.

Law school training usually takes 3 years and requires courses such as contracts, criminal law, and property law. The second and third years may be devoted to specialized courses for law in the public service sector. These include constitutional law, family law, and workers' compensation. Environmental lawyers should also take courses in environmental law and have a good technical grasp of environmental science.

To practice law you must be admitted to the bar in the state in which you want to practice. In most states admission to the bar requires graduation from law school and passing the bar examination.

Getting the Job

During law training, students can assist attorneys undertaking pro bono work (services donated for the public good). Many law firms and government agencies send representatives to law schools to recruit graduating students. Students with good grades

Working Conditions

Public service lawyers may be required to work long hours, especially during emergency situations. Outside of working hours, lawyers must spend time keeping up with new laws and court decisions in their areas of interest.

Public service lawyers may also have to travel to carry out their legal duties in certain situations.

Earnings and Benefits

Public service lawyers may make a financial sacrifice when they accept jobs in government agencies or legal aid offices. Environmental lawyers earn only 55% to 80% of the usual $175 to $200 an hour received by other specialty lawyers. Salaries for government lawyers, for example, average about $62,000 a year. They also receive paid holidays, health and life insurance, and pension benefits.

Where to Go for More Information

American Bar Association
750 North Lake Shore Drive
Chicago, IL 60611
(312) 988-5000

Librarian, Public

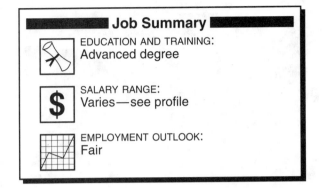

Job Summary

EDUCATION AND TRAINING:
Advanced degree

SALARY RANGE:
Varies—see profile

EMPLOYMENT OUTLOOK:
Fair

Definition and Nature of the Work

Public librarians make information available to the community they serve. This information can be in the form of books, books on tape, compact discs, government documents, films, audiotapes or videotapes, and even computer software. Jobs range from selecting and ordering print and nonprint materials to using them in a variety of ways to serve the public. Some librarians may develop materials and programs especially designed to meet the needs expressed by their patrons. Librarians who work closely with the community are knowledgeable about the interests of their patrons. Some librarians do not work closely with the public. Others are administrators who work with government and community leaders. Public libraries and library systems vary widely in scope and size, according to the needs and financial resources of the community to which they are connected. Librarians' duties vary accordingly.

Large libraries offer librarians a chance to specialize. Among the librarians who have little contact with the public are *acquisitions librarians*. These librarians read reviews of new materials and often examine sample copies. They order and process new materials for the library and are familiar with companies that supply a variety of materials, including out-of-print books and videotapes. *Catalogers* describe books according to their subject matter and assign subject headings and classification numbers for card catalogs or on-line catalog terminals. Original cataloging is often unnecessary because it is readily available from the Library of Congress, the national library of the United States. Catalogers or their helpers prepare books for filing on shelves according to the system used by the particular library. The Dewey decimal and the Library of Congress classification systems are the ones most commonly used in public libraries.

Reference librarians, unlike catalogers, deal directly with library users. They help people research specific pieces of information by either looking up facts or referring people to useful sources. They handle reference questions in person and over the telephone. These librarians also use computerized information services to provide answers to questions or lists of book and periodical sources on particular topics. Reference librarians usually have a special desk in the reference or information section. They may also be responsible for suggesting titles to be acquired for the reference collection.

Some librarians work with specific segments of the community. *Children's librarians* and *youth services librarians* are trained to meet the needs of young people. Librarians in the children's section often prepare displays and conduct weekly story hours designed to interest children in books and library services. They may also have film programs. Youth services librarians work mainly with junior and senior high school students, helping them learn to use libraries and their resources. They can aid young people in finding books for pleasure, vocational guidance, and reference for school-related projects. *Bookmobile librarians* work from vans especially designed as mobile libraries. They travel to outlying neighborhoods that lack adequate library services. Librarians select books according to the needs of the community the bookmobile serves. They often supply books or other materials from a central library in response to requests from their bookmobile patrons. Other community outreach librarians may serve special groups, such as those living in nursing homes or housing projects.

Some libraries are staffed by only two or three people. These librarians may combine the duties of all of the above specialists. Large library systems are generally administered by sizable staffs. *Library administrators* are responsible for the operation and continued funding of their libraries.

Education and Training Requirements

Librarians generally need a master's degree in library science. Graduate programs usually last 1 year and include a summer of study. About 120 schools offer such programs, and currently 60 of these are accredited by the American Library Association. Library school students take basic courses in the history of books and printing, intellectual freedom, reference tools, and user services. Because most libraries now have automated systems, almost all

library schools offer courses in information storage and retrieval, microcomputer technology, and the use of on-line information retrieval systems. Advanced courses may be taken in specialties such as children's or adult services; classification, cataloging, indexing, and abstracting; library administration; library automation; and archives. Some schools offer doctoral programs in library science. A doctorate is often a prerequisite for top administrators in large library systems. Undergraduate study in the liberal arts, including English, foreign languages, data processing, and business, may prove helpful. Also useful is part-time library work as a technical or clerical assistant. Some graduate schools offer 2-year work-study programs that enable students to get work experience while they are in school.

Getting the Job

Your school placement office can give you information about job openings and applications. Both private and state employment offices sometimes list library openings. Library associations in many states have job hotlines that list openings on a recorded telephone message. You can also write directly to public libraries in your community. Professional library journals and local newspapers list job openings in their want ad sections. The Sunday edition of *The New York Times* lists library positions that are available throughout the country.

Advancement Possibilities and Employment Outlook

Librarians can advance within their own library system or they may choose to move to a larger or more specialized kind of library. Most top-level jobs are administrative and often require a doctoral degree. Librarians with doctoral degrees may also become teachers of library science.

Employment of librarians is expected to grow more slowly than average for all occupations through the year 2005. This is due to an anticipated reduction of local government expenditures for library services. Competition for positions should be stiff; most openings that become available each year will be to replace librarians who retire or leave the field.

Working Conditions

Public libraries, particularly newer facilities, are generally pleasant and quiet places to work. The specific duties affect the conditions of work. For example, catalogers spend most of their day working in one place, while reference librarians move about the library helping people to find information. Reference librarians work under pressure when patrons need information quickly. Most librarians work between 35 and 40 hours a week, including some evenings and weekends.

Earnings and Benefits

Salaries of public librarians vary largely by location and size of library and by a librarian's level of ed-

ucation and experience. Starting salaries for graduates of library school master's degree programs accredited by the American Library Association average $23,800 a year in public libraries. The average annual salary for federal government librarians in all positions, including supervisory and managerial, is $44,500. Most public librarians can expect paid vacations of 3 or 4 weeks a year, as well as paid holidays, sick leave benefits, and health and pension plans.

Where to Go for More Information

American Library Association
50 East Huron Street
Chicago, IL 60611
(312) 944-6780

Librarian, School

Job Summary

EDUCATION AND TRAINING:
College plus training

SALARY RANGE:
Starting—$25,400 to $27,400
Average—$34,000 to $42,000

EMPLOYMENT OUTLOOK:
Varies—see profile

Definition and Nature of the Work

School librarians introduce students to the school library and teach them how to use it. Elementary schools, junior and senior high schools, and colleges and universities all employ school librarians. Librarians select and order books and other materials that will support the curriculum of the school or college. They are responsible for maintaining the collection so that items are easily accessible to their patrons. Frequently they are also responsible for audiovisual materials and equipment. They sometimes prepare exhibits.

Actual duties vary with the size of the library and the needs of the students. High school libraries are generally larger than those in elementary schools because older students need more extensive resources for research. Elementary and secondary school librarians may work alone, while librarians in colleges and universities may be part of sizable staffs that include other librarians, technical assistants, and clerks. In large libraries assistants catalog

new books, shelve returned books, repair damaged books, and take care of bindery procedures. In small libraries these tasks are done by professional librarians.

Elementary school librarians teach basic library skills, often in regularly scheduled classes in the library. They may teach students how to distinguish among various kinds of books, such as fiction, nonfiction, poetry, and biography, and how to use the classification system for finding books in the library. They encourage use of the library for information and recreation, while making it an interesting and important part of the students' school day. In an effort to interest students in reading, librarians may conduct story hours for the younger students and arrange other special programs for those in the higher grades.

Secondary school librarians teach more sophisticated skills to older students. Most students begin to learn research techniques in junior and senior high school. Secondary school librarians may hold orientation sessions for individual classes to explain the use of card catalogs or catalog access terminals, reference books, and indexes to periodicals. They help individual students by suggesting specific sources or ways of finding information. Sometimes librarians set up exhibits designed to make students aware of some of the library's holdings. Such exhibits may coordinate with historical events or holidays. Some school libraries contain many audiovisual materials. The school librarian may need to have training in this area.

College and university librarians work in relatively large libraries suited to the research needs of both students and faculty. Libraries on this level usually have large staffs of librarians who work in a number of specializations. Librarians in technical services order, process, and catalog new materials. These procedures are generally automated to a greater or lesser degree, depending on the size and budget of the library. Librarians in user services work closely with students and faculty. They direct users to helpful sources and also find specific pieces of information. They often conduct bibliographic instruction classes to teach library research methods. Many new on-line computer services available for reference may require that librarians also be trained in computer information searching techniques. Some universities have separate libraries for the various disciplines offered by the institution. There may be, for example, one library for general use, one for technical and scientific subjects, and an art library that may include an extensive slide collection. Some academic librarians develop subject bibliographies to direct patrons to the many different sources and forms of information in the library. Often libraries exchange materials through on-line interlibrary loan networks to make still more information available to the academic community. Librarians who work in specialized libraries may

need expertise in the subject in addition to a degree in library science. They are sometimes required to have a second master's degree in the subject field. Library administrators and head librarians supervise all library operations.

Education and Training Requirements

Elementary and secondary school librarians may need to be certified both as librarians and as teachers in their states. To be certified as a school librarian you generally must earn either a bachelor's or a master's degree in library science and pass a written examination. Since educational requirements vary from state to state and change frequently, you should check the current requirements in your state before making any decisions.

Most college and university librarians have a master's degree in library science. Top administrative posts, however, generally go to those who have a doctoral degree. Librarians who work in large university libraries are frequently required to have a second master's degree in the subject area of the faculty they represent. Some academic libraries may also require proficiency in a foreign language. Rare

book librarians may need special training in that field, as well as a second advanced degree. Because of the many automated systems in academic libraries, librarians should be familiar with computerized information retrieval systems and on-line catalogs.

Getting the Job

College and graduate school placement offices usually list library openings. You can apply directly to private schools and public school boards. Newspapers sometimes list openings for librarians; the Sunday edition of *The New York Times* advertises positions that are available throughout the country. The *Chronicle of Higher Education* is a good place to look for librarian openings in colleges and universities. Professional library journals also list job openings in the field, as do private employment agencies that specialize in education. Many professional associations have telephone hotlines that list openings on prerecorded messages.

Advancement Possibilities and Employment Outlook

School librarians can advance by furthering their education. Graduate programs offer both master's and doctoral degrees in library science. With higher degrees or with a second-subject master's, school librarians may transfer to large college or university libraries or become library administrators. School librarians may also become teachers at library schools. Competition will be keen in schools, colleges, and universities. Growth in the number of new positions will depend largely on the extent of public funding for education. Replacement positions will be available each year as librarians retire or leave the field. In certain urban areas, such as New York City, there will be a strong demand for children's and young adult specialists in school and public libraries through the year 2005.

Working Conditions

Libraries are generally quiet, pleasant places to work. Working hours vary with each school, but elementary and high school librarians usually work the same hours that teachers do, while college and university librarians often work 35- to 40-hour weeks with some evening and weekend hours.

Earnings and Benefits

Salaries vary with the individual school, its location, and the librarian's education and experience. Starting salaries average about $27,400 for public school librarians and $25,400 for college and university librarians. The average salary of experienced school librarians is about $34,000 to $42,000 a year. Benefits include paid holidays, long vacations, health insurance, and pension plans.

Where to Go for More Information

American Library Association
50 East Huron Street
Chicago, IL 60611
(312) 944-6780

National Education Association of the U.S.
1201 Sixteenth Street, NW
Washington, DC 20036-3290
(202) 833-4000

Librarian, Special

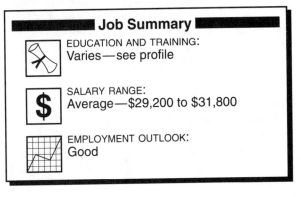

■■■■■ **Job Summary** ■■■■■

EDUCATION AND TRAINING:
Varies—see profile

SALARY RANGE:
Average—$29,200 to $31,800

EMPLOYMENT OUTLOOK:
Good

Definition and Nature of the Work

Special librarians make information on specific subjects available to people in industry, commerce, and government. Librarians acquire and organize data that are required by their employers. Librarians may work in institutions as large as the National Library of Medicine or as small as a two- or three-person office. The growth of computer storage and retrieval of information has changed this field radically. Many positions deal primarily or even exclusively with research through on-line data base searching. Special librarians help people find information and see that needed materials are easily accessible.

The main difference between special librarians and all other librarians is that special librarians serve a particular organization and specialize in the subject area that suits the needs of that organization. They work in public institutions as well as in private businesses, such as television stations, advertising agencies, and law firms. Some librarians work solely with medical books and periodicals in hospital libraries, while others work in museums with such materials as filmstrips, slides, prints, and art history books. In some libraries the librarian is responsible for translating material into English from a foreign language. These librarians may also abstract and index articles, research papers, or books. Since special librarians deal with one subject in depth, they must be very knowledgeable in that particular field. Sometimes they do research for their companies and present their findings in a report to the staff. They also assist staff members who are conducting research.

Special librarians are usually free to reorganize traditional library procedures to adapt them to their specialized needs. Many special libraries have several staff positions. They are supervised by a *head librarian*, who is in charge of planning the budget, hiring personnel, and handling important correspondence. *Library assistants* often do the routine tasks of filing, checking in materials, and taking inventory. Others work in circulation or take care of subscription and book orders. In small libraries one or two staff members can often handle all the duties.

Some graduate students take part in work-study arrangements that allow them to work part time while attending school. Graduate study often includes foreign language courses, as well as the study of library procedures, on-line data base searching, information science, and library automation. Volunteer and part-time or summer work in libraries can prove useful for people who plan to become librarians.

Education and Training Requirements

The education required of special librarians is entirely up to the employer. Sometimes a high school diploma plus some experience is sufficient for the job. However, some employers look for a master's degree in library science combined with a strong background or an advanced degree in a specific field. Writing skill and knowledge of computer operations are often necessary. Art museum librarians generally need a college major in art history and a master's degree in library science. Librarians in large technical libraries usually need a master's or doctoral degree in a relevant field and a library science degree.

Getting the Job

The placement office of your college is a good source of job openings. The want ads in newspapers and professional journals may offer job leads. You can also apply directly to firms and agencies that have special libraries. Government jobs usually require that you apply to take the necessary civil service examination. The Special Libraries Association has local telephone hotlines for listing job openings in various parts of the country.

Advancement Possibilities and Employment Outlook

Advancement generally depends on the librarian's educational background and continuing education in the field. Those with a doctoral degree may advance to become head librarians or library administrators.

The employment outlook is good because of the increase in the number of special libraries. In some areas of the country there are more jobs than there are librarians qualified to fill them. This trend is expected to continue through the year 2005.

Working Conditions

The atmosphere in libraries is generally pleasant and quiet. Special librarians, however, must sometimes work under considerable pressure, especially when information is needed quickly. Librarians should be knowledgeable and well-organized people. Their workweek is typically 35 to 40 hours long.

Earnings and Benefits

Salary depends on the librarian's education and experience as well as on the budget limitations of the employing organization. Special librarians with 1 to 5 years of experience earn average annual salaries of about $29,200 to $31,800. Special library managers earn an average of $45,200 a year. Librarians can expect between 2 and 4 weeks of paid vacation and sick leave. Benefits usually include health insurance and pension plans.

Where to Go for More Information

American Library Association
50 East Huron Street
Chicago, IL 60611
(312) 944-6780

American Society for Information Science
8720 Georgia Avenue, Suite 501
Silver Spring, MD 20910-3602
(301) 495-0900

Special Libraries Association
1700 Eighteenth Street, NW
Washington, DC 20009
(202) 234-4700

Marriage and Family Counselor

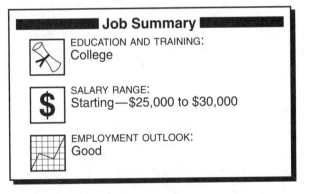

Job Summary

EDUCATION AND TRAINING:
College

SALARY RANGE:
Starting—$25,000 to $30,000

EMPLOYMENT OUTLOOK:
Good

Definition and Nature of the Work

Marriage and family counselors offer therapy to people who have problems. Counselors help clients understand themselves and their relationships with others. The aim of counseling is to help clients use their new understanding to develop better relationships. Counselors work in mental health centers and clinics, in hospitals, and for social service agencies. Others have private practices.

Many approaches are used in conducting marriage counseling. Marriage counselors speak with the husband and wife at the same time although they may have some sessions with the husband or wife alone. Some marriage counselors see married couples in groups. They may also see groups of husbands or groups of wives. Whatever method is used, the goal is the same. Many marital problems arise because the couples do not understand each other. Counselors strive to increase this understanding. Perhaps a couple is considering divorce when they come to the counselor. The counselor will work to see whether a reconciliation is possible. If it is not possible, the counselor may suggest a trial separation.

Family counselors work with entire families or with individual family members. Even when a counselor speaks with only one person, the orientation of the therapy includes the client's parents and siblings or spouse and children. Here, too, the counselor helps clients communicate with others to aid in improving troubled relationships.

The nature of the work may vary depending on the particular place of employment. Counselors in private practice, for example, may specialize in one or two kinds of problems. Such counselors may refer clients to other counselors if clients' problems are outside their area of expertise. Counselors who work in clinics may work in teams. They may consult with their colleagues on special cases. Some clinics employ counselors with special qualifications to take on the most difficult cases.

Education and Training Requirements

An increasing number of states have instituted formal licensing requirements for marriage and family counselors. Counselors employed in private practice may not have a degree, although most have at least a master's degree. Some people with a bachelor's degree work as counselors for social service agencies. Some counselors are psychologists or psychiatrists.

While in college take courses in sociology, social work, psychology, and modern foreign languages. To get a position for which there is stiff competition graduate work is necessary. Many schools offer graduate programs in marriage and family counseling. Some counselors specialize in social work and psychology.

Getting the Job

Newspapers and professional journals advertise counseling positions in their classified sections. School placement offices list openings too. Applicants can also write directly to local agencies, hospitals, and clinics. If you wish to work for a government agency, apply to take the necessary civil service test. Many students make future job contacts while doing field work for courses in social work and psychology.

Advancement Possibilities and Employment Outlook

Marriage and family counselors can become self-employed or work as directors of departments or agencies. They can also further their training by getting a doctoral degree or by taking further postgraduate courses. Counselors who have a great deal of experience may become trainers and teachers of new counselors.

Increased demand for marriage and family counseling should result in moderate growth in the employment of these workers through the year 2005. Despite recent cutbacks in government support of many social service programs, some growth is expected in public sector jobs as well as in opportunities for counselors in private practice.

Working Conditions

Counselors work in offices where they can speak with their client in private or in groups. Some counselors in private practice have offices in their own homes. Working hours vary since many counselors combine part-time jobs in social service agencies

with private practice. Agency work often includes 2 or 3 evenings a week, especially in marriage counseling, because clients work during the day. Counselors in private practice can regulate their own schedule, although they too usually have some evening and weekend sessions.

The work can be very demanding. Counselors must always give their complete attention to their clients' difficulties.

Earnings and Benefits

Pay scales vary considerably. Beginning counselors employed in public agencies or clinics often earn starting salaries ranging from about $25,000 to $30,000 a year, depending on their educational background. Experienced counselors with a master's degree generally earn $35,000 to $40,000 a year. Psychologists and psychiatrists in this field earn higher salaries. Counselors in private practice also often have higher earnings once they become established. Benefits for counselors employed by government agencies or other large public or private organizations usually include paid holidays and vacations, health insurance, and pension plans.

Where to Go for More Information

American Association for Marriage and Family
   Therapy
1100 Seventeenth Street, NW, Tenth Floor
Washington, DC 20036
(202) 452-0109

Parole Officer

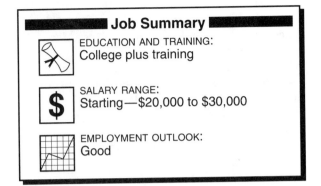

Job Summary

EDUCATION AND TRAINING:
College plus training

SALARY RANGE:
Starting—$20,000 to $30,000

EMPLOYMENT OUTLOOK:
Good

Definition and Nature of the Work

Parole officers help people who have served time in prison return to society. They work with prisoners who are eligible for parole. Parole is the conditional release of prisoners from prison before their sentences have been completed. Prisoners become eligible for parole after they show progress in rehabilitation programs. Such progress is demonstrated by obeying prison rules, performing prison jobs well, and completing therapy programs. The prison parole boards decide which prisoners have made enough progress to be released. They try to identify those prisoners who will not repeat their crimes. Most parole officers work for state parole departments. Some officers are employed by counties or at the federal level by the United States Board of Parole.

Some parole officers work inside correctional institutions. They prepare reports for the parole board. These reports include the details of the prisoners' lives before prison, of their prison years, and of their home situations. The officers try to give the parole board some idea of whether the prisoners' families will be helpful to the released prisoners. Parole officers provide information about the job prospects a prisoner might have if released. Based on the parole officers' reports and interviews with the prisoners and their families, the board chooses certain prisoners for release.

Other parole officers work in the field with parolees, or prisoners who have been released. They may be assisted by parole aides or parole officer trainees. The first thing ex-convicts need is a job. Parole officers help their clients find jobs. Officers also lend emotional support to parolees as they meet the challenges of returning to their communities. For example, ex-convicts are often held suspect by employers and co-workers. Parole officers try to help convicts by talking to their employers and explaining that the parolees need a chance to make

a living if they are to function as honest citizens. Other convicts may have financial problems. Parole officers are familiar with community services and welfare benefits so that they can direct ex-convicts to agencies that can provide further support.

Generally, parolees continue in rehabilitation programs such as basic education, job training, or therapy. Parole officers assist clients in finding schools and job training or therapy programs. For instance, former drug addicts may need to be enrolled in programs that help them to stay off drugs. In addition, parolees can also be placed in halfway houses or community centers where people on parole live together in small groups to share their experiences and lend each other support. These halfway houses are sometimes supervised by parole officers with the help of drug therapists, psychiatrists, and social workers.

Parolees must visit their officers regularly so that their progress can be evaluated. Parole officers question their clients at these sessions to make sure that they are not breaking the parole rules in any way. If a parolee breaks the rules, such as by violating a law or by associating with bad company, the parole officer may recommend that the parole be revoked. Then the parole board may send the parolee back to prison.

Education and Training Requirements

You generally must have a bachelor's degree to become a parole officer. Majors in either sociology, psychology, criminology, or corrections are appropriate. In addition, many employing agencies including the United States Board of Parole require 1 or 2 years of experience in a correctional institution or other social agency or a master's degree in sociology or psychology. Parole officer trainees receive on-the-job training under the supervision of experienced parole officers and the senior parole officer.

Getting the Job

Contact state, federal, or county parole boards to ask about job openings. Arrange to take the required federal or state civil service test. If you do field work for college courses in social work you may come in contact with people who can help you find a job when you graduate. Job openings are often listed at college placement offices.

Advancement Possibilities and Employment Outlook

Advancement opportunities are good for parole officers. There are many chances for qualified people to advance to jobs as administrators and department heads. They may become the directors of special projects or units.

The need for new parole officers will be great due to the increasing numbers of people who are serving prison terms and will become eligible for parole. However, opportunities depend on the extent of public funding. Many states and counties as well as the federal government will expand their parole departments through the year 2005 if funding permits.

Working Conditions

Field parole officers do much of their work independently. They interview clients and go out into the community to find jobs for parolees. All parole officers are under pressure to present a positive image of the parole system to the community. Parole officers make a great effort to help ex-prisoners solve their psychological problems. Caseloads may be heavy. Officers often work more than 40 hours a week. They sometimes make evening or weekend appointments with parolees who work or who have emergency problems.

Earnings and Benefits

Earnings vary depending on the location of the employer. Beginning parole officers average about $20,000 to $30,000 a year. Supervisors and directors earn much higher salaries. Most parole officers receive paid holidays and vacations, health insurance, and pension plans.

Where to Go for More Information

American Correctional Association
8025 Laurel Lakes Court
Laurel, MD 20707
(301) 206-5100

American Federation of State, County and Municipal
  Employees
1625 L Street, NW
Washington, DC 20036
(202) 452-4800

National Council on Crime and Delinquency
685 Market Street, Suite 620
San Francisco, CA 94105
(415) 896-6223

Political Consultant

Job Summary

EDUCATION AND TRAINING:
College

SALARY RANGE:
Varies—see profile

EMPLOYMENT OUTLOOK:
Very good

Definition and Nature of the Work

Political consultants, or lobbyists, work behind the scenes to promote the election of certain candidates or the interests of certain groups. The consultant plans the strategy, coordinates the campaign staff, and arranges meetings to publicize the candidate or cause.

The corporate lobbyist may specialize in representing the company to the federal or state government. Lobbyists try to persuade government officials to understand their company's problems, and they may advise and participate in marketing the company's products to government departments. Lobbyists also discuss such issues as taxation and regulation with the members of Congress and other senior officials.

Education and Training Requirements

College majors in political science, communication, English, or foreign languages will be useful for the political consultant. Other fields of study important to this career are economics, business, law, and sociology.

Volunteer work for local politicians or interest groups will give you experience and helpful contacts. A master's degree in government policy-making or public administration may be supplemented by part-time work on a campaign staff or in a congressperson's local office.

Getting the Job

Volunteer and part-time work during school and college will be a good springboard for finding full-time employment. Jobs in the personnel and public

relations divisions of companies may lead to corporate lobbying positions. Many trade and professional associations have well-established lobbying offices and regularly hire new personnel.

Advancement Possibilities and Employment Outlook

As local, state, and federal political contests become more complex, candidates increasingly rely on campaign consultants to manage their overall organization. While there may be more jobs at the local level during election time, state and federal representatives often employ full-time political consultants in Washington and the state capitals.

Corporate lobbying has been on the rise since 1980. Smaller companies that cannot afford full-time lobbyists hire outside lobbyists who are experts on specific issues. Specialization has opened up new advancement possibilities for many political consultants who have set up their own political consulting firms.

The outlook for political consultants is very good, although competition will be keen for those in beginning positions or those who are starting their own consulting firms.

Working Conditions

Political consultants work at an energetic pace arguing the case of their candidate or cause. They spend a considerable amount of time on the telephone and in face-to-face contact with legislators and other officials. They must be skilled in dealing with people. During an election campaign the consultant often travels ahead of the candidate, organizing meetings, interviews, and publicity. The job is varied and often requires evening and weekend work.

Earnings and Benefits

Entry-level political consultants may receive payment for out-of-pocket expenses and low wages.

Starting salaries range from $26,000 to $31,000 a year. However, as word of energetic and successful strategies gets around, candidates and corporations will offer higher wages and benefits. A Washington lobbyist for a corporation may receive $50,000 to $75,000 or more a year. Corporation employees also receive pension and vacation benefits. Self-employed consultants must arrange these for themselves.

Where to Go for More Information

American Association of Political Consultants
900 Second Street, NE, Suite 204
Washington, DC 20002
(202) 371-9585

Probation Officer

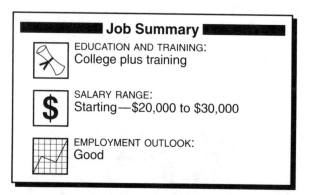

Job Summary

EDUCATION AND TRAINING:
College plus training

SALARY RANGE:
Starting—$20,000 to $30,000

EMPLOYMENT OUTLOOK:
Good

Definition and Nature of the Work

Probation officers are appointed by the courts to help people whom the courts decide need guidance. Probation officers counsel their clients and help them in a variety of ways. Officers generally work in the adult, juvenile, or family divisions of probation departments. They work for state or county courts. Others work at the federal level in the Probation Office of the United States District Court.

Some of the people whom probation officers supervise are on probation. These people have been convicted of a crime and are placed on probation instead of or in addition to being given a prison sentence. An individual placed on probation must see the officer regularly. The officer examines what the client has been doing. The probation officer may recommend entering a job-training program or enrolling in a school. Clients on probation must obey certain rules, such as avoiding bad company

and informing the probation officer of any change of address. If clients violate the rules of probation, officers report it to the judge. The judge may then revoke the probation, extend the period of probation, or impose a fine. Sometimes probation officers go to court to present information to the judge.

Some of the probation officers' clients are not on probation. For example, children may be placed under an officer's supervision if they have done something that is wrong but that would not be a crime if done by an adult.

Pretrial investigations are an important part of probation officers' work. Many people accused of crimes are investigated before they are brought to trial. The officers must decide whether it is in the best interest of society and the individuals to hold a trial. Because trials are very costly, court systems try to find alternative ways of dealing with alleged criminals. Probation officers interview the alleged criminals and their families and co-workers. The officers may believe that it is unlikely the accused will ever commit another crime. They may recommend to the judge that these people be placed under supervision instead of going to trial. The officers hope that their direction will prevent their clients from being accused of a crime again.

Probation officers also conduct the presentence investigations. They investigate the character, background, and criminal record of people who have been tried and convicted of crimes. Then they make recommendations to the judge concerning sentences. Officers may recommend prison sentences, probation, or a combination of the two. Probation officers must consider possible harmful effects on society if certain people are not imprisoned.

Probation officers also conduct bail investigations. People who are arrested may be released pending trial if they pay a sum of money to the court. This money, called bail, is returned if they appear at the trial. Probation officers may recommend that a person be released on high or low bail or without bail, depending on whether or not the officers think it is likely that the accused will appear at the trial.

Officers who work in family divisions may do custody investigations. In cases in which parents are separating or getting a divorce, both may want the children. Officers interview members of the family and recommend custody, living, and visitation arrangements to the judge.

Some probation officers who work in large probation offices may specialize in one aspect of probation work such as job placement. Some work in rural districts where there are few clients. These officers often work on all kinds of probation problems. Clients on probation are sometimes placed in halfway houses where they live together and work or go to school in the community. Some probation officers work in these halfway houses along with other professionals such as psychiatrists and social workers.

Education and Training Requirements

You must have a bachelor's degree to become a probation officer. Preferred majors are sociology, psychology, and criminology. Many probation offices and courts require that you have 1 or 2 years of experience working in a social welfare agency or correctional institution. Some offices prefer to hire people with a master's degree in one of the behavioral sciences. Probation officers are trained on the job by experienced officers.

Getting the Job

Most jobs in probation are at the county level. Contact your local probation office for information on job openings. You must pass a civil service test to get the job. If you are interested in working for probation offices at the federal level, arrange to take the necessary civil service exam. Then contact the federal probation offices to ask about current openings. Also check for job listings with your college placement office.

Advancement Possibilities and Employment Outlook

There are good advancement opportunities in probation work. Officers receive regular promotions and salary increases by passing civil service tests. Probation officers may go on to supervise other probation officers, or they may become the chief probation officer or the director of a probation department. Some probation officers go on to related jobs in government.

The employment outlook for probation officers is good since many officers will be needed to handle the increasing number of cases coming before the courts. Increased opportunities for probation officers, however, depend on public funding.

Working Conditions

Probation officers generally work 40 hours a week. Their hours may be irregular. They sometimes make weekend or evening appointments with probationers who work. The probation officer's job can be emotionally demanding since the officer must help the clients solve a wide range of personal problems.

Earnings and Benefits

Salaries vary widely depending on experience and location. The state, county, and federal governments have different pay scales. Beginning salaries for probation officers average about $20,000 to $30,000 a year. Benefits include paid holidays and vacations, health and life insurance, and retirement plans.

Where to Go for More Information

American Federation of State, County and Municipal
   Employees
1625 L Street, NW
Washington, DC 20036
(202) 452-4800

National Council on Crime and Delinquency
685 Market Street, Suite 620
San Francisco, CA 94105
(415) 896-6223

Rehabilitation Counselor

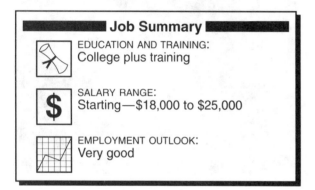

Job Summary

EDUCATION AND TRAINING:
College plus training

SALARY RANGE:
Starting—$18,000 to $25,000

EMPLOYMENT OUTLOOK:
Very good

Definition and Nature of the Work

Rehabilitation counselors help disabled people receive the training, support, and opportunities they need in order to lead more self-sufficient and normal lives at home and, if possible, on the job. They assist individuals who have mental, emotional, or physical handicaps. It is the counselor's responsibility to evaluate the individual and to arrange for a rehabilitation program that is suited to his or her needs, interests, and capabilities. This program may include medical care, occupational therapy, and job placement.

To find a suitable program for their client, counselors study medical and job histories and confer with doctors and therapists. They also talk to the client and his or her family.

Many counselors work for publicly funded agencies. Other places of employment include hospitals, schools, and rehabilitation facilities.

The work requires patience, perseverance, and initiative. The ability to interact well with people is essential since a rehabilitation counselor must be able to relate not only to clients but also to their families and prospective employers.

Education and Training Requirements

Some employers require that rehabilitation counselors have a master's degree in rehabilitation counseling, counseling and guidance, or counseling psychology. Others hire those with a bachelor's degree in rehabilitation services, counseling, psychology, or a related field. Many employers require that rehabilitation counselors be certified. Certification standards are set by the Commission on Rehabilitation Counselor Certification.

Getting the Job

Since roughly one-third of all rehabilitation counselors are employed by public service organizations, vacancies may be listed in state or federal civil service bulletins. Doing volunteer work in the field may give you some experience and contacts that will help you find a job.

Advancement Possibilities and Employment Outlook

Counselors may become directors of rehabilitation programs or self-employed consultants. The employment outlook is very good because the trend toward helping the disabled become more independent and productive is likely to continue. Moreover, both the government and private industry are showing an increased commitment to helping these individuals become members of the work force.

Working Conditions

The job generally entails some field work, visiting the homes of clients, and meeting with members of the business community to promote employment for the disabled or to locate training programs. Re-habilitation counselors are sometimes assigned to the job sites of disabled employees to help acclimate them to the work situation. Although they generally work fairly conventional hours, counselors may perform a diverse range of tasks, from preparing marketing presentations for corporations to locating voice boards to help clients speak. Therefore, a good counselor must be highly versatile.

Earnings and Benefits

Entry-level salaries are approximately $18,000 to $25,000, while experienced counselors in the highest-paying positions may earn over $41,000.

Rehabilitation counselors who are employed by government agencies or private businesses usually receive paid vacations, holidays, and medical insurance. Self-employed counselors must provide their own benefits.

Where to Go for More Information

National Association of Rehabilitation Facilities
1910 Association Drive, Suite 200
Reston, VA 22091
(703) 648-9300

National Rehabilitation Association
633 South Washington Street
Alexandria, VA 22314
(703) 836-0850

Religious Vocation

▬ Job Summary ▬

EDUCATION AND TRAINING:
Varies—see profile

SALARY RANGE:
Varies—see profile

EMPLOYMENT OUTLOOK:
Varies—see profile

Definition and Nature of the Work

Religious vocations are unlike all others. People enter religious vocations primarily for spiritual reasons. The three main spiritual vocations, or callings, are as Protestant *ministers*, Catholic *priests*, and Jewish *rabbis*. There are other spiritual groups, but Protestants, Catholics, and Jews constitute the largest religious groups in the country. Members of the ordained Christian clergy and the Jewish rabbinate are the religious leaders of the community. They are responsible for the sacred activities of their religious group. Ministers, priests, and rabbis perform many services that are common to all denominations. They preside over religious services, conduct weddings and funerals, counsel members of their congregations, and deliver sermons. Other activities are based on the beliefs and practices of the individual religions. Rabbis, for example, read the Torah, and priests hear confessions. Ministers, priests, and rabbis are sometimes assisted by members of their congregations. Some religious groups

belong to religious communities. They serve as teachers and counselors and may perform other jobs including maintenance work. A great number of lay employees—people who have not had formal authorization for their religious vocations—assist in clerical matters, social work, and administration.

Education and Training Requirements

Requirements vary according to the particular faith and specific vocation. Clergy and rabbis usually must study 3 to 5 years after receiving their bachelor's degree. Some Protestant faiths, however, have no formal educational requirements for their ministers. All ministers, priests, and rabbis, however, must have a thorough knowledge of the rites and beliefs of their group.

Training for religious vocations may begin in high school. Prospective priests study Latin. Those interested in Jewish vocations study Hebrew. All religious vocations emphasize modern-language study. Many individuals seeking religious vocations attend high schools and colleges with religious affiliations.

Those interested in religious vocations who do not wish to become ministers, priests, or rabbis will not need as much formal education. The range of jobs is too broad to generalize about the requirements. As a rough guide, however, lay employees require the same training as those performing similar tasks without religious affiliation. For example, the educational requirements for someone interested in working for a Christian youth group will be the same as those for a secular social worker with similar responsibilities.

are assisted by *deacons*. The duties of ministers, priests, and rabbis may include participating in interfaith services, organizing community activities, and working with community leaders on secular, or nonreligious, matters such as raising funds for building a hospital. Most Protestant and Jewish denominations permit women to serve as ministers or rabbis, but the Catholic church does not ordain women as priests.

Not all high-ranking religious vocations involve working with a congregation. Some priests, for example, work as teachers or scholars. Various aspects of social work are open to people desiring religious vocations. There is also missionary work, which involves providing religious and social assistance to developing societies overseas. *Chaplains* serve people's spiritual needs at armed services bases and in hospitals and schools.

There are religious vocations other than those of ministers, priests, and rabbis. Roman Catholic *nuns* are members of religious orders. Frequently they work as teachers. Their other jobs include nursing and social service work. Roman Catholic *brothers*

Getting the Job

Many people who are interested in religious vocations are assigned to their positions by religious officials. People interested in a religious vocation should contact their religious leaders for career counseling. Many people begin by working as assistants in their own congregations. Lay employees, such as social workers, who perform jobs similar to those in the secular world generally find jobs the same way their secular counterparts do.

Advancement Possibilities and Employment Outlook

As they become more experienced, priests, rabbis, and ministers take on greater responsibilities. Priests may become bishops or cardinals. Religious teachers may advance within their colleges or seminaries to more prestigious teaching positions. Lay workers and members of the clergy sometimes take on administrative jobs in religious institutions.

The outlook varies according to the religious denomination. The number of positions for rabbis and ministers is growing slowly. There are additional opportunities in social institutions with religious affiliations. There has been an increasing demand for Catholic priests that should continue through the year 2005.

Working Conditions

Conditions vary according to the faith and vocation. Rabbis, priests, and ministers are involved with their vocations 24 hours a day. Some lay employees, on the other hand, work only part time. Religious vocations may involve working in majestic cathedrals, ghettos, jungles in foreign countries, hospitals, or any other place a religious message is needed.

The living situations vary also. Catholic priests, nuns, and brothers are not permitted to marry. They usually live with others of their order. A good part of the day is spent working with people, but time is also needed for prayer, meditation, and study.

Earnings and Benefits

Salaries are generally lower than in other fields of work. Payment differs with the individual congregation—a wealthy church or temple can afford to pay more. Many members of the clergy receive free housing, utilities, and benefits such as health and retirement plans.

Catholic priests receive an average of $9,000 a year in addition to having free room and board in the parish rectory. Protestant ministers receive an estimated average income of about $25,000 to $29,000 a year. Rabbis earn $38,000 to $60,000 a year, although some senior rabbis earn more. Extra income may be earned by performing special services such as marriages.

Where to Go for More Information

Association of Theological Schools in the United
    States and Canada
10 Summit Park Drive
Pittsburgh, PA 15275-1103
(412) 788-6505

National Council of the Churches of Christ in the
    U.S.A.
475 Riverside Drive, Room 880
New York, NY 10115
(212) 870-2141

School Administrator

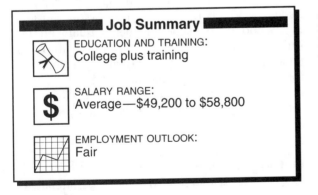

Job Summary

EDUCATION AND TRAINING:
College plus training

SALARY RANGE:
Average—$49,200 to $58,800

EMPLOYMENT OUTLOOK:
Fair

Definition and Nature of the Work

School administrators direct all aspects of school life. They work on several levels of control: as administrators for the federal and state governments, as superintendents working for local school boards, and as principals of individual schools.

Federal and *state school administrators* work in government departments of education. Federal administrators develop academic standards and pro-

grams and allocate funds to the schools. State administrators interpret state policy governing school lunches, teaching standards, and student transportation. They run large education departments with many staff members.

School superintendents head school districts that are made of several schools. District size varies considerably; districts may include from 2 to 800 schools. Superintendents carry out the school boards' decision on such matters as budget, hiring procedure, curriculum, and the expansion of facilities. They also keep track of their districts' needs and examine school policies to see that they are both efficient and effective. Superintendents may help the school board draw up the districts' budgets or make budgeting decisions with state and federal school administrators.

Superintendents are in charge of setting and administering their districts' policies on hiring and curriculum management. For example, superintendents may decide what textbooks will be used in classes. Superintendents of small districts work

closely with each school and its faculty; those who are responsible for many schools have contact primarily with their staff of assistant superintendents.

School principals administer individual schools. Principals draw up the school's budget and see that the school's policies on curriculum, discipline, and teaching are carried out. They are also in charge of the school's physical maintenance. In addition, they maintain contact with students and parents. Depending on the size of their schools, principals may have staffs of assistant principals in charge of curriculum or discipline for various grades. Like superintendents, school principals represent their schools to the community. They may write papers for publication, distribute school awards, and attend meetings and conferences. As administrators they act as links between the school and the community.

Education and Training Requirements

The educational requirements vary. Administrators should combine teaching experience with training in school administration. Most administrators have had college courses in education, economics, business, and sociology. In most cases administrators need a master's degree plus at least 2 years of teach-

ing experience. Although not all principals have a master's degree, most have taken courses in school administration. Some urban school principals are required to have a doctoral degree. These requirements vary according to the grade level and location of the school. Many school principals work as assistant principals for several years before advancing. School district superintendents usually are required to have completed graduate study in educational administration, preferably at the doctoral level. Both superintendents and principals must meet the specific certification requirements that are set by the state in which they are employed.

Getting the Job

Openings for school principals and superintendents are announced by local school boards. State departments of education and both public and private placement bureaus also list openings in educational administration. If you are interested in working for the state or federal government apply to take the appropriate civil service examination. Inexperienced civil service workers generally begin in middle-management positions and advance to higher government posts through length of service and by taking further examinations.

Advancement Possibilities and Employment Outlook

School principals may become school superintendents. Superintendents may go on to more challenging jobs in larger districts or with the state or federal government. The top posts in government are generally filled by appointment. Outstanding workers in the civil service may be chosen for these jobs. Administrators on all levels may be chosen to head special and experimental programs for government and for private companies that create educational materials.

Little growth in the employment of school administrators is expected through the year 2005. The number of available positions may decrease somewhat in some areas as school systems are reorganized. Most openings will occur to replace administrators who retire or leave their jobs for other reasons. Competition among job seekers is likely to be keen.

Working Conditions

School administrators generally work long hours. Principals are often expected to be at school when there are after-school functions such as concerts or sporting events. Superintendents spend extra time attending meetings and traveling. All administrators are on call in case of emergencies; their jobs carry pressure as well as prestige. They are often called on to make difficult decisions. Administrators should enjoy working with people. They must also be efficient and responsible in their work.

Earnings and Benefits

Salaries vary with the individual administrator's education and experience as well as with the location and size of the school or district. Salaries for assistant principals currently average $49,200 a year. Superintendents average about $58,800 a year. School administrators can expect paid holidays and vacations of between 2 and 4 weeks a year. They also receive health insurance and pension plans.

Where to Go for More Information

American Association of School Administrators
1801 North Moore Street
Arlington, VA 22209
(703) 528-0700

American Counseling Association
5999 Stevenson Avenue
Alexandria, VA 22304
(703) 823-9800

National Education Association of the U.S.
1201 Sixteenth Street, NW
Washington, DC 20036-3290
(202) 833-4000

School Counselor

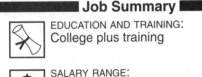

Job Summary

EDUCATION AND TRAINING:
College plus training

SALARY RANGE:
Starting—$24,000
Average—$38,500 to $42,500

EMPLOYMENT OUTLOOK:
Very good

Definition and Nature of the Work

School counselors help students make decisions that affect their personal and academic development. Counselors help students choose the courses they will take. Counselors also work with students who are experiencing personal and family problems. School counselors, who are sometimes called guidance counselors, work in both public and private schools. They work in elementary schools, junior high schools, and senior high schools. Counselors work as part of a team that includes classroom teachers, school psychologists, school nurses, and community groups. Counselors also meet with parents and parent groups.

Counselors who work in junior and senior high schools may spend much of their time helping students decide what they will do after high school graduation. As early as junior high school, students must choose courses that will enable them to get the training they need for the jobs they want. For example, students who plan to learn a trade may need a technical background, while business courses may best suit the career plans of others. Counselors encourage students to set goals and stick to them. To understand students' interests and abilities counselors may administer tests such as occupational interest tests. In addition, counselors make

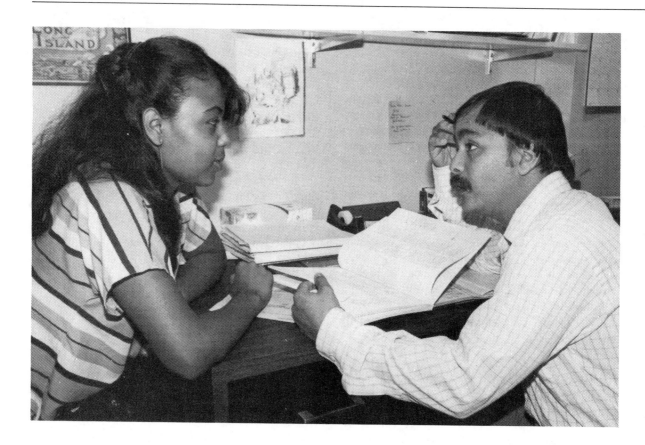

available to students scholarship information, training manuals, and catalogs of schools that offer advanced training.

Counselors who work in elementary schools work mainly with students who have special problems getting along in the classroom. Usually classroom teachers refer such students to counselors for guidance. Counselors provide special assistance to physically handicapped students and to those from troubled families. Students who get into trouble in the community are also counseled.

In addition to speaking to students individually, counselors may hold group sessions. In some schools guidance is a regularly scheduled class. Counselors may use this time to present specific materials to the class, or they may allow the students to choose the subject for discussion.

Education and Training Requirements

Check the educational requirements in your state before making any definite plans that affect your schooling. Requirements vary widely from state to state and change frequently. In general, states demand that counselors have certification, which requires 1 to 5 years of graduate training. Some states also require teaching certification. An undergrad-

uate major in psychology, education, or the liberal arts may be useful. Graduate students study group dynamics, testing, counseling, and statistics.

Getting the Job

Graduate school placement offices usually have a list of job openings. You can also write directly to the superintendent of schools in the district in which you would like to work. In addition, professional associations and journals may offer job leads. Newspaper want ads may list openings; the Sunday edition of *The New York Times* carries advertisements for educational positions all over the country. Private employment agencies that specialize in placing workers in educational jobs may be able to help you. In some areas counselors are assigned to schools when they are certified.

Advancement Possibilities and Employment Outlook

School counselors are already at the top of their profession. Some specialize in a certain area of guidance, such as vocational counseling. They may become the coordinator for their school in their area of expertise. Others take on supervisory jobs or become administrators for the school system.

The number of jobs for school counselors is expected to grow faster than average through the year 2005 as student enrollments increase. Counselors will also be needed to provide crisis and preventive counseling, particularly in secondary schools. Counselors should expect to face considerable competition for jobs.

Working Conditions

Full-time school counselors work longer hours than teachers do because they often meet with students and parents before and after school. Some counselors work part time or combine counseling with teaching duties. Generally, counselors have their own offices so that they can conduct their interviews in private. Counselors must be able to relate well to all kinds of people. Patience, resourcefulness, and stability are important qualities for school counselors.

Because the school year runs from September to June, counselors may take the summer months as paid vacation. Some have the opportunity to earn extra money during the summer by working in their schools or at other jobs. Counselors also have long winter and spring breaks. Many school counselors belong to labor unions.

Earnings and Benefits

Starting salaries for school counselors average $24,000 a year, but vary depending on the counselor's qualifications and the geographic location. Experienced school counselors earn from $38,500 to $42,500 a year. Benefits include paid holidays and vacations, sick leave, health insurance, and retirement plans.

Where to Go for More Information

American School Counselor Association
5999 Stevenson Avenue
Alexandria, VA 22304
(703) 823-9800

School Media Specialist

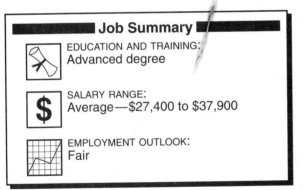

Job Summary

EDUCATION AND TRAINING:
Advanced degree

SALARY RANGE:
Average—$27,400 to $37,900

EMPLOYMENT OUTLOOK:
Fair

Definition and Nature of the Work

School media specialists advise school personnel on the use of nonprint media. Films, audiotapes, filmstrips, film loops, and slide presentations are all nonprint media. School media specialists may work either for an individual school or for a school district. Those who work in individual schools help teachers plan programs for their classes. For example, a media specialist may consult with a history teacher about the maps, tapes, and filmstrips available for an American history project. Media specialists also help plan the school's curriculum. They conduct workshops for teachers on the use of media in the classroom. They know what equipment is available for school use from the state and district offices. They also supervise the purchase of equipment and resources for the school. Many specialists work in school libraries.

Specialists at the district level have administrative duties. They plan the use of audiovisual materials for all the schools in a given district. They also make policy decisions about the use of media in schools. For example, they may help school superintendents make presentations to school boards. Sometimes they are in charge of the schools' libraries as well.

School media specialists are experts on the tools and techniques of media production and presentation. Some media specialists put their training and experience to work producing new educational materials for publishing firms.

Education and Training Requirements

Requirements vary widely from state to state. Furthermore, requirements change frequently. Before you decide on a course of study, be sure to check the requirements of the state in which you want to teach. School media specialists generally need a master's degree in educational media or a master's degree in another field of education and coursework in media. In some states teacher certification, teaching experience, and experience working as a media specialist are required.

Getting the Job

Your school placement office may be able to help you find a job. Private employment agencies that specialize in the field of education may offer job leads. In some areas you are assigned to a post when you are certified. You can also apply directly to school boards. Want ads in local newspapers may list openings; furthermore, the Sunday edition of *The New York Times* carries want ads for educational positions all over the country.

Advancement Possibilities and Employment Outlook

Specialists can advance from positions at the school level to posts at the district level or to jobs as heads of media for several school districts. Those with a doctoral degree can find jobs as college teachers. Some specialists advance to state posts in the department of education. They may become directors of curriculum or media programming.

Little growth is anticipated in the employment of school media specialists through the year 2005. Opportunities in this relatively small field will depend largely on the extent of public funding for education. However, corporations that maintain in-house libraries may offer some additional job opportunities for the media specialist.

Working Conditions

Many specialists who work at the school level combine media work with teaching. Their schedule follows that of other teachers. Sometimes their work involves handling heavy projection equipment. District media specialists and state workers work less often in the actual production of programs. However, their hours may be longer because they often attend late meetings and conferences.

Earnings and Benefits

Salaries vary with each state. School workers earn salaries comparable to those of teachers. District supervisors earn slightly higher wages. School media specialists currently earn salaries ranging from $27,400 to $37,900 a year. Benefits generally include paid holidays and vacations, health insurance, and pension plans. Media specialists often may receive tenure during their years as full-time teachers. Tenure protects employees from being fired without exceptional cause.

Where to Go for More Information

American Federation of Teachers
555 New Jersey Avenue, NW
Washington, DC 20001
(202) 879-4400

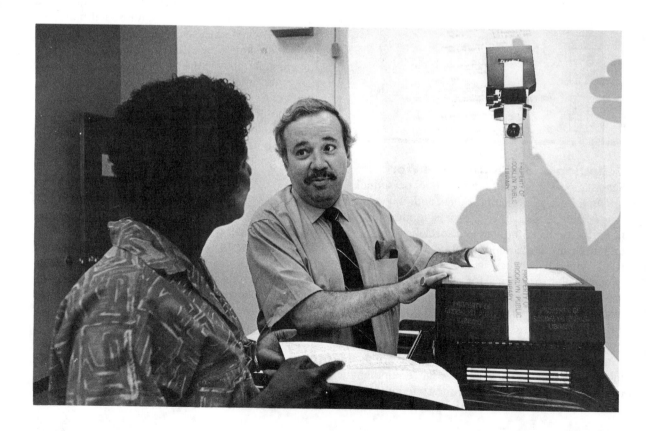

American Library Association
50 East Huron Street
Chicago, IL 60611
(312) 944-6780

Association for Educational Communications and
    Technology
1025 Vermont Avenue, NW, Suite 820
Washington, DC 20005
(202) 347-7834

International Communications Industries Association
3150 Spring Street
Fairfax, VA 22031-2399
(703) 273-7200

National Education Association of the U.S.
1201 Sixteenth Street, NW
Washington, DC 20036-3290
(202) 833-4000

Social Worker

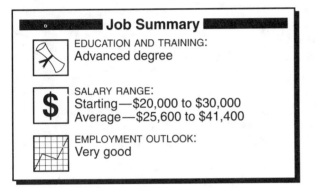

Job Summary

EDUCATION AND TRAINING:
Advanced degree

SALARY RANGE:
Starting—$20,000 to $30,000
Average—$25,600 to $41,400

EMPLOYMENT OUTLOOK:
Very good

Definition and Nature of the Work

Social workers help people with problems related to poverty, sickness, family matters, and individual crises. They provide guidance and counseling. They work in public welfare agencies, private social service agencies, school systems, hospitals, clinics, and recreation and rehabilitation centers. Their clients include children who have family or school problems, elderly people who have no one to care for them, and others who need help to solve their problems.

The services that social workers provide include finding foster homes for children and helping families who have been victimized by floods and other disasters. Sometimes social workers help their clients obtain government funds and services. Social workers help clients seek treatment for illness, obtain additional education, and find homemaking services when needed. They also conduct courses on child care and begin legal action in cases of child abuse.

Social workers who are employed in school systems work with students who are having difficulties. In trying to discover the root of a particular problem, they meet with the student and his or her parents and teachers. If social workers cannot handle the case, they refer it to an appropriate agency. Many work in conjunction with juvenile courts. Social workers employed by hospitals help patients

adjust to disabilities. They also counsel the patients' families. A small number of social workers are employed as teachers or researchers.

There are three approaches to social work: casework, group work, and community organization work. Most social workers use a combination of these methods. Caseworkers have conferences with individuals and families. For instance, they may help families stricken by the death of a parent. Group work involves helping people who have problems in common through recreation, guidance, and rehabilitation. Social workers meet with groups of unwed mothers, alcoholics, drug addicts, and elderly people to help them solve their problems through discussions and well-planned activities. Through community organization work social workers set up religious, civic, and political groups that are needed in an area of a city or town. For example, they may set up programs to find jobs for idle high school students.

One special group of social workers are *psychiatric social workers*. They may work at the same agencies and institutions as other social workers, but their emphasis is on psychological problems. Psychiatric social workers are usually a part of a team of specialists. In most agencies they work under the direction of a psychiatrist or psychologist.

Education and Training Requirements

For most positions a master's degree in social work is required, although a limited number of jobs are available for those with a bachelor's degree. Social workers who teach or do research generally hold a doctoral degree.

When in college you should major in sociology, psychology, or another social science and take courses in related areas such as economics, child studies, education, and political science. Graduate school courses generally include human growth and development, social welfare policies, and methods

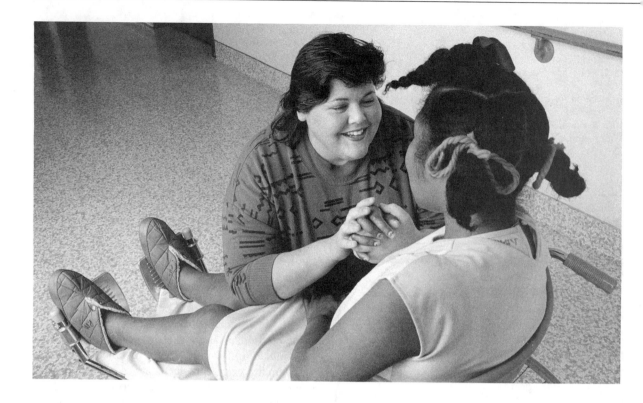

of social work. Most graduate schools offer work-study programs that will enable you to get work experience in an agency, hospital, or school.

New workers generally learn from experienced workers for the first few months on the job. After 2 years of supervised experience you may be eligible for membership in the Academy of Certified Social Workers, which is administered by the National Association of Social Workers. Membership is not required, but it is prestigious.

Psychiatric social workers must have a master's degree in psychiatric social work. Their academic requirements are similar to those of social workers, but there is a heavier concentration in psychology. A good part of their training during graduate school is spent in field work supervised by clinical psychologists.

Getting the Job

Your school placement office may be able to help you find a job. You may also apply directly to agencies for which you would like to work. Newspaper want ads and professional journals offer job leads. Private employment agencies that specialize in placing professional workers may help you. If you are interested in a government job, apply to take the necessary civil service test. Many job contacts are made by students doing field work for college courses.

Advancement Possibilities and Employment Outlook

Experienced social workers holding a master's degree may become senior caseworkers, case supervisors, or chief social workers, or they may take on administrative jobs. Those holding a doctoral degree may become university teachers or researchers.

The employment outlook for social workers is very good through the year 2005. Many openings will occur to replace workers who retire or leave their jobs for other reasons. Competition may exist in major metropolitan areas, however. Job prospects will be best for holders of graduate degrees.

Working Conditions

Social workers are employed in many places. Cities, suburbs, and rural areas all need social workers in schools, hospitals, offices, agencies, jails, and courts. While social work jobs are generally challenging and fulfilling, at times they can be quite frustrating. Many people are afraid to share their problems, and some cases may be difficult to handle. Frequently important work cannot be accomplished because agencies do not have the money for supplies and services. Social workers must be mature and sensitive to handle their responsibilities. Although they usually work 35 to 40 hours a week, they are sometimes required to work overtime. They generally receive compensatory time off for extra hours.

Earnings and Benefits

Salaries vary widely with education, experience, and location. Social workers with a bachelor's degree earn starting salaries averaging about $20,000 a year. Beginning social workers with a master's degree average about $30,000 a year. Experienced social workers earn average salaries of between $25,600 and $41,400 a year. Social workers in teaching, research, and administrative positions, as well as those employed by cities and large urban counties, earn considerably more than those employed by state agencies. Benefits generally include paid holidays and vacations, health insurance, and pension plans.

Where to Go for More Information

American Federation of State, County and Municipal
    Employees
1625 L Street, NW
Washington, DC 20036
(202) 452-4800

Council on Social Work Education
1600 Duke Street, Suite 300
Alexandria, VA 22314
(703) 683-8080

National Association of Social Workers
750 First Street, NE
Washington, DC 20002-4241
(202) 408-8600

Teacher, College

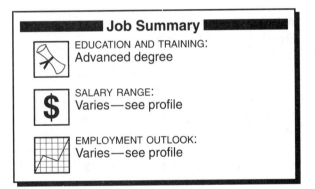

Job Summary

EDUCATION AND TRAINING:
Advanced degree

SALARY RANGE:
Varies—see profile

EMPLOYMENT OUTLOOK:
Varies—see profile

Definition and Nature of the Work

The job of teacher at the college and university level involves much more than teaching. As experts in their subject area, college teachers set the standards for the research conducted in their discipline. They also write articles and books in addition to teaching classes on the graduate and undergraduate levels. Teachers work at four-year colleges, two-year junior and community colleges, and graduate and professional schools. Some teach in evening and continuing education programs.

Colleges and universities are composed of many different departments such as music, psychology, and computer science. Most teachers work in one department and specialize in one phase of their discipline. They usually teach from two to four courses each semester. Teachers usually combine many different methods of teaching, but most use some form of lecture and discussion. In addition, teachers read student papers and correct examinations. They hold office hours so that students may discuss their work. Teachers also act as advisers to students who are majoring in their departments. Some teachers combine teaching with administrative duties. For example, a physics teacher at a small college might also be the dean of students. Other college teachers work part time as consultants to educational organizations and other groups that can use their special knowledge.

Although all college teachers may be called professors in the general sense, there are distinct ranks in the profession. *Instructors* rank lowest; they usually have no job security and may have no voice in determining curriculum or setting university policy. Instructors usually teach undergraduates. *Assistant professors* and *associate professors* are more experienced. They teach undergraduates and, at some schools, graduate students. They may be active in university administrative affairs and set the curriculum for their own courses. *Full professors* are the most highly ranked teachers. They may serve as department heads as well as teach.

Education and Training Requirements

College teachers must have a master's or a doctoral degree. Many junior and community colleges hire teachers who have a master's degree. Four-year

oratory classes that are part of a professor's large lecture classes. Teaching assistantships provide graduate students with financial aid and college teaching experience.

Getting the Job

Your school placement bureau may be able to help you find a teaching position. Often professors help their students find jobs. Because they know teachers at other colleges, they are in a good position to know about openings before they are announced. You can apply directly to teaching institutions for jobs. Professional journals often list openings in a specific field, and the Sunday edition of *The New York Times* is a clearinghouse for teaching jobs all over the world. The *Chronicle of Higher Education,* a weekly newspaper, also lists hundreds of positions. You may be able to find a job through a private employment agency that specializes in placing teachers.

Advancement Possibilities and Employment Outlook

Instructors may become assistant professors, associate professors, and then full professors after many years of experience. Teachers usually need a doctoral degree to get positions as associate professors. The requirement for promotion varies from place to place; some colleges look for excellence in teaching while others require teachers to write extensively for publication. Experienced and well-qualified teachers often are given tenure at their colleges. Having tenure generally constitutes a permanent appointment; tenured professors cannot be dismissed without exceptional cause. Professors can also advance by accepting jobs at more prestigious colleges or by becoming department heads. They may choose to take administrative posts; for example, some become college presidents.

colleges and universities employ teachers who have a master's degree as instructors, but they usually expect these teachers to complete their doctoral degree. Many teachers finish the requirements for their doctoral degree while they work.

A master's degree generally requires between 1 and 3 years of graduate work beyond college. To complete a doctoral degree, between 2 and 6 years of work beyond the master's are required. High school and college courses in foreign languages are helpful because many graduate programs require that students be able to read foreign languages. Graduate students take in-depth courses in their field. For a master's degree, a master's thesis and written and oral examinations may be required. Requirements for a doctoral degree include more course work, oral examinations, and a book-length paper, called a dissertation, which is based on original research.

Many graduate students work as teaching assistants for at least 1 year. Some teach their own classes. Others lead small discussion groups or conduct lab-

Over 812,000 people work as full- and part-time college teachers. The employment outlook varies with each field. Although a higher percentage of people are attending college now than ever before, the general decline in population has caused the total number of students to decline. However, the number of people holding doctoral degrees has increased, so there are more people competing for teaching jobs. Most openings arise when teachers advance, retire, or leave the field. Teachers in the sciences, as well as those with administrative skills, generally will have the best opportunities.

Working Conditions

Teachers spend from 12 to 16 hours a week in class. Their schedules change each semester. Office hours, faculty meetings, advising, and class preparation account for between 30 and 40 additional hours a week. Teachers enjoy a certain degree of freedom because they can arrange their own schedules around their class time. Since the school year runs from September to May, teachers may use the other months to do research or take summer teaching jobs. Because research projects, especially those in the sciences, may be funded by private and government money, teachers may have to compete for available funds. In colleges in which the pressure to publish is strong, research may take up much of the teacher's time. Teachers with established reputations may be asked to spend semesters as visiting professors at other colleges. Many college teachers belong to labor unions.

Earnings and Benefits

Salaries vary widely with rank and with the individual college. Instructors average about $27,700 a year. Assistant professors earn about $36,800, while associate professors earn about $44,100. Salaries for full professors range from $52,000 to over $67,000 a year. Some teachers increase their income by working as consultants.

Benefits also vary. Teachers are usually paid over a 12-month period that includes the time they do not teach. Most receive health insurance and pension plans. Some colleges offer tenured teachers sabbatical leave every seventh year. During leaves, professors are relieved from teaching duties to devote all of their time to research. Some colleges provide housing at reduced prices.

Where to Go for More Information

American Association of Community Colleges
One Dupont Circle, NW, Suite 410
Washington, DC 20036
(202) 728-0200

American Association of University Professors
1012 Fourteenth Street, NW, Suite 500
Washington, DC 20005
(202) 737-5900

American Council on Education
One Dupont Circle, NW, Suite 800
Washington, DC 20036
(202) 939-9300

National Education Association of the U.S.
1201 Sixteenth Street, NW
Washington, DC 20036-3290
(202) 833-4000

Teacher, Elementary and Preschool

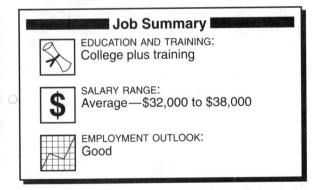

Job Summary

EDUCATION AND TRAINING:
College plus training

SALARY RANGE:
Average—$32,000 to $38,000

EMPLOYMENT OUTLOOK:
Good

Definition and Nature of the Work

Elementary and preschool teachers instruct children from the nursery school level through the sixth grade. Preschool teachers work with the young children in nursery schools and kindergartens. *Nursery school teachers* teach children who are two to four years old. Nursery school teachers concentrate on the social skills; they teach children to share and communicate with others their own age. They also help children learn practical skills such as tying their own shoes. Nursery school teachers keep their pupils occupied with activities that include music, games, and storybooks.

Kindergarten teachers have many of the same goals. They help their five-year-old pupils learn to play and communicate with others. In kindergarten students are introduced to subjects they will pursue in later grades. They learn arithmetic by means of counting games and begin to read the letters on building blocks. Teachers at the preschool level have little difficulty keeping their students occupied. Their aim is to provide constructive outlets for their students' curiosity. Since young children generally go to school only a few hours a day, their teachers may have two separate classes, one in the morning and one in the afternoon.

Elementary school teachers generally have the same class for the whole school day. They teach students the basic skills they will need throughout their school years: reading, writing, arithmetic, and simple concepts in science. Some teachers who participate in team-teaching programs specialize in one subject, such as science or arithmetic, which they teach to several groups of students. A few, such as *remedial reading teachers*, are specialists who work with small groups of students who need special attention.

Other specialists include *bilingual teachers,* who concentrate on improving their students' English-language skills. They may also teach other subjects in their students' native language. *ESL* (English as a second language) *teachers* teach English to students who have not been exposed to the language at all. *Special education teachers* teach the handicapped, retarded, and mentally disturbed. Special education teachers usually teach diverse groups because students are placed in special education classes regardless of grade. *Homebound teachers* give lessons to students who are unable to attend school regularly because of health problems. Teachers of the homebound go to students' homes to teach.

Teachers on both the preschool and elementary levels attend meetings of the school board and parent-teacher association. Furthermore, teachers meet regularly with parents to tell them about their children's progress and to determine how students' home environments affect their development in school.

Education and Training Requirements

Teachers who work in public schools must be certified in the state in which they teach. In many states private and parochial school teachers must be certified to work. Certification requirements in most states include minimum educational standards as well as satisfactory performance on written examinations. Kindergarten and elementary school teachers need a bachelor's degree, including coursework in education and student-teaching experience. Some school districts require a master's degree. Nursery school teachers generally need at least a bachelor's degree as well as experience working in early childhood education.

Since requirements vary, you should know the standards in your state and the preferences of local school boards before making any decisions regarding your education. Teachers who work in special areas of education generally need the most training.

Getting the Job

Your college placement office may help you find a teaching position. Some teachers' associations also offer help in finding academic positions. You can write directly to the superintendents of school districts in which you want to teach. In some school districts teachers are assigned to schools when they pass the certification examinations. Newspaper want ads often list openings for teachers.

Advancement Possibilities and Employment Outlook

As teachers become more experienced, they may find advancement in the form of higher pay. Some become specialists in areas such as remedial reading. Teachers may become the directors of special educational projects in their school districts. Others become administrators such as teacher supervisors or principals, or go on to teach at colleges of education. These positions sometimes require further education. Nursery school teachers may go on to teach kindergarten and elementary classes if they complete the necessary educational requirements.

The employment outlook for elementary and preschool teachers is generally expected to grow somewhat through the year 2005. Openings will occur to replace teachers who retire or leave their profession for other reasons. Job prospects are expected to improve owing to a rising birth rate and corresponding enrollment increases in preschools and the lower grades. While enrollment may increase, opportunities will vary throughout the country according to funding availability in different school systems.

Working Conditions

Working conditions vary from school to school. The job can be tiring, even for teachers who love children. The pace of activity is especially high in the early grades. Unruly students can make teaching difficult. However, teachers find personal satisfaction by watching their students make progress.

Nursery school teachers may work only half a day. Elementary school teachers usually work with the same class the whole school day, whereas kindergarten teachers generally work with two classes, one in the morning and one in the afternoon. Although preparation periods are built into the workday, teachers also spend extra time preparing lessons and grading papers at home. Teachers sometimes attend late meetings. Since the school year runs from September to June, teachers may have to look for positions in summer schools or find other jobs. Some spend their summers taking courses to improve their skills. Many teachers belong to labor unions.

Earnings and Benefits

Salaries vary widely with each school depending on its location and the teacher's education. The earnings of public elementary school teachers average about $32,000 to $38,000 a year. Experienced teachers may earn as much as $45,000 a year. Salaries of preschool and kindergarten teachers average about $19,000 to $26,000 a year. Benefits vary, but elementary and preschool teachers can usually expect paid holidays and vacations, health insurance, and pension plans.

Where to Go for More Information

American Counseling Association
5999 Stevenson Avenue
Alexandria, VA 22304
(703) 823-9800

American Federation of Teachers
555 New Jersey Avenue, NW
Washington, DC 20001
(202) 879-4400

National Association for the Education of Young
   Children
1509 Sixteenth Street, NW
Washington, DC 20036-1426
(202) 232-8777

National Education Association of the U.S.
1201 Sixteenth Street, NW
Washington, DC 20036-3290
(202) 833-4000

Teacher, Secondary School

Job Summary

EDUCATION AND TRAINING:
College plus training

SALARY RANGE:
Average—$33,000 to $39,000

EMPLOYMENT OUTLOOK:
Very good

Definition and Nature of the Work

Secondary school teachers instruct students in junior and senior high schools. They conduct classes in academic subjects or teach courses such as mechanical drawing and woodworking in which specific skills are learned. In addition, they organize extracurricular activities such as sports and social groups and meet with other teachers to plan courses that use new methods and materials. Teachers work as part of a team that includes school administrators, school counselors, and school psychologists. Teachers work closely with parents and parent groups and with community and social work agencies.

Junior high school teachers instruct students in the seventh, eighth, and ninth grades, while *high school teachers* teach the tenth, eleventh, and twelfth grades. In some school districts junior high schools have been replaced by middle or intermediate schools, which students enter at a somewhat earlier age. *Intermediate school teachers* may teach the fifth through eighth grades.

Secondary school teachers generally teach between four and seven classes a day. Teachers usually conduct classes only in their field of interest. English, mathematics, science, and history are academic subjects taught in all schools. Some teachers specialize in foreign languages, computer sciences, mathematics, music, or art. In addition to subject classes, teachers may be assigned to homeroom classes and study halls. In homeroom attendance is taken and school business handled. Teachers in study halls must maintain order so that students can study in a quiet atmosphere.

Physical education teachers teach gym classes. These teachers concentrate on improving students' strength and motor skills. Teachers may administer physical fitness and posture tests and set up exercise programs to meet students' needs. Specific sports such as softball and basketball may also be taught. Physical education teachers generally serve as

coaches for one or more sports teams after school hours.

Some teachers have special skills in certain areas of teaching. *Special education teachers* teach the handicapped, retarded, and mentally disturbed. *ESL* (English as a second language) *teachers* teach English to students who have not been exposed to the language at all. *Bilingual teachers* work to improve their students' skills in English. They may also teach other subjects such as mathematics and history in their students' native language. *Homebound* teachers give lessons to students who are unable to attend school regularly because of health problems. Teachers of the homebound go to students' homes to teach.

Education and Training Requirements

Teachers who work in public secondary schools must be certified in their state; in many states private and parochial school teachers also must be certified. Certification requirements include a bachelor's degree, usually in the subject to be taught, student teaching experience, and coursework in education. Many states now require teachers to possess or be working toward a master's degree at the time of certification. Requirements vary from state to state and change frequently. Check the requirements in your state before making any decisions that affect your schooling. Usually teachers must pass written and sometimes oral examinations in order to be certified.

Getting the Job

Your school placement office may list job openings. You may apply directly to the principal of a school or superintendent of a district in which you would like to teach. Some professional journals and teachers' organizations list job openings. Private employment agencies that specialize in education may offer job leads. The Sunday edition of *The New York Times* carries want ads for openings all over the country. Want ads in local newspapers may also list openings. In some areas teachers are assigned to schools when they are certified.

Advancement Possibilities and Employment Outlook

Teachers may become heads of their departments. Teachers may also take on administrative and counseling duties as school counselors, assistant prin-

cipals, principals, and school superintendents. Most of these positions require at least a master's degree; some require a doctoral degree as well.

About 1,263,000 people are employed as secondary school teachers. Employment is expected to grow faster than the average, due to a strong increase in the number of 14- to 17-year-olds through the year 2005. Competition for jobs may be keenest in suburban areas, however. Jobs will be most plentiful in central cities and rural areas. Teachers in the natural and physical sciences, mathematics, special education, and vocational subjects are likely to find jobs more easily than teachers in other fields.

Working Conditions

Working conditions vary somewhat with each subject taught. While most teachers work with 10 to 30 students per class, music teachers may work with one student at a time. Teaching is physically strenuous; most teachers stand most of the day and may suffer from voice strain. Hours vary, but most teachers are in school between 9 and 3 o'clock each day. Teachers also work at home, and some spend additional time at school in meetings and supervising extracurricular activities such as drama productions or sports events. Generally secondary school teachers do not work during the summer months; many use this free time to earn additional income. Many teachers belong to labor unions.

Earnings and Benefits

Teachers' salaries vary with education, length of service, and location of the school. The average annual salary for secondary school teachers is about $33,000 to $39,000. Urban schools tend to pay higher salaries than those in rural areas. Teachers with a master's or doctoral degree earn much more than those who have only a bachelor's degree.

Teachers receive unusually long paid vacations and holidays as well as health insurance and pension plans. Some schools offer sabbatical leave after several years of employment.

Where to Go for More Information

American Counseling Association
5999 Stevenson Avenue
Alexandria, VA 22304
(703) 823-9800

American Federation of Teachers
555 New Jersey Avenue, NW
Washington, DC 20001
(202) 879-4400

National Education Association of the U.S.
1201 Sixteenth Street, NW
Washington, DC 20036-3290
(202) 833-4000

Teacher, Vocational Education

Job Summary

EDUCATION AND TRAINING:
High school plus training

SALARY RANGE:
Average—$24,000 to $34,000

EMPLOYMENT OUTLOOK:
Very good

Definition and Nature of the Work
Vocational education teachers instruct students in vocational and occupational subjects that teach specific skills. These subjects may include secretarial skills, computer technology, cosmetology, drafting, commercial art, plumbing, automotive mechanics,

practical nursing, and electronics. Vocational education teachers may work in public or private high schools, in community colleges, or in privately owned trade schools. They may also work in special teaching facilities run by noneducation organizations such as companies and labor unions.

Some teachers specialize in one subject, while others teach a variety of subjects. In addition to teaching the material and evaluating students' knowledge and performance, teachers are sometimes responsible for placing students in actual work settings and monitoring their progress.

Education and Training Requirements
A college degree generally is not required for vocational education instructors, but they usually have to pass a licensing examination that verifies their

expertise in the subject they plan to teach. Many have extensive job experience in their fields of instruction. Some teachers, especially those who are in rapidly changing technological fields, continue to take courses throughout their teaching careers.

Getting the Job

Jobs are often advertised in the newspapers. Some teachers break into the field as teaching assistants in vocational programs. These positions are sometimes given to vocational program graduates who place at or near the top of their class. These assistants divide their time between teaching and working in industry.

Advancement Possibilities and Employment Outlook

Vocational education teachers may advance to administrative positions such as principal or superintendent, but this move often requires additional education credentials.

The employment outlook is very good because the field currently is suffering from a lack of teachers. This trend is apt to continue because qualified vocational education teachers can earn considerably more money for their expertise by working in industry, and many are choosing to do so.

Working Conditions

The hours are fairly regular, but teachers usually have to prepare lessons and grade tests on their own time. Teachers whose place of employment follows the conventional 10-month school year do not work during the summer months.

Earnings and Benefits

Vocational education teachers earn annual salaries of approximately $24,000 to $34,000. Teaching assistants may earn as much as 90% of a teacher's salary. Benefits generally include vacations, sick pay, and health and life insurance. Some employers may offer tuition reimbursement programs for employees who wish to attend college.

Where to Go for More Information

American Vocational Association
1410 King Street
Arlington, VA 22314
(703) 683-3111

Urban and Regional Planner

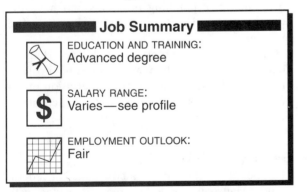

Job Summary

EDUCATION AND TRAINING:
Advanced degree

SALARY RANGE:
Varies—see profile

EMPLOYMENT OUTLOOK:
Fair

Definition and Nature of the Work

Urban planners design new communities and develop programs for revitalizing and expanding existing cities. Regional planners are engaged in the same kind of work on a much larger scale; their work involves states, large regional areas, and, sometimes, entire countries. Planners renovate slums, expand cities, modernize transportation systems, and devise ways to properly distribute public facilities such as schools and parks. Their major concern is to unify the social, economic, and physical development of an area so that it will be functional for its citizens. Also, planners find ways to attract industries to move to an area in order to create jobs for residents.

Urban and regional planning projects generally begin with a request from a city or state official to develop a new community or renovate an area that is run-down. Planners gather information about the area's economic and social climate, projected population growth or decline, and plans for industrial development. To get a cross section of public opinion, planners meet with representatives of community groups, government, public agencies, and labor and business organizations. Planners consider the area's current problems as well as needs that are likely to arise in the future. For example, an expected rise in an area's population will create a greater need for electrical power. Foreseeing this need, planners try to determine ways in which the necessary power can be generated without creating pollution.

Once the data are collected, teams of planners study the information and arrive at decisions. Then they draw up proposals and submit them to the area's planning commission or to government officials for approval. If approval is given, construction or renovation begins. Planners usually supervise the work through its completion. Projects may take many years to complete.

Most planners work for city, county, state, federal, or regional agencies. Some work for large construction companies and architectural firms. Others work as consultants or hold teaching or research positions. Planners also work for international organizations that plan projects in developing nations.

Education and Training Requirements

Most employers prefer to hire planners who have a master's degree or some graduate training in urban planning. A few jobs may be available to people who have a bachelor's degree. In college it is best to major in architecture, public administration, landscape architecture, or civil engineering. You should also take courses in related fields such as political science, economics, and geography.

With a bachelor's degree in architecture or engineering, you may be able to earn a master's degree in 1 year. Many programs take 2 to 3 years to complete. In graduate school you will learn to analyze and solve planning problems and have the opportunity to do part-time field work in an office or agency.

Recent graduates expand their skills on the job. Generally they begin by working on small projects or aspects of projects under the supervision of experienced workers. As planners gain practical experience they take on more responsibility.

Getting the Job

Most people begin work at a city, state, or federal agency. Many cities have planning commissions with technical staffs and special agencies for urban renewal or neighborhood conservation programs. For a government job you must pass a civil service test and meet the necessary educational and experience requirements. There are many opportunities for regional planners in other countries. Private employment agencies that specialize in placing professionals may be able to help you find a job. You may apply directly to private and international organizations for which you would like to work.

Advancement Possibilities and Employment Outlook

Urban and regional planners can advance to become project directors. Some choose to take on more challenging projects that offer them greater responsibility.

The job outlook for urban and regional planners is fair through the year 2005. There is a growing demand for experts trained in environmental, economic, and energy planning. However, increases in the number of people entering this relatively small field may result in stiff competition for available jobs.

Working Conditions

Urban and regional planning is highly rewarding work. Workers find satisfaction not only in knowing that they help others but also in seeing projects through from conception to the physical reality. There are, however, some disadvantages. Lack of funds or disapproval from government officials can be discouraging. Planners must be patient because their ideas may take many years to implement. Planners must be both creative and flexible when proposals must be modified to suit the government's needs. They must be able to handle detail as well as have the tenacity to follow problems through until they are solved. Planners work both indoors and outdoors. Planners generally work 35 to 40 hours a week, although those in positions of great responsibility may work many more hours. Consulting planners set their own hours.

Earnings and Benefits

Salaries vary widely with education, experience, and the location of the work. Salaries are generally higher in larger cities. Starting salaries for urban and regional planners range from about $18,000 to $28,000 a year. The salaries of experienced planners range from $36,000 to $65,000, depending on the size of the company for which they work. Consultants' fees are paid on an hourly basis and generally depend on their previous experience and reputation. Benefits generally include paid holidays and vacations, health insurance, and pension plans.

Where to Go for More Information

American Federation of State, County and Municipal
    Employees
1625 L Street, NW
Washington, DC 20036
(202) 452-4800

American Planning Association
1776 Massachusetts Avenue, NW, Suite 400
Washington, DC 20036-1997
(202) 872-0611

United States Government Federal Information
    Center
Phone number in local directory.

Vocational Counselor

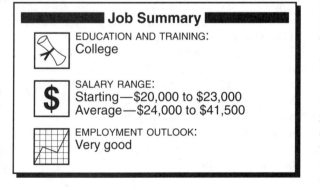

```
■■■■■ Job Summary ■■■■■
  EDUCATION AND TRAINING:
  College

  SALARY RANGE:
  Starting—$20,000 to $23,000
  Average—$24,000 to $41,500

  EMPLOYMENT OUTLOOK:
  Very good
```

Definition and Nature of the Work

Vocational counselors, sometimes called employment counselors, help people find employment that suits their needs and skills. They provide a link between people looking for work and employers.

Because people are not always aware of their capabilities, counselors often help clients decide on career goals. To do this counselors must have a good awareness of their clients' potential and also know what skills are in demand in the job market. Unlike agents who work for profit-making employment agencies, these counselors work for organizations that provide vocational counseling free of charge. Counselors work in state employment offices, veterans' programs, colleges and universities, and private and government-sponsored social service agencies. Those who work with the mentally ill and physically disabled are called *rehabilitation counselors*. In colleges and universities they may be called *college placement counselors*.

Counselors first interview their clients to find out about their goals, past work experience, and potential. Counselors may administer achievement,

aptitude, and occupational preference tests. In state employment offices and some other agencies, an employment interviewer collects this information for the employment counselor, who advises the clients. In some agencies the counselor performs all of these duties.

Some people are fully qualified for employment, and it is up to the counselors to contact prospective employers. This is often the case in college placement offices. Clients who seek help from social service organizations, on the other hand, usually have had some difficulty in finding or holding jobs. Counselors may work with these clients over a period of several months. Clients may be handicapped or considered too old to start work. They may lack sufficient training or have a history of alcoholism or drug abuse. Some have faced prejudice because of their race or sex. Those who have been out of work for a long time may be too discouraged to do well at employment interviews. Counselors work to solve the problems of the particular individual. They may place clients in training programs that will help

them develop marketable skills. They may refer clients to other social service organizations that can help them solve the problems that cause their joblessness. For example, a counselor might refer a handicapped client to a physical rehabilitation center. Counselors may coach clients so that they are able to perform well at interviews.

School counselors in junior and senior high schools sometimes serve as vocational counselors. They may help students find part-time or summer jobs or place them in full-time positions after graduation. However, they concentrate on preparing students for the job market. They help students choose careers and get the education and training they need for the jobs they want.

Education and Training Requirements

A bachelor's degree is the minimum requirement for counselors, although many employers require a master's degree in vocational counseling, social work, sociology, or a related field. Many agencies seek to have at least 1 staff member with a doctoral degree in a counseling-related field. A background in interviewing and testing procedures is useful. Most agencies give on-the-job training to teach new workers counseling methods and to acquaint them with the goals and procedures of the particular agency. Experience with personnel and administrative work may be helpful.

Getting the Job

The placement office of your school may help you find a job. You can also write directly to agencies for which you would like to work. Professional journals and organizations often list job openings in their publications. State and private employment agencies and newspaper want ads may offer job leads. If you are interested in a government job, apply to take the appropriate civil service test.

Advancement Possibilities and Employment Outlook

Vocational counselors may take on supervisory or administrative jobs in their agencies. Those who work in schools and colleges may move up to higher positions in the school administration. Some become consultants to government and industry. Others teach counseling in colleges and graduate schools. Counselors may be required to have a doctoral degree to teach in colleges or to reach the highest administrative jobs.

The employment outlook for vocational counselors is very good. Because of the restructuring of the American work force, many workers, especially in manufacturing, will lose their jobs and require career counseling. However, opportunities in this field can be affected by changes in federal funding

levels. Applicants are likely to face some competition for counseling jobs.

Working Conditions

Counselors must be able to communicate clearly and listen carefully. They must be aware of the changing employment scene as well as of various training programs. To keep up with their field, counselors may spend many extra hours reading papers and bulletins. They generally work in small offices where they can talk with people in private. Sometimes counselors leave the office to talk to employers or to visit training centers. Vocational counselors work 35 to 40 hours a week. Sometimes they put in extra hours during the evening or on weekends.

Earnings and Benefits

Salaries vary with experience, level of education, and the size and location of the employer. Salaries for beginning vocational counselors employed in state employment services average about $20,000 to $23,000 a year. Experienced vocational counselors earn between $24,000 and $41,500 a year. Benefits generally include paid holidays and vacations, health insurance, and pension plans.

Where to Go for More Information

American Counseling Association
5999 Stevenson Avenue
Alexandria, VA 22304
(703) 823-9800

American Federation of State, County and Municipal
  Employees
1625 L Street, NW
Washington, DC 20036
(202) 452-4800

Further Reading and Resources

General Career Information—Books

Exploring the Working World

Recommended

The Encyclopedia of Careers and Vocational Guidance, 9th ed., 4 vols., William E. Hopke, et al., eds. New York: Ferguson, 1993. Comprehensive source. Volume 1 is an overview of various fields. Volumes 2, 3, and 4 provide specific information for professional, administrative, technical, engineering, media, and health care careers.

Occupational Outlook Handbook, United States Department of Labor. Washington, DC: United States Government Printing Office, revised biennially. Expands on the *Dictionary of Occupational Titles*. Groups jobs into similar categories. Discusses the nature of the work, the employment outlook, and earnings.

VGM's Careers Encyclopedia, 3rd ed., Craig T. Norback, ed. Lincolnwood, IL: VGM Career Horizons/NTC Publishing Group, 1991. A one-volume guide to 180 careers.

Aid to Career Decisions, D. Arthur. San Diego, CA: Windsong, 1991.

American Almanac of Jobs and Salaries, John W. Wright and Edward J. Dwyer. New York: Avon Books, rev. 1993.

America's Fastest Growing Jobs: A Complete Guide. New York: Gordon Press, 1992.

Career Action Plan, William M. Bloomfield. Bloomington, IL: Meridian Education, 1989.

Career Briefs series. Largo, FL: Careers, Inc. Series of leaflets on many occupations; these are available separately and are revised regularly.

Career Discovery Encyclopedia, C. J. Summerfield, ed., 6 vols. Chicago: Ferguson, 1993.

Career Employment Opportunities Directory, 2nd ed., 4 vols. Santa Monica, CA: Ready Reference Press.

Career Summary series. Largo, FL: Careers, Inc. Series of cards on hundreds of jobs, available separately. Updated regularly.

The Complete Guide to Public Employment, 3rd ed., Ronald Krannich. Manassas, VA: Impact Publications, 1993.

Dictionary of Occupational Titles, 4th ed., United States Department of Labor. Washington, DC: United States Government Printing Office, rev. 1991.

Exploring Careers: The World of Work and You, J. Michael Farr and JoAnn Amore. Indianapolis, IN: JIST Works, 1989.

Great Careers: The Fourth of July Guide to Careers, Internships, and Volunteer Opportunities in the Nonprofit Sector, Devon C. Smith, ed. Garrett Park, MD: Garrett Park Press, 1990.

The Harvard Guide to Careers, 3rd ed., Martha P. Leape and Susan M. Vacca. Cambridge, MA: Harvard University Press, 1991.

Job Search Kit, Thomas R. Wims. Lanham, MD: Roberts Publications, 1992.

Jobs '95, Kathryn Petras. New York: Simon & Schuster, annual.

Jobs Rated Almanac Two, Les Krantz. New York: Pharos Books, rev. 1992.

National Job Bank, 1994, Carter Smith. Boston: Adams, 1993.

Occu-Facts: Facts on Over 565 Careers, Elizabeth Handville, ed. Largo, FL: Careers, Inc., 1989.

Occupational Mini-Brief series. Moravia, NY: Chronicle Guidance Publications. Series of leaflets, available separately.

Occupational Outlook series. Washington, DC: United States Government Printing Office. Briefs, separately published.

Occupational Outlook Quarterly. Washington, DC: Occupational Outlook Service, Bureau of Labor Statistics, current since 1956. Quarterly.

Occupational Projections and Training Data: A Statistical Supplement to the Occupational Outlook Handbook. United States Department of Labor. Washington, DC: United States Government Printing Office, revised biennially.

Professional Careers Sourcebook, 3rd ed. Detroit: Gale, 1993.

Top Professions: The 100 Most Popular, Dynamic, and Profitable Careers in America Today, Nicholas Basta. Princeton, NJ: Peterson's Guides, 1989.

Vocational Careers Sourcebook, Hill, et al. Detroit: Gale, 1992.

Education and Training Opportunities

Recommended

The following four sources are basic directories of information on colleges and universities. They include general information on each school, its address, a listing of the programs offered, the size of the institution, and costs for tuition.

Barron's Top Fifty: An Inside Look at America's Best Colleges, 2nd ed., 2 vols., Tom Fischgrund, ed. Hauppauge, NY: Barron's Educational Series, revised regularly.

The College Blue Book. New York: Macmillan Publishing Co., revised regularly.

Lovejoy's College Guide, Charles T. Straughn and Barbarasue Straughn, ed. New York: Prentice Hall, revised regularly.

Peterson's Guide to Four-Year Colleges, Susan Dilts and Mark Zidzik, eds. Princeton, NJ: Peterson's Guides, revised regularly.

American Universities and Colleges. Hawthorne, NY: De Groyter, revised regularly.

America's Lowest Cost Colleges, 8th ed., Nicholas A. Roes. Barryville, NY: NAR Publications, 1993.

Barron's Guide to Graduate Business Schools, Eugene Miller, ed. Hauppauge, NY: Barron's Educational Series, revised regularly.

Barron's Guide to Law Schools. Hauppauge, NY: Barron's Educational Series, revised regularly.

Barron's Guide to Medical and Dental Schools, Saul Wischitzer, ed. Hauppauge, NY: Barron's Educational Series, 1993.

Bear's Guide to Earning College Degrees Non-Traditionally, 11th ed., John Bear. Benicia, CA: C&B Publishing, 1994.

Chronicle Vocational School Manual, Patricia Hammon, ed. Moravia, NY: Chronicle Guidance Publications, annual.

College Applications and Essays: A How-To Handbook, 2nd ed., Susan D. Van Raalte. New York: Prentice Hall, 1993.

College Comes Sooner Than You Think!, Bonnie Featherstone and Jill Reilly. Dayton, OH: Ohio Psychology Press, 1990.

The College Comparison Guide, Killiaen V. Townsend. Athens, GA: Agee Publishers, 1992.

The College Costs and Financial Aid Handbook, College Board Staff. New York: The College Board, annual.

College Financial Aid Annual, College Research Group of Concord, MA. New York: Prentice Hall, annual.

The College Guide for Parents, Charles Shields. New York: The College Board, rev. 1988.

The College Handbook. New York: The College Board, revised regularly.

College Planning for Gifted Students, 2nd ed., Sandra L. Berger. Reston, VA: Council for Exceptional Children, 1994.

Directory of Internships, Work Experience Programs and On-the-Job Training Opportunities, 2nd ed. Santa Monica, CA: Ready Reference Press.

Four Years: A Knucklehead's Guide to College Life, Russ Clemenza. Midland Park, NJ: Knuthouse, rev. 1990.

Free Money for College: A Guide to More Than 1000 Grants and Scholarships for Undergraduate Study, 3rd ed., Laurie Blum. New York: Facts on File, 1994.

Getting into College: A Guide for Students and Parents, Frank Leana. New York: Farrar, Strauss, & Giroux, 1990.

The Gourman Report: A Rating of Undergraduate Programs in American and International Universities, 7th ed., Jack Gourman. Los Angeles, CA: National Education Standards, 1989.

How to Prepare for the American College Testing Assessment-Act Program, 9th ed., George Ehrenhaft, et al. Hauppauge, NY: Barron's Educational Series, 1991.

Index of Majors and Graduate Degrees. New York: The College Board, annual.

Insider's Guide to the Colleges, Yale Daily News Staff, ed. New York: St. Martin's Press, annual.

National Guide to Educational Credit for Training Programs, American Council on Education. Phoenix, AZ: Oryx Press, rev. 1994.

Peterson's Competitive Colleges, 1994–95, 3rd ed., Susan C. Dilts, ed. Princeton, NJ: Peterson's Guides, 1994.

Peterson's Guide to College Admissions: Getting into the College of Your Choice, 5th ed., R. Fred Zuker. Princeton, NJ: Peterson's Guides, 1991.

Peterson's Guide to Graduate and Professional Programs, Book 1: An Overview, Amy Lefferts, ed. Princeton, NJ: Peterson's Guides, revised regularly.

Peterson's Guide to Two-Year Colleges, Susan Dilts, ed. Princeton, NJ: Peterson's Guides, revised regularly.

Peterson's Paying Less for College, 12th ed. Princeton, NJ: Peterson's Guides, 1994.

Student Access Guide to America's Top 100 Internships, 1995, Mark Oldman. New York: Random House, 1994.

Students, Courses, and Jobs: The Relationship Between Higher Education and the Labor Market, J. L. Brennan. Washington, DC: Taylor and Francis, 1993.

A Student's Guide to College Admissions: Everything Your Guidance Counselor Has No Time to Tell You, Harlow Unger. New York: Facts on File, rev. 1991.

The Ultimate College Shopper's Guide, Heather Evans and Deidre Sullivan. Redding, MA: Addison-Wesley, 1992.

Vocational Education for People with Handicaps, Robert Gaylord-Ross. Mountain View, CA: Mayfield, 1988.

Vocational Education in the Nineteen Nineties II: A Sourcebook for Strategies, Methods, and Materials, Craig Anderson and Lary C. Rampp. Ann Arbor, MI: Prakken Publications, 1993.

Vocational Education: Status in 2-Year Colleges and Early Signs of Change. Upland, PA: Diane Publishing Company, 1994.

Career Goals

Recommended

Personal Career Consultant: A Step-by-Step Guide to Finding a Successful and Satisfying Career, Lehman and Shapiro. New York: Prentice Hall, 1988.

What Color Is Your Parachute?, Richard N. Bolles. Berkeley, CA: Ten Speed Press, revised annually. One of the best sources for career changers and job hunters. Workbook style with exercises to identify skills and interests. Provides comprehensive list of sources including books, agencies, and associations.

Career Anchors: Discovering Your Real Values, Edgar H. Schein. San Diego, CA: Pfeiffer & Co., rev. 1990.

Career Choices: A Guide for Teens and Young Adults, Mindy Bingham and Sandy Stryker. Santa Barbara, CA: Academic Innovations, 1990.

Career Choices and Changes: A Guide for Discovering Who You Are, What You Want, and How to Get It, Mindy Bingham and Sandy Stryker. Santa Monica, CA: Academic Innovations, 1992.

Career Development: Taking Charge of Your Career, 2nd ed., Monica E. Breidenbach. Englewood Cliffs, NJ: Prentice Hall, 1992.

Career Directions, Donna J. Yena. Burr Ridge, IL: Richard D. Irwin, Inc., 1993.

Career Exploration: A Self-Paced Approach, 2nd ed., Charlie Mitchell, et al. Dubuque, IA: Kendall/Hunt, 1992.

The Career Finder: Pathways to Over 1500 Entry-Level Jobs, Lester Schwartz and Irv Brechner. New York: Ballantine Books, 1990.

Career Planning, Martin Mini. Dubuque, IA: Kendall/Hunt, 1994.

Career Planning and Development for College Students and Recent Graduates, John E. Steele and Marilyn S. Morgan. Lincolnwood, IL: NTC Publishing Group, 1991.

Career Planning Q's and A's: A Handbook for Students, Parents, and Professionals, Paul Phifer. Garrett Park, MD: Garrett Park Press, 1990.

Career Planning Today, Randall Powell. Dubuque, IA: Kendall/Hunt, 1994.

Career Workbook: A Tool for Self-Discovery, Marcia A. Perkins-Reed. Portland, OR: High Flight Press, 1989.

Careers Checklist, Arlene S. Hirsch. Lincolnwood, IL: NTC Publishing Group, 1991.

Chronicle Career Index 1994–95, Harriet Scarry, ed. Moravia, NY: Chronicle Guidance Publications, 1994.

College Board Guide to Jobs and Career Planning, 2nd ed., Joyce Slayton Mitchell. New York: College Board, 1994.

College Majors and Careers: A Resource Guide for Effective Life Planning, Phil Phifer. Garrett Park, MD: Garrett Park Press, rev. 1993.

Discover What You're Best At, Barry Gale. New York: Simon & Schuster, rev. 1990.

Guide to Careers Without College, Kathleen S. Abrams. New York: Watts, 1988.

Self-Assessment and Career Development, 3rd ed., James G. Clawson, et al. Englewood Cliffs, NJ: Prentice Hall, 1991.

Getting the Job and Getting Ahead

Recommended

The Complete Job-Search Handbook, Howard Figler. New York: Henry Holt & Co., rev. and expanded 1988. Basic career skills are described and their development and use explained; a positive approach with helpful tips.

The After College Guide to Life, Carole B. Everett and Tracy C. Harkins. Severna Park, MD: Alcove Press, 1993.

Almanac of American Employers, Jack W. Plunkett. Boerne, TX: Corporate Jobs Outlook, rev. 1993.

Fast Track to the Best Job: How to Launch a Successful Career Right Out of College, Bruce J. Bloom. Scarsdale, NY: Blazer Books, 1991.

From School to Work, J. J. Littrell. South Holland, IL: Goodheart-Willcox Co., 1991.

Get the Job You Want: Successful Strategies for Selling Yourself in the Job Market, Signe A. Dayhoff. New Boston, NH: Brick House Publishing, 1990.

Getting Hired in the 'Nineties, 2nd ed., Vicki Spina. Schaumburg, IL: Corporate Image Publications, 1992.

Getting the Job You Want . . . Now!, David H. Roper. New York: Warner Books, 1994.

Job-Finder's Workbook, Chet Muklewicz and Michael Bender. Austin, TX: PRO-ED, 1988.

Job Hotlines U.S.A. 1994–95: The National Telephone Directory of Employer Joblines, Steven A. Wood. Harleysville, PA: Career Communications.

Job Hunter's Yellow Pages, 1994–95: The National Directory of Employment Services, Stephen A. Wood. Harleysville, PA: Career Communications Group.

Jobsearch: The Complete Manual for Job Seekers, 2nd ed., H. Lee Rust. New York: AMACOM, 1990.

Job Search Handbook: The Basics of a Professional Job Search, John Noble. Boston: Adams, Inc., 1988.

Job Search Organizer, Jack O'Brien. Washington, DC: Miranda Associates, 1990.

Job Search That Works, Rick Lamplugh. Los Altos, CA: Crisp Publications, 1991.

Job Seeker's Guide to Private-Public Companies, 4 vols., Charity A. Dorgan. Detroit: Gale, 1993–1995.

Job Seeker's Guide to Success, Atley Host and Cheryl McCann, eds. Minneapolis, MN: Discovery Press, 1990.

Job Seeker's Workbook, Lee A. Boerner. Menomonie, WI: Material Development Center, 1988.

Mentoring at Work: Developmental Relationships in Organizational Life, Kathy E. Kram. Lanham, MD: University Press of America, 1988.

The Student's Guide to Finding a Superior Job, 2nd ed., William A. Cohen. San Diego, CA: Pfeiffer & Co., 1993.

Surviving in the Workplace, Earl Harrell and Cassandra Harrell. Milwaukee: ET Publishing Co., 1993.

Telesearch: Direct Dial the Best Job of Your Life, John Truitt. Ann Arbor, MI: Books Demand UMI.

Work-At-Home Sourcebook, 5th ed., Lynie Arden. Boulder, CO: Live Oak Publications, 1994.

Resumes and Interviews

Recommended

Damn Good Resume Guide, Yana Parker. Berkeley, CA: Ten Speed Press, rev. 1989. Describes how to write a functional resume.

Job Resumes, J. I. Biegeleisen. New York: Berkley Publishing Group, 1991.

The Perfect Resume, Max Eggert. Avenel, NJ: Random House Value, rev. 1994.

Better Resumes for Executives and Professionals, 2nd ed., Robert F. Wilson. Hauppauge, NY: Barron's Educational Series, 1991.

Complete Resume Guide, 4th ed., Marian Faux. New York: Prentice Hall General Reference & Travel, 1991.

Designing Creative Resumes, Gregg Berryman. Los Altos, CA: Crisp Publications, rev. 1991.

Job Interviews, McVey and Associates Staff. Englewood Cliffs, NJ: Cambridge Books, 1988.

Job Interviews That Mean Business, David R. Eyler. New York: Random House, 1992.

Knock 'Em Dead: The Ultimate Job Seeker's Handbook, Martin J. Yate. Boston: Adams, rev. 1994.

Resume Adviser: How to Write and Design a Professional Resume, Thomas M. Sherman and Craig A. Stephen. Scottsdale, AZ: Barrister House, 1992.

Resume Handbook, 2nd ed., BMCC Coop Staff. Dubuque, IA: Kendall/Hunt, 1993.

Resume Handbook, 2nd ed., Arthur Rosenberg and David Hizer. Boston: Adams, Inc., 1990.

The Resume Kit, 2nd ed., Richard H. Beatty. New York: John Wiley & Sons, 1991.

Resume Power: Selling Yourself on Paper, Tom Washington. Bellevue, WA: Mount Vernon Press, 1990.

Resume Writing: A Comprehensive How-to-Do-It Guide, 4th ed. Burdette E. Bostwick. New York: John Wiley & Sons, 1990.

Resume Writing Made Easy, 4th ed., Lola M. Coxford. Gorsuch Scarisbrick, 1991.

Resumes for Better Jobs, 6th. ed., Lawrence D. Brennan. Englewood Cliffs, NJ: Prentice Hall, 1994.

Resumes That Work, 2nd ed., Loretta D. Foxman. New York: John Wiley & Sons, 1992.

Successful Interviewing, Andrew Ambraziejus. Stamford, CT: Longmeadow Press, 1992.

Your Resume: Key to a Better Job, 5th ed., Leonard Corwen. New York: Prentice Hall General Reference & Travel, 1993.

Mid-Career Options

Recommended

Career Change: Everything You Need to Know to Meet New Challenges and Take Control of Your Career. Lincolnwood, IL: NTC Publishing Group, 1995.

Career Burnout: Causes and Cures, Ayala Pines and Elliot Aronson. New York: Free Press, 1988.

Career Redirections for Adults. Portland, OR: Northwest Regional Educational Library.

Careering and Re-Careering for the 1990's: The Complete Guide to Planning Your Future, 2nd ed., Ronald L. Krannich. Manassas, VA: Impact, 1991.

Getting a Job After 50, John S. Morgan. Princeton, NJ: Petrocelli Books, 1990.

Guide for the Employee Who Is Losing His or Her Job, Dorri Jacobs. New York: Programs on Change, 1992.

Guide for the Employee Who Is to Be Relocated, Dorri Jacobs. New York: Programs on Change, 1992.

Guide for the Employee Who Is Up for a Promotion, 3rd ed., Dorri Jacobs. New York: Programs on Change, 1992.

Equality of Opportunity

Recommended

Coping with Sexual Harassment, Beryl Black, ed. New York: The Rosen Publishing Group, rev. 1992. Helpful in giving direct ways to respond to and prevent sexual harassment at work.

Routes into the Mainstream: Career Choices of Women and Minorities, Sue E. Berryman. Columbus, OH: Center On Education and Training For Employment, 1988.

The Black Resource Guide, 10th ed. Washington, DC: Black Resource Guide, 1992.

Coping with Discrimination, Gabrielle Edwards. New York: The Rosen Publishing Group, rev. 1992.

Directory of Career Resources for Minorities. Santa Monica, CA: Ready Reference Press.

Equal Opportunity. Hauppauge, NY: Equal Opportunity Publications, published 3 times a year.

Every Woman's Guide to Career Success, Denise Dudley. Mission, KS: Skill Path Publications, rev. 1991.

Exploring Non-Traditional Jobs for Women, Rose Neufield. New York: The Rosen Publishing Group, rev. 1989.

Financial Aid for Minorities. Garrett Park, MD: Garrett Park Press, 1994.

Financial Aid for the Disabled and Their Families, 1994–1996, 6th ed., Gail A. Schlachter and R. David Weber. San Carlos, CA: Reference Services Press, 1994.

Resume Guide for Women of the Nineties, Kim Marino. Berkeley, CA: Ten Speed Press, 1992.

Women and Work, Susan Bullock. Atlantic Highlands, NJ: Humanities Press, 1994.

Lists and Indexes of Career and Vocational Information

Career Index, Gretchen S. Baldauf. Westport, CT: Greenwood Press, 1990.

The Career Source Encyclopedia, Career Associates Staff. Danbury, CT: Grolier, 1993.

Chronicle Career Index. Moravia, NY: Chronicle Guidance Publications, annual publication.

Dictionary of Holland Occupational Codes (DHOC), 2nd ed., Gary D. Gottfredson and John L. Holland. Lutz, FL: Psychological Assessment Resources, 1989.

Dictionary of Occupational Titles, United States Department of Labor. Washington, DC: United States Government Printing Office, rev. 1991.

Monthly Catalog of United States Government Publications. Washington, DC: United States Government Printing Office, monthly publication.

Vertical File Index. New York: Wilson, monthly publication.

Where the Jobs Are: A Comprehensive Directory of 1200 Journals Listing Career Opportunities, S. Norman Feingold and Glenda Ann Hansard-Winkler. Garrett Park, MD: Garrett Park Press, 1989.

Where to Start Career Planning: Essential Resource Guide for Career Planning and Job Hunting, 8th ed., Pamela L. Feodoroff and Carolyn Lloyd Lindquist. Princeton, NJ: Peterson's Guides (distr.), 1991.

General Career Information—Audiovisual Materials

Exploring the Working World

Career Assessment. Video; student worksheets; guide. Charleston, WV: Cambridge Job Search.

Career Choice: A Lifelong Process. Video; guide. Mount Kisco, NY: Guidance Associates.

Career Cluster Decisions. Video; guide. Charleston, WV: Cambridge Job Search.

Career Exploration: A Job Seeker's Guide to the OOH, DOT, and GOE. Video. Charleston, WV: Cambridge Job Search.

Career Goals: The Window to Success. Video; student workbook. Mansfield, OH: Opportunities for Learning, Inc.

Career Plan. Video; guide. Charleston, WV: Cambridge Job Search.

Career Planning: Putting Your Skills to Work. 2 videos; guide. Mansfield, OH: Opportunities for Learning, Inc.

Career Planning Steps. Video. Charleston, WV: Cambridge Job Search.

Career Self-Assessment: Where Do You Fit? Video; guide. Mount Kisco, NY: Guidance Associates.

Career Values: What Really Matters to You? Video; guide. Mount Kisco, NY: Guidance Associates.

Investigating the World of Work. Video; manual. Charleston, WV: Cambridge Job Search.

Jobs for the 21st Century. Video; guide. Mount Kisco, NY: Guidance Associates.

Kaleidoscope of Careers. 5 videos; manual. Mansfield, OH: Opportunities for Learning, Inc.

Learning for Earning. Video; guide. Charleston, WV: Cambridge Job Search.

Me and Jobs. Video; student workbooks; manual. Mansfield, OH: Opportunities for Learning, Inc.

New Tomorrows. Video. Mansfield, OH: Opportunities for Learning, Inc.

Occupational Preparation. Video; manual. Charleston, WV: Cambridge Job Search.

Preparing for the Jobs of the 1990s: What You Should Know. Video; guide. Mount Kisco, NY: Guidance Associates.

School-to-Work Transition. Video; guide. Charleston, WV: Cambridge Job Search.

Self-Awareness and Your Career Options. Video; manual. Charleston, WV: Cambridge Job Search.

Setting Career Goals the Video Way. Video. Charleston, WV: Cambridge Job Search.

The Ten Fastest Growing Careers: Jobs for the Future. Video; guide. Mount Kisco, NY: Guidance Associates.

Voyage: An Introduction to Career/Life Planning. Video. Mansfield, OH: Opportunities for Learning, Inc.

Where Do You Want to Work? Video. Mansfield, OH: Opportunities for Learning, Inc.

Why Work? Working for a Living. Video. New York: Educational Design, Inc.

Your Future: Planning Through Career Exploration. Video. Bloomington, IL: Meridian Education Corporation.

Your Interests: Related to Work Activities. Video. Bloomington, IL: Meridian Education Corporation.

Your Temperaments: Related to Work Situations. Video. Bloomington, IL: Meridian Education Corporation.

Getting the Job and Getting Ahead

Communicating on the Job. Video. Bowling Green, KY: Southern School Media.

The Complete Video Guide to Job Hunting. Video. Charleston, WV: Cambridge Job Search.

Dialing for Jobs. Video. Mansfield, OH: Opportunities for Learning, Inc.

Finding a Company That's Right for You. Video. Mansfield, OH: Opportunities for Learning, Inc.

Getting a Good Start. Video; guide. Bloomington, IL: Meridian Education Corporation.

Getting Along on the Job: Interpersonal Work Skills. Video. Mansfield, OH: Opportunities for Learning, Inc.

Given the Opportunity: A Guide to Interaction in the Workplace. Video. Bloomington, IL: Meridian Education Corporation.

If At First . . . How To Get a Job and Keep It. Video. Mount Kisco, NY: Vocational Media Associates.

If You Really Want to Get Ahead . . . Video. Mansfield, OH: Opportunities for Learning, Inc.

The Interview. Video. Olathe, KS: RMI Media Productions.

Interview Techniques and Resume Tips for the Job Applicant. Video. Mansfield, OH: Opportunities for Learning, Inc.

Job Survival Kit. Video. Charleston, WV: Cambridge Job Search.

Job Survival Skills: Working With Others. Video. Mount Kisco, NY: Vocational Media Associates.

Keeping Your Job. Video. Olathe, KS: RMI Media Productions.

Learning Seed's Job Search Strategies. Video. Lake Zurich, IL: The Learning Seed.

Locating Potential Employers. Video. Olathe, KS: RMI Media Productions.

Making It On Your First Job. Video. Olathe, KS: RMI Media Productions.

Moving Up or Out. Video. Lake Zurich, IL: The Learning Seed.

Power Interviewing. Video. Charleston, WV: Cambridge Job Search.

Resumes That Get Interviews. Video. Mount Kisco, NY: Vocational Media Associates.

Sell Yourself: Successful Job Interviewing. Video. Lake Zurich, IL: The Learning Seed.

Shhh! I'm Finding a Job: The Library and Your Self-Directed Job Search. Video; guide. Charleston, WV: Cambridge Job Search.

Tough Times: Finding the Jobs. Video. Charleston, WV: Cambridge Job Search.

Unemployment: A Plan of Action. Video. Mansfield, OH: Opportunities for Learning, Inc.

The Video Resume Writer. Video. Charleston, WV: Cambridge Job Search.

What Employers Expect. Video. Bowling Green, KY: Southern School Media.

Your Resume and Other Job Search Skills. Video; guide. Mansfield, OH: Opportunities for Learning, Inc.

General Career Information—Computer Software

The Cambridge Career Counseling System. 2 disks for IBM. Charleston, WV: Cambridge Job Search.

Career Area Interest Checklist. Disk for Apple or IBM. Bloomington, IL: Meridian Education Corporation.

Career Compass. Disk for IBM. Bloomington, IL: Meridian Education Corporation.

Career Compusearch. Disk for Apple or IBM. Bloomington, IL: Meridian Education Corporation.

Career Counselor. Disk for Apple. Mansfield, OH: Opportunities for Learning, Inc.

Career Development Plan. 2 disks for IBM. Charleston, WV: Cambridge Job Search.

Career Directions. Disk for IBM. Charleston, WV: Cambridge Job Search.

Career Finder. Disk for Apple or IBM. Bloomington, IL: Meridian Education Corporation.

Career Match. Disk for Apple or IBM. Charleston, WV: Cambridge Job Search.

Career Scan V. Disk for Apple or IBM. Mansfield, OH: Opportunities for Learning, Inc.

Career System 2000. 7 disks for Apple. Mansfield, OH: Opportunities for Learning, Inc.

Careers of the Future. 3 disks for Apple or IBM. Mansfield, OH: Opportunities for Learning, Inc.

Computerized Career Assessment and Planning. 8 disks for Apple. Mansfield, OH: Opportunities for Learning, Inc.

Computerized Career Information System. 5 disks for Apple or IBM. Mansfield, OH: Opportunities for Learning, Inc.

Computerized Dictionary of Occupational Titles. 16 disks for IBM. Largo, FL: Careers, Inc.

Emerging Occupations. Disk for Apple or IBM. Mansfield, OH: Opportunities for Learning, Inc.

Encyclopedia of Careers and Vocational Guidance. CD-ROM. Largo, FL: Careers, Inc.

How to Win Your Job Search. Disk for IBM. Charleston, WV: Cambridge Job Search.

Interview Skills of the Future. CD-ROM for Apple. Charleston, WV: Cambridge Job Search.

Job Hunter's Survival Kit. 2 disks for Apple or IBM. Mansfield, OH: Opportunities for Learning, Inc.

Job-O. Disk for Apple or IBM. Mansfield, OH: Opportunities for Learning, Inc.

Job Search Skills for the 21st Century. CD-ROM for Apple. Charleston, WV: Cambridge Job Search.

Jobs in Today's World. Disk for Apple or IBM. Mansfield, OH: Opportunities for Learning, Inc.

Life and Career Planning: The Future Is Yours. Disk for Apple or IBM. Mansfield, OH: Opportunities for Learning, Inc.

MSPI: Exploring Career Goals and College Courses. Disk for Apple or IBM. Charleston, WV: Cambridge Job Search.

Multimedia Career Center. 2 CD-ROMs. Bloomington, IL: Meridian Education Corporation.

The Multimedia Career Path. CD-ROM for Apple. Charleston, WV: Cambridge Job Search.

The Multimedia Guide to Occupational Exploration. 2 CD-ROMs. Bloomington, IL: Meridian Education Corporation.

Occu-Facts 2000. Disk for Apple or IBM. Largo, FL: Careers, Inc.

Occupational Outlook Handbook on CD-ROM. CD-ROM for IBM. Largo, FL: Careers, Inc.

The Perfect Resume. 2 disks for IBM. Mansfield, OH: Opportunities for Learning, Inc.

Resume Express: The Multimedia Guide. CD-ROM for Apple. Charleston, WV: Cambridge Job Search.

The Right Job Application. Disk for IBM. Charleston, WV: Cambridge Job Search.

Successful Interviewing. Disk for Apple or IBM. Mansfield, OH: Opportunities for Learning, Inc.

Career and Vocational Information on Public and Community Services

General

Books

Recommended

Washington Information Directory, 1994–1995, Washington, DC: Congressional Quarterly, updated annually. Lists organizations, including directors and executive officers.

Careers in Counseling and Human Development, Brook B. Collison and Nancy J. Garfield, eds. Alexandria, VA: American Counseling Association, 1990.

Doing Well by Doing Good: The Complete Guide to Careers in the Nonprofit Sector, Terry M. McAdam. Detroit, MI: Fund Raising Institute, 1991.

Jobs and Careers with Nonprofit Organizations, Ron Krannich. Manassas Park, VA: Impact Publications, 1992.

Opportunities in Nonprofit Organization Careers, Adrian A. Paradis. Lincolnwood, IL: NTC Publishing Group, 1994.

Audiovisual Materials

Exploring Career Areas: Humanitarian. Video. Bloomington, IL: Meridian Education Corporation.

Family, Social, & Human Services. Video. Bloomington, IL: Meridian Education Corporation.

Video Career Library: Public & Personal Service. Video. Bowling Green, KY: Southern School Media.

The Video GOE: Humanitarian. Video. Bowling Green, KY: Southern School Media.

We the People: Careers in Public Service. Video. Mansfield, OH: Opportunities for Learning, Inc.

Armed Services

Books

America's Top Military Careers: The Official Guide to Occupations in the Armed Forces, JIST Editorial Staff. Indianapolis, IN: JIST Works, 1993.

Exploring Careers in the Military Services, Robert W. McDonald. New York: The Rosen Publishing Group, rev. 1991.

Guide to Military Careers, Robert E. Dunbar. New York: Franklin Watts, 1992.

Opportunities in Military Careers, Adrian Paradis. Lincolnwood, IL: NTC Publishing Group, 1989.

Law Enforcement

Books

■■

Recommended

Law Enforcement Career Guide: Practical Guide to Finding Police Employment, 5th ed., Jackye Bundschu. Winter Haven, FL: Harvest Communications, 1993.

Careers in Law Enforcement and Security, Paul Cohen and Shari Cohen. New York: The Rosen Publishing Group, rev. 1994.

Opportunities in Law Enforcement and Criminal Justice, James Stinchcomb. Lincolnwood, IL: NTC Publishing Group, rev. 1990.

Audiovisual Materials

The Career Builders Video Series: Law Enforcement. Video. New York: Educational Design, Inc.

Profiles: People and Jobs—Service Occupations #2. Video. Bloomington, IL: Meridian Education Corporation. Includes profiles of guard and corrections officer.

Video Career Library: Public & Personal Service. Video. Bloomington, IL: Meridian Education Corporation. Includes profiles of police officer and corrections officer.

Vocational Visions: Personal Service Cluster. Video. Mount Kisco, NY: Guidance Associates. Includes profile of law enforcement worker.

Work-A-Day America: Law Enforcement. Video. Mansfield, OH: Opportunities for Learning, Inc.

Legal Work

Books

Best Resumés for Attorneys, Joan Fondell and Mary J. Russo. New York: John Wiley & Sons, 1994.

Career Choices for Students of Law. New York: Walker & Company, rev. 1990.

Careers in Civil Litigation. Chicago: American Bar Association, 1990.

Careers in Entertainment Law. Chicago: American Bar Association, 1990.

Careers in International Law. Chicago: American Bar Association, 1993.

Careers in Law, Gary Munneke. Lincolnwood, IL: NTC Publishing Group, 1992.

Criminal Justice Careers Guidebook. New York: Gordon Press, 1991.

Directory of Legal Employers 1994. Washington, DC: National Association for Law Placement, 1994.

Federal Careers for Attorneys: A Guide to Legal Careers in over 80 Practice Fields, 2nd ed., Richard L. Hermann, Linda P. Sutherland, Jeanette Sobajian, and Beth Fishkin, eds. Washington, DC: Federal Reports, 1991.

From Here to Attorney: The Ultimate Guide to Excelling in Law School and Launching Your Legal Career, Robert J. Arnett III, Arthur Coon, and Michael DeGeronimo. Belmont, CA: Professional Publications, 1993.

Law as a Career. Chicago: American Bar Association, 1992.

Legal Assistant, Jack Rudman. Syosset, NY: National Learning Corporation, 1991.

Life Outside the Law Firm: Non-Traditional Careers for Paralegals, Karen Treffinger. Albany, NY: Delmar Publishers, 1995.

Now Hiring: Government Jobs for Lawyers. Chicago: American Bar Association, 1990.

Opportunities in Law Careers, Gary A. Munneke. Lincolnwood, IL: NTC Publishing Group, 1994.

Opportunities in Paralegal Careers, Alice Fins. Lincolnwood, IL: NTC Publishing Group, 1990.

Paralegal: An Insider's Guide to the Fastest Growing Occupations of the 1990s, 2nd ed., Barbara Bernardo. Princeton, NJ: Peterson's Guides, 1993.

Paralegal Career Guide, Chere B. Estrin. New York: Wiley Law Publications, 1992.

The Prelaw Handbook. Washington, DC: National Association for Law Placement, updated annually.

Public, Civil, and Social Services

Books

Recommended

Find a Federal Job Fast: How to Cut the Red Tape and Get Hired, 3rd ed., Ronald L. Krannich and Caryl R. Krannich, eds. Manassas Park, VA: Impact Publications, 1995.

United States Government Manual, Office of the Federal Register, National Archives and Records Administration Staff, ed. Lanham, MD: Bernan Press, updated annually. A directory of all the offices that make up the federal government.

Career Advancement for Women in the Federal Service: An Annotated Bibliography and Resource Book, Lynn C. Ross. New York: Garland Publishing, 1993.

Career Choices for Students of Political Science and Government. New York: Walker & Company, rev. 1990.

Careers in International Affairs, Maria Pinto Carland and Daniel H. Spatz, Jr., eds. Washington, DC: Georgetown University, Institute for the Study of Diplomacy, rev. 1991.

The Complete Guide to Public Employment, 3rd. ed., Ron Krannich. Manassas Park, VA: Impact Publications, 1993.

Continuing Education for Gerontological Careers, Roberta A. Greene. Alexandria, VA: Council on Social Work Education, 1988.

Directory of Colleges and Universities with Accredited Social Work Degree Programs. Alexandria, VA: Council on Social Work Education, 1994.

Federal Personnel Guide, 1995 Edition, Kenneth D. Whitehead, ed. Chevy Chase, MD: Key Communications Group, 1995.

Government Job Finder, 2nd ed., Donald Lauber. River Forest, IL: Planning/Communications, 1994.

Government Jobs: The New Employment Manual, 3rd rev. ed., Richard M. Zink. Dearborn, MI: Zinks International Career Guidance, 1994.

Guide to Careers in World Affairs, Foreign Policy Association Staff and Pamela Gerard, eds. Manassas Park, VA: Impact Publications, 1993.

The Harvard College Guide to Careers in Government and Politics, Lynn Bracken Wehnes. Cambridge, MA: Harvard University, Office of Career Services, 1992.

How to Get a Federal Job, 7th ed., David E. Waelde. Washington, DC: Fedhelp Publications, 1989.

Occupational Therapy and Mental Health: Principles, Skills and Practice, Jennifer Creek, ed. New York: Churchill Livingstone, 1990.

Opportunities in Counseling and Development Careers, Neale J. Baxter and Mark O. Toch. Lincolnwood, IL: NTC Publishing Group, 1994.

Opportunities in Federal Government Careers, 2nd ed., Neale J. Baxter. Lincolnwood, IL: NTC Publishing Group, 1992.

Opportunities in Social Work Careers, Renee Wittenberg. Lincolnwood, IL: NTC Publishing Group, 1988.

Summary Information on Master of Social Work Programs, Council on Social Work Education Staff. Alexandria, VA: Council on Social Work Education, updated annually.

VGM's Handbook of Government and Public Service Careers, Annette Selden, ed. Lincolnwood, IL: NTC Publishing Group, 1994.

Working for Your Uncle: Complete Guide to Finding a Job with the Federal Government, Federal Jobs Digest Staff. Ossining, NY: Breakthrough Publications, 1993.

Audiovisual Materials

Career Success Series: Fire Fighting and Prevention. Video. Mansfield, OH: Opportunities for Learning, Inc.

Career Success Series: Social Work. Video. Mansfield, OH: Opportunities for Learning, Inc.

Careers in Child Development. Olathe, KS: RMI Media Productions.

Day in a Career Series: Social Worker. Video. Charleston, WV: Cambridge Job Search.

Profiles: People and Jobs—Professional Specialty Occupations #1. Video. Bloomington, IL: Meridian Education Corporation. Includes profiles of social worker and human services worker.

Religious Careers

Books

Clergy Assessment and Career Development, Richard A. Hunt, John E. Hinkle, Jr., and Newton H. Malony. Nashville, TN: Abingdon Press, 1990.

Opportunities in Religious Service Careers, John O. Nelson. Lincolnwood, IL: NTC Publishing Group, 1988.

Audiovisual Materials

Video Career Library: Social Sciences. Video. Bloomington, IL: Meridian Education Corporation. Includes profile of clergy.

Teaching—Library Science

Books

Becoming a Teacher of Young Children, Margaret Lay-Dopyera and John Dopyera. New York: McGraw-Hill, 1992.

Career Portraits: Teaching, Marjorie Eberts and Margaret Gisler. Lincolnwood, IL: NTC Publishing Group, 1995.

Careers for Bookworms and Other Literary Types. Lincolnwood, IL: NTC Publishing Group, 1990.

Careers in Child Care, Marjorie Eberts. Lincolnwood, IL: NTC Publishing Group, 1994.

Careers in the Classroom: When Teaching Is More Than a Job, Sylvia M. Yee. New York: Columbia University, Teachers College Press, 1990.

Careers in Education, Roy A. Edelfelt and Blythe Camenson. Lincolnwood, IL: NTC Publishing Group, 1993.

Careers in Teaching, Robert Shockley and Glenn W. Cutlip. New York: The Rosen Publishing Group, rev. 1994.

Extending the Librarian's Domain: A Survey of Emerging Occupational Opportunities for Librarians and Information Professionals. Washington, DC: Special Libraries Association, 1994.

Guide to Career Opportunities for Special Librarians and Information Professionals, 1991. Washington, DC: Special Libraries Association, 1991.

How to Find Jobs Teaching Overseas, 2nd ed., Jim Muckle. Sebastopol, CA: KSJ Publishing Company, 1992.

How to Get a Job in Education, 2nd ed., Joel Levin. Boston, MA: Bob Adams, 1994.

Opportunities in Library and Information Science, Kathleen Heim and Margaret Myers. Lincolnwood, IL: NTC Publishing Group, 1992.

Opportunities in Teaching Careers, Janet Fine. Lincolnwood, IL: NTC Publishing Group, 1989.

Resumes for Education. Lincolnwood, IL: NTC Publishing Group, 1992.

Teach Abroad: The Complete International Guide to Teaching Opportunities Overseas, Central Bureau Staff. London: Kuperard, 1993.

Teaching. Lincolnwood, IL: NTC Publishing Group, 1995.

Audiovisual Materials

Career Encounters: Teaching. Video. Bowling Green, KY: Southern School Media.

Career Success Series: Elementary Education. Video. Mansfield, OH: Opportunities for Learning, Inc.

Culture and Conscience—Careers in Education, Culture, and Social Sciences. Video. Mansfield, OH: Opportunities for Learning, Inc.

Education. Video. New York: Educational Design, Inc.

Inside Teaching: Exploring Styles. Video. Olathe, KS: RMI Media Productions.

Video Career Library: Education. Video. Bowling Green, KY: Southern School Media.

Video Guide to Occupational Exploration: Leading and Influencing II. Video. Mansfield, OH: Opportunities for Learning, Inc. Includes profile of education.

Directory of Institutions Offering Career Training

The information in this directory was generated from the IPEDS (Integrated Postsecondary Education Data System) database of the U.S. Department of Education. It includes only regionally or nationally accredited institutions offering postsecondary occupational training in public and community services. Because college catalogs and directories of colleges and universities are readily available elsewhere, this directory does not include institutions that offer only bachelor's and advanced degrees.

Armed Services

ALABAMA

John C Calhoun State Community
College
P.O. Box 2216
Decatur 35609-2216

TEXAS

Wayland Baptist University
1900 West Seventh
Plainview 79072

WEST VIRGINIA

The University of Charleston
2300 MacCorkle Ave. SE
Charleston 25304

Custodial Services

CALIFORNIA

Center for Employment Training-Gilroy
7800 Arroyo Circle
Gilroy 95020

Center for Employment Training-Spring
St.
426 Spring St.
Los Angeles 90013

Center for Employment Training-Vernon
2947 East 44th St.
Vernon 90058

Center for Employment Training-Salinas
330 Griffin St.
Salinas 93901

Center for Employment Training-Santa
Ana
120 West Fifth St.
Santa Ana 92701

ILLINOIS

Illinois Valley Community College
2578 East 350th Rd.
Oglesby 61348

MINNESOTA

Minnesota Riverland Technical
College-Faribault Campus
1225 Southwest Third St.
Faribault 55021

Northeast Metro Technical College
3300 Century Ave. N
White Bear Lake 55110

PENNSYLVANIA

Philadelphia Elwyn Institute
4040 Market St.
Philadelphia 19104-3003

Fire Control Technology

ALABAMA

Chattahoochee Valley Community
College
2602 College Dr.
Phenix City 36869

Community College of the Air Force
Maxwell Air Force Base
Montgomery 36112

Jefferson State Community College
2601 Carson Rd.
Birmingham 35215-3098

ALASKA

University of Alaska-Anchorage
3211 Providence Dr.
Anchorage 99508

University of Alaska-Fairbanks
Signers Hall
Fairbanks 99775

ARIZONA

Glendale Community College
6000 West Olive Ave.
Glendale 85302

Mesa Community College
1833 West Southern Ave.
Mesa 85202

Phoenix College
1202 West Thomas Rd.
Phoenix 85013

Pima Community College
2202 West Anklam Rd.
Tucson 85709-0001

Yavapai College
1100 East Sheldon St.
Prescott 86301

ARKANSAS

Black River Technical College
Hwy. 304, P.O. Box 468
Pocahontas 72455

CALIFORNIA

Allan Hancock College
800 South College Dr.
Santa Maria 93454

American River College
4700 College Oak Dr.
Sacramento 95841

Bakersfield College
1801 Panorama Dr.
Bakersfield 93305-1299

Butte College
3536 Butte Campus Dr.
Oroville 95965

Cabrillo College
6500 Soquel Dr.
Aptos 95003

Chabot College
25555 Hesperian Blvd.
Hayward 94545

College of San Mateo
1700 West Hillsdale Blvd.
San Mateo 94402

Columbia College-Columbia
P.O. Box 1849
Columbia 95310

Crafton Hills College
11711 Sand Canyon Rd.
Yucaipa 92399-1799

El Camino College
16007 Crenshaw Blvd.
Torrance 90506

Fresno City College
1101 East University Ave.
Fresno 93741

Long Beach City College
4901 East Carson St.
Long Beach 90808

Merced College
3600 M St.
Merced 95348-2898

Mission College
3000 Mission College Blvd.
Santa Clara 95054-1897

Monterey Peninsula College
980 Fremont Blvd.
Monterey 93940-4799

Mount San Antonio College
1100 North Grand
Walnut 91789

Oxnard College
4000 South Rose Ave.
Oxnard 93033

Rancho Santiago College
17th at Bristol
Santa Ana 92706

Rio Hondo College
3600 Workman Mill Rd.
Whittier 90601-1699

San Diego Miramar College
10440 Black Mountain Rd.
San Diego 92126-2999

Santa Rosa Junior College
1501 Mendocino Ave.
Santa Rosa 95401-4395

Shasta College
P.O. Box 496006
Redding 96049

Sierra College
5000 Rocklin Rd.
Rocklin 95677

COLORADO

Aims Community College
P.O. Box 69
Greeley 80632

Arapahoe Community College
2500 West College Dr.
Littleton 80160-9002

Red Rocks Community College
13300 West Sixth Ave.
Golden 80401

FLORIDA

Broward Community College
225 East Las Olas Blvd.
Fort Lauderdale 33301

Daytona Beach Community College
1200 Volusia Ave.
Daytona Beach 32114

Edison Community College
8099 College Pkwy. SW
Fort Myers 33906-6210

Florida Community College at
Jacksonville
501 West State St.
Jacksonville 32202

Indian River Community College
3209 Virginia Ave.
Fort Pierce 34981

Lake County Area Vocational-Technical
   Center
2001 Kurt St.
Eustis 32726

Lewis M Lively Area
   Vocational-Technical Center
500 North Appleyard Dr.
Tallahassee 32304

Miami-Dade Community College
300 Northeast Second Ave.
Miami 33132

Palm Beach Community College
4200 Congress Ave.
Lake Worth 33461

Pasco-Hernando Community College
36727 Blanton Rd.
Dade City 33525-7599

Sarasota County Technical Institute
4748 Beneva Rd.
Sarasota 34233-1798

Seminole Community College
100 Weldon Blvd.
Sanford 32773-6199

South Technical Education Center
1300 Southwest 30th Ave.
Boynton Beach 33426-9099

William T McFatter Vocational
   Technical Center
6500 Nova Dr.
Davie 33317

GEORGIA

Dekalb College
3251 Panthersville Rd.
Decatur 30034

HAWAII

Honolulu Community College
874 Dillingham Blvd.
Honolulu 96817

ILLINOIS

City College of Chicago-Chicago
   City-Wide College
226 West Jackson Blvd.
Chicago 60606-6997

College of Du Page
Lambert Rd. and 22nd St.
Glen Ellyn 60137

Illinois Central College
One College Dr.
East Peoria 61635

Investigations Institute
2155 Stonington Ave.
Hoffman Estates 60195-2057

Joliet Junior College
1216 Houbolt Ave.
Joliet 60436

Lincoln Land Community College
Shepherd Rd.
Springfield 62194-9256

Moraine Valley Community College
10900 South 88th Ave.
Palos Hills 60465-0937

Prairie State College
202 Halsted St.
Chicago Heights 60411

Southeastern Illinois College
3575 College Rd.
Harrisburg 62946

INDIANA

Indiana Vocational Technical
   College-Central Indiana
One West 26th St.
Indianapolis 46206-1763

IOWA

Des Moines Community College
2006 Ankeny Blvd.
Ankeny 50021

Kirkwood Community College
P.O. Box 2068
Cedar Rapids 52406

KANSAS

Johnson County Community College
12345 College Blvd.
Overland Park 66210-1299

LOUISIANA

Delgado Community College
615 City Park Ave.
New Orleans 70119

Louisiana State University-Eunice
P.O. Box 1129
Eunice 70535

MAINE

Southern Maine Technical College
Fort Rd.
South Portland 04106

MASSACHUSETTS

Bristol Community College
777 Elsbree St.
Fall River 02720

Middlesex Community College
Springs Rd.
Bedford 01730

North Shore Community College
One Ferncroft Rd.
Danvers 01923

Tad Technical Institute
45 Spruce St.
Chelsea 02150

MICHIGAN

Delta College
University Center 48710

Henry Ford Community College
5101 Evergreen Rd.
Dearborn 48128

Lansing Community College
419 North Capitol Ave.
Lansing 48901-7210

Macomb Community College
14500 Twelve Mile Rd.
Warren 48093-3896

MINNESOTA

Duluth Technical College
2101 Trinity Rd.
Duluth 55811

MISSOURI

Saint Louis Community College-Forest
   Park
5600 Oakland Ave.
Saint Louis 63110

NEBRASKA

Southeast Community College-Lincoln
   Campus
8800 O St.
Lincoln 68520

NEVADA

Community College of Southern Nevada
3200 East Cheyenne Ave.
Las Vegas 89030

Truckee Meadows Community College
7000 Dandini Blvd.
Reno 89512

NEW HAMPSHIRE

New Hampshire Technical College at
   Laconia
Prescott Hill Rte. 106
Laconia 03246

NEW JERSEY

Mercer County Community College
1200 Old Trenton Rd.
Trenton 08690

NEW YORK

Corning Community College
Spencer Hill
Corning 14830

Monroe Community College
1000 East Henrietta Rd.
Rochester 14623

Onondaga Community College
Rte. 173
Syracuse 13215

Suffolk County Community
   College-Ammerman Campus
533 College Rd.
Selden 11784

NORTH CAROLINA

Central Piedmont Community College
P.O. Box 35009
Charlotte 28235

Guilford Technical Community College
P.O. Box 309
Jamestown 27282

OHIO

Columbus State Community College
550 East Spring St., P.O. Box 1609
Columbus 43216

Lakeland Community College
7700 Clocktower Dr.
Mentor 44060-7594

Lawrence County Joint Vocational School
Rte. 2 Getaway
Chesapeake 45619

University of Akron-Main Campus
302 Buchtel Common
Akron 44325-4702

OKLAHOMA

Oklahoma State University-Oklahoma
   City
900 North Portland
Oklahoma City 73107

OREGON

Chemeketa Community College
P.O. Box 14007
Salem 97309-7070

Portland Community College
P.O. Box 19000
Portland 97280-0990

RHODE ISLAND

Community College of Rhode Island
400 East Ave.
Warwick 02886-1805

Providence College
River Ave. and Eaton St.
Providence 02918

TEXAS

Austin Community College
5930 Middle Fiskville Rd.
Austin 78752

Collin County Community College
2200 West University
McKinney 75070

Houston Community College System
22 Waugh Dr., P.O. Box 7849
Houston 77270-7849

San Antonio College
1300 San Pedro Ave.
San Antonio 78284

Tarrant County Junior College District
1500 Houston St.
Fort Worth 76102

WASHINGTON

Bates Technical College
1101 South Yakima Ave.
Tacoma 98405

Spokane Community College
North 1810 Greene Ave.
Spokane 99207

WISCONSIN

Blackhawk Technical College
P.O. Box 5009
Janesville 53547

Fox Valley Technical College
1825 North Bluemound Dr.
Appleton 54913-2277

Milwaukee Area Technical College
700 West State St.
Milwaukee 53233

Northeast Wisconsin Technical College
2740 West Mason St., P.O. Box 19042
Green Bay 54307-9042

Wisconsin Area Vocational Training and
   Adult Education System District
   Number Four
3550 Anderson St.
Madison 53704

Legal Services Technology

ALABAMA

Gadsden State Community College
P.O. Box 227
Gadsden 35902-0227

George C Wallace State Community
College-Hanceville
801 Main St. NW, P.O. Box 2000
Hanceville 35077-2000

James H. Faulkner State Community
College
1900 U.S. Hwy. 30 S
Bay Minette 36507

John C Calhoun State Community
College
P.O. Box 2216
Decatur 35609-2216

Phillips Junior College
4900 Corporate Dr.
Huntsville 35805

Samford University
800 Lakeshore Dr.
Birmingham 35229

ALASKA

Alaska Junior College
800 East Dimond Blvd.
Anchorage 99515

Charter College
2221 East Northern Lights Blvd.
Anchorage 99508

University of Alaska-Anchorage
3211 Providence Dr.
Anchorage 99508

ARIZONA

Academy Business College
3320 West Cheryl Dr.
Phoenix 85051

American Institute of Court Reporting
3443 North Central Ave.
Phoenix 85012

Lamson Business College
6367 East Tanque Verde Rd.
Tucson 85715

Lamson Junior College
1980 West Main
Mesa 85201

Lamson Junior College
2701 West Bethany Home Rd.
Phoenix 85017

Paralegal Institute
3602 West Thomas Rd.
Phoenix 85061-1408

Phoenix College
1202 West Thomas Rd.
Phoenix 85013

Pima Community College
2202 West Anklam Rd.
Tucson 85709-0001

Sterling School, Inc.
801 East Indian School Rd.
Phoenix 85014

ARKANSAS

Westark Community College
P.O. Box 3649
Fort Smith 72913

CALIFORNIA

American River College
4700 College Oak Dr.
Sacramento 95841

Catherine College, Inc.
8155 Van Nuys Blvd.
Panorama 91402

Century Business College
3325 Wilshire Blvd.
Los Angeles 90010

Century Schools
2665 Fifth Ave.
San Diego 92103

Cerritos College
11110 Alondra Blvd.
Norwalk 90650

City College of San Francisco
50 Phelan Ave.
San Francisco 94112

Coastline Community College
11460 Warner Ave.
Fountain Valley 92708

College of the Redwoods
7351 Tompkins Hill Rd.
Eureka 95501-9302

College of the Sequoias
915 South Mooney Blvd.
Visalia 93277

De Anza College
21250 Stevens Creek Blvd.
Cupertino 95014

El Camino College
16007 Crenshaw Blvd.
Torrance 90506

Fresno City College
1101 East University Ave.
Fresno 93741

Fullerton College
321 East Chapman Ave.
Fullerton 92632-2095

Humphreys College
3600 Sisk Rd.
Modesto 95356

Kensington College
2428 North Grand Ave.
Santa Ana 92701

Merit College
7101 Sepulveda Blvd.
Van Nuys 91405

Napa Valley College
2277 Napa Vallejo Hwy.
Napa 94558

Newbridge College
700 El Camino Real
Tustin 92680

Pasadena City College
1570 East Colorado Blvd.
Pasadena 91106

Phillips College-Inland Empire Campus
4300 Central Ave.
Riverside 92506

Phillips Junior College
8520 Balboa Blvd.
Northridge 91325

Phillips Junior College L A South
One Civic Plaza
Carson 90745

Phillips Junior College-Condie Campus
One West Campbell Ave.
Campbell 95008

Platt College-Ontario
2920 Inland Empire Blvd.
Ontario 91764

Rancho Santiago College
17th at Bristol
Santa Ana 92706

Rio Hondo College
3600 Workman Mill Rd.
Whittier 90601-1699

Saint Mary's College of California
P.O. Box 3554
Moraga 94575

San Joaquin College of Law
3385 East Shields Ave.
Fresno 93726

Sawyer College at Ventura
2101 East Gonzales Rd.
Oxnard 93030

Skyline College
3300 College Dr.
San Bruno 94066

Southern California College of Business
and Law
595 West Lambert Rd.
Brea 92621

Southwestern College
900 Otay Lakes Rd.
Chula Vista 92010

University of Northern
California-Lorenzo Patino School Law
727-1/2 J St.
Sacramento 95814-2501

University of San Francisco
2130 Fulton St.
San Francisco 94117-1080

University of West Los Angeles
1155 West Arbor Vitae St.
Inglewood 90301

Watterson College
1165 East Colorado Blvd.
Pasadena 91106

Watterson College Pacific
2030 University Dr.
Vista 92083

Watterson College Pacific
815 North Oxnard Blvd.
Oxnard 93030

West Los Angeles College
4800 Freshman Dr.
Culver 90230

West Valley College
14000 Fruitvale Ave.
Saratoga 95070

COLORADO

Arapahoe Community College
2500 West College Dr.
Littleton 80160-9002

Blair Junior College
828 Wooten Rd.
Colorado Springs 80915

College of the Canons
Forge Rd. Industrial Park, P.O. Box 1180
Canon City 81212

Community College of Aurora
16000 East Centre Tech Pkwy.
Aurora 80011-9036

Community College of Denver
P.O. Box 173363
Denver 80217

Denver Paralegal Institute
1401 19th St.
Denver 80202-1213

Denver Paralegal Institute-Colorado
Springs
105 East Vermijo Ave.
Colorado Springs 80903

Pikes Peak Community College
5675 South Academy Blvd.
Colorado Springs 80906-5498

CONNECTICUT

Branford Hall Career Institute
Nine Business Park Dr.
Branford 06405

Briarwood College
2279 Mount Vernon Rd.
Southington 06489

Connecticut Institute for Paralegal Studies
26 Sixth St.
Stamford 06905

Huntington Institute, Inc.
193 Broadway
Norwich 06360

Manchester Community College
60 Bidwell St., P.O. Box 1045
Manchester 06040-1046

Mattatuck Community College
750 Chase Pkwy.
Waterbury 06708

Morse School of Business
275 Asylum St.
Hartford 06103

Norwalk Community Technical College
188 Richards Ave.
Norwalk 06854

Sacred Heart University
5151 Park Ave.
Fairfield 06432-1023

Teikyo Post University
800 Country Club Rd., P.O. Box 2540
Waterbury 06723-2540

The Corporate Education Center, Inc.
2A Ives St.
Danbury 06810

University of Bridgeport
380 University Ave.
Bridgeport 06601

University of Hartford
200 Bloomfield Ave.
West Hartford 06117

DELAWARE

Delaware Technical and Community
College-Southern Campus
P.O. Box 610
Georgetown 19947

The Career Institute
711 Market St. Mall
Wilmington 19801

FLORIDA

American Institute for Paralegal Studies,
Inc.-Tampa
University of Tampa
Tampa 33606

Broward Community College
225 East Las Olas Blvd.
Fort Lauderdale 33301

Daytona Beach Community College
1200 Volusia Ave.
Daytona Beach 32114

Florida Community College at
Jacksonville
501 West State St.
Jacksonville 32202

Gulf Coast Community College
5230 West Hwy. 98
Panama City 32401

Hillsborough Community College
P.O. Box 31127
Tampa 33631-3127

Indian River Community College
3209 Virginia Ave.
Fort Pierce 34981

International College
2654 Tamiami Trail E
Naples 33962

Jones College-Jacksonville
5353 Arlington Expwy.
Jacksonville 32211

Keiser College of Technology
1500 Northwest 49th St.
Fort Lauderdale 33309

Legal Career Institute
7289 Garden Rd.
Riviera Beach 33404

Legal Career Institute
5225 West Broward Blvd.
Fort Lauderdale 33317

Manatee Community College
5840 26th St. W
Bradenton 34207

Miami-Dade Community College
300 Northeast Second Ave.
Miami 33132

Okaloosa-Walton Community College
100 College Blvd.
Niceville 32578

Orlando College
5500-5800 Diplomat Circle
Orlando 32810

Palm Beach Community College
4200 Congress Ave.
Lake Worth 33461

Paralegal Careers, Inc.
1211 North Westshore
Tampa 33607

Pensacola Junior College
1000 College Blvd.
Pensacola 32504

Saint Petersburg Junior College
P.O. Box 13489
Saint Petersburg 33733

Santa Fe Community College
3000 Northwest 83rd St.
Gainesville 32601

Seminole Community College
100 Weldon Blvd.
Sanford 32773-6199

South College
1760 North Congress Ave.
West Palm Beach 33409

Southern College
5600 Lake Underhill Rd.
Orlando 32807

Tallahassee Community College
444 Appleyard Dr.
Tallahassee 32304-2895

Tampa College
3319 West Hillsborough Ave.
Tampa 33614

Tampa College-Lakeland
1200 U.S. Hwy. 98 S
Lakeland 33801

Tampa College-Pinellas
15064 U.S. Hwy. 19 N
Clearwater 34624

Valencia Community College
P.O. Box 3028
Orlando 32802

Webster College, Inc.
5623 U.S. Hwy. 19 S
New Port Richey 34652

GEORGIA

Athens Area Technical Institute
U.S. Hwy. 29 N
Athens 30610-0399

HAWAII

Kapiolani Community College
4303 Diamond Head Rd.
Honolulu 96816

IDAHO

Lewis-Clark State College
Eighth Ave. and Sixth St.
Lewiston 83501

New Careers College of Business and
   Technology
2410 Bank Dr.
Boise 83705

ILLINOIS

Elgin Community College
1700 Spartan Dr.
Elgin 60123

Illinois Central College
One College Dr.
East Peoria 61635

MacCormac College
506 South Wabash
Chicago 60605

Midstate College
244 Southwest Jefferson
Peoria 61602

Robert Morris College
180 North Lasalle St.
Chicago 60601

Sanford-Brown College
3237 West Chain of Rocks Rd.
Granite 62040

South Suburban College
15800 South State St.
South Holland 60473

William Rainey Harper College
1200 West Algonquin Rd.
Palatine 60067-7398

Woodridge Business Institute
1310 Mercantile Dr.
Highland 62249

INDIANA

Ball State University
2000 University Ave.
Muncie 47306

Indiana Vocational Technical
   College-Central Indiana
One West 26th St.
Indianapolis 46206-1763

Professional Career Institute
2611 Waterfront Pkwy. & East Dr.
Indianapolis 46214-2028

Sawyer College-Hammond
6040 Hohman Ave.
Hammond 46320

Sawyer College-Merrillville Branch
3803 East Lincoln Hwy.
Merrillville 46410

University of Indianapolis
1400 East Hanna Ave.
Indianapolis 46227

Vincennes University
1002 North First St.
Vincennes 47591

IOWA

American Institute of Commerce
2302 West First St.
Cedar Falls 50613

Des Moines Community College
2006 Ankeny Blvd.
Ankeny 50021

Kirkwood Community College
P.O. Box 2068
Cedar Rapids 52406

Teikyo Marycrest University
1607 West 12th St.
Davenport 52804-4096

KANSAS

Johnson County Community College
12345 College Blvd.
Overland Park 66210-1299

Kansas City Kansas Community College
7250 State Ave.
Kansas City 66112

The Brown Mackie College
8000 West 110th St.
Overland Park 66210

The Brown Mackie College
126 South Santa Fe St.
Salina 67402-1787

Washburn University of Topeka
1700 College Ave.
Topeka 66621

Wichita State University
1845 Fairmount
Wichita 67260

KENTUCKY

Eastern Kentucky University
Lancaster Ave.
Richmond 40475

Kentucky Career Institute
8095 Connector Dr., P.O. Box 143
Florence 41022-0143

Midway College
512 Stephens St.
Midway 40347-1120

Sullivan College
3101 Bardstown Rd.
Louisville 40205

University of Louisville
South Third St.
Louisville 40292-0001

LOUISIANA

Baton Rouge College
2834 South Sherwood Forest
Baton Rouge 70816

Jefferson College
12 Westbank Expwy.
Gretna 70053

McNeese State University
4100 Ryan St.
Lake Charles 70609

Nicholls State University
University Station
Thibodaux 70310

Phillips Junior College
822 South Clearview Pkwy.
New Orleans 70123

Southern Technical College
303 Rue Louis XIV
Lafayette 70508

Tulane University of Louisiana
6823 Saint Charles Ave.
New Orleans 70118

MAINE

Beal College
629 Main St.
Bangor 04401

Casco Bay College
477 Congress St.
Portland 04101

MARYLAND

Abbie Business Institute
5310 Spectrum Dr.
Frederick 21701

Anne Arundel Community College
101 College Pkwy.
Arnold 21012

Baltimore City Community College
2901 Liberty Heights Ave.
Baltimore 21215

Dundalk Community College
7200 Sollers Point Rd.
Dundalk 21222

Frederick Community College
7932 Opossumtown Pike
Frederick 21702

Hagerstown Business College
18618 Crestwood Dr.
Hagerstown 21742

Montgomery College of Takoma Park
Takoma Ave. and Fenton St.
Takoma Park 20912

Prince Georges Community College
301 Largo Rd.
Largo 23701-1243

Villa Julie College
Green Spring Valley Rd.
Stevenson 21153

MASSACHUSETTS

Aquinas College at Milton
303 Adams St.
Milton 02186

Bay Path College
588 Longmeadow St.
Longmeadow 01106

Becker College-Worcester
61 Sever St.
Worcester 01615-0071

Fisher College
118 Beacon St.
Boston 02116

Kinyon-Campbell Business School
59 Linden St.
New Bedford 02740

Kinyon-Campbell Business School
1041 Pearl St.
Brockton 02401

Massachusetts Bay Community College
50 Oakland St.
Wellesley Hills 02181

Middlesex Community College
Springs Rd.
Bedford 01730

Mount Ida College
777 Dedham St.
Newton Centre 02159

North Shore Community College
One Ferncroft Rd.
Danvers 01923

Northern Essex Community College
Elliott Way
Haverhill 01830-2399

Quincy College
34 Coddington St.
Quincy 02169

Stonehill College
Washington St.
North Easton 02357

MICHIGAN

Academy of Court Reporting
26111 Evergreen Rd.
Southfield 48076-4481

American Education Centers
26075 Woodward Ave.
Huntington Woods 48070

American Institute for Paralegal Studies,
Inc.
17515 West Nine Mile Rd.
Southfield 48075

Delta College
University Center 48710

Ferris State University
901 South State St.
Big Rapids 49307

Gogebic Community College
East 4946 Jackson Rd.
Ironwood 49938

Great Lakes Junior College of Business
310 South Washington Ave.
Saginaw 48607

Henry Ford Community College
5101 Evergreen Rd.
Dearborn 48128

Jackson Community College
2111 Emmons Rd.
Jackson 49201

Kellogg Community College
450 North Ave.
Battle Creek 49017

Lansing Community College
419 North Capitol Ave.
Lansing 48901-7210

Macomb Community College
14500 Twelve Mile Rd.
Warren 48093-3896

Montcalm Community College
2800 College Dr.
Sidney 48885

Mott Community College
1401 East Court St.
Flint 48503

Northwestern Michigan College
1701 East Front St.
Traverse City 49684

Oakland Community College
2480 Opdyke Rd.
Bloomfield Hills 48304-2266

Oakland University
Rochester Hills 48309-4401

Professional Careers Institute
23300 Greenfield Ave.
Oak Park 48237

Southwestern Michigan College
58900 Cherry Grove Rd.
Dowagiac 49047-9793

University of Detroit-Mercy
P.O. Box 19900
Detroit 48219-0900

MINNESOTA

Inver Hills Community College
5445 College Trail
Inver Grove Heights 55076

North Hennepin Community College
7411 85th Ave. N
Brooklyn Park 55445

Northland Community College
Hwy. 1 E
Thief River Falls 56701

MISSISSIPPI

Mississippi Gulf Coast Community
College
Central Office, P.O. Box 67
Perkinston 39573

Phillips Junior College
2680 Insurance Center Dr.
Jackson 39216

Phillips Junior College
942 Beach Dr.
Gulfport 39507

MISSOURI

Drury College
900 North Benton Ave.
Springfield 65802

Missouri Western State College
4525 Downs Dr.
Saint Joseph 64507

Northwest Missouri Community College
4315 Pickett Rd.
Saint Joseph 64503-1635

Penn Valley Community College
3201 Southwest Trafficway
Kansas City 64111

Phillips Junior College
1010 West Sunshine
Springfield 65807

Rockhurst College
1100 Rockhurst Rd.
Kansas City 64110

Saint Louis Community College-Forest
Park
5600 Oakland Ave.
Saint Louis 63110

Sanford-Brown Business College
12006 Manchester Rd.
Des Peres 63131

Vattenott College
3925 Industrial Dr.
Saint Ann 63074

Watterson College-Saint Louis Missouri
3323 South Kings Hwy.
Saint Louis 63139

Webster University
470 East Lockwood
Saint Louis 63119

William Jewell College
500 College Hill
Liberty 64068

MONTANA

College of Great Falls
1301 Twentieth St. S
Great Falls 59405-4996

May Technical College
P.O. Box 127
Billings 59103

May Technical College-Great Falls
1807 Third St. NW
Great Falls 59404

Missoula Vocational Technical Center
909 South Ave. W
Missoula 59801

NEBRASKA

College of Saint Mary
1901 South 72nd St.
Omaha 68124

Institute of Computer Science
808 South 74th Place
Omaha 68114

Metropolitan Community College Area
P.O. Box 3777
Omaha 68103

Nebraska College of Business
3636 California St.
Omaha 68131

NEVADA

Community College of Southern Nevada
3200 East Cheyenne Ave.
Las Vegas 89030

Morrison College/Reno Business College
140 Washington St.
Reno 89503

NEW HAMPSHIRE

Hesser College
Three Sundial Ave.
Manchester 03103

McIntosh College
23 Cataract Ave.
Dover 03820

New Hampshire Technical College at
Nashua
505 Amherst St.
Nashua 03061-2052

New Hampshire Technical Institute
11 Institute Dr.
Concord 03301

NEW JERSEY

Bergen Community College
400 Paramus Rd.
Paramus 07652

Brookdale Community College
Newman Springs Rd.
Lincroft 07738-1599

Burlington County College
Rte. 530
Pemberton 08068

Cittone Institute
523 Fellowship Rd.
Mount Laurel 08054

Cumberland County College
College Dr., P.O. Box 517
Vineland 08360

Horizon Institute of Paralegal Studies
453 North Wood Ave.
Linden 07036

Katharine Gibbs School
80 Kingsbridge Rd.
Piscataway 08854

Mercer County Community College
1200 Old Trenton Rd.
Trenton 08690

Middlesex County College
155 Mill Rd., P.O. Box 3050
Edison 08818-3050

Omega Institute
Rte. 130 South Cinnaminson Mall
Cinnaminson 08077

Sussex County Community College
Commission
College Hill
Newton 07860

NEW MEXICO

Albuquerque Career Institute
111 Wyoming NE
Albuquerque 87123

Albuquerque Technical-Vocational
Institute
525 Buena Vista SE
Albuquerque 87106

San Juan College
4601 College Blvd.
Farmington 87402

Santa Fe Community College
South Richards Ave. P.O. Box 4187
Santa Fe 87502-4187

NEW YORK

Betty Owen Schools, Inc.
350 Fifth Ave.
New York 10118

Broome Community College
P.O. Box 1017
Binghamton 13902

Corning Community College
Spencer Hill
Corning 14830

Erie Community College-City Campus
121 Ellicott St.
Buffalo 14203

Herkimer County Community College
Reservoir Rd.
Herkimer 13350-1598

Nassau Community College
One Education Dr.
Garden City 11530

National Academy for Paralegal Studies,
Inc.
28 Industrial Dr., P.O. Box 907
Middletown 10940

Rennert Bilingual
Two West 45th St.
New York 10036

Schenectady County Community College
Washington Ave.
Schenectady 12305

Suffolk County Community
College-Western Campus
Crooked Hill Rd.
Brentwood 11717

Suffolk County Community
College-Ammerman Campus
533 College Rd.
Selden 11784

The Sobelsohn School
370 Seventh Ave.
New York 10001

Tompkins-Cortland Community College
170 North St.
Dryden 13053

NORTH CAROLINA

Cape Fear Community College
411 North Front St.
Wilmington 28401

Carteret Community College
3505 Arendell St.
Morehead City 28557

Central Carolina Community College
1105 Kelly Dr.
Sanford 27330

Central Piedmont Community College
P.O. Box 35009
Charlotte 28235

Coastal Carolina Community College
444 Western Blvd.
Jacksonville 28546-6877

Davidson County Community College
P.O. Box 1287
Lexington 27293

Durham Technical Community College
1637 Lawson St.
Durham 27703

Fayetteville Technical Community
College
2201 Hull Rd.
Fayetteville 28303

Forsyth Technical Community College
2100 Silas Creek Pkwy.
Winston-Salem 27103

Guilford Technical Community College
P.O. Box 309
Jamestown 27282

Johnston Community College
P.O. Box 2350
Smithfield 27577-2350

Kings College
322 Lamar Ave.
Charlotte 28204

Pitt Community College
Hwy. 11 S, P.O. Drawer 7007
Greenville 27835-7007

Rockingham Community College
P.O. Box 38
Wentworth 27375-0038

Southwestern Community College
275 Webster Rd.
Sylva 28779

Western Piedmont Community College
1001 Burkemont Ave.
Morganton 28655-9978

NORTH DAKOTA

Interstate Business College
520 East Main Ave.
Bismarck 58501

OHIO

Academy of Court Reporting-Columbus
630 East Broad St.
Columbus 43215

Academy of Court Reporting-Akron
2930 West Market St.
Akron 44333

Academy of Court Reporting
614 Superior Ave. NW
Cleveland 44113

American Institute for Paralegal Studies,
Inc.
400 East Second St.
Dayton 45401

American Institute for Paralegal Studies,
Inc.
3200 Chagrin Blvd.
Pepper Pike 44124-5974

American Institute for Paralegal Studies,
Inc.
1216 Sunburg Rd.
Columbus 43219

American Institute for Paralegal Studies,
Inc.
2020 Easton St.
Canton 44720

American Institute for Paralegal Studies,
Inc.
1231 West Kemper Rd.
Cincinnati 45240

American Institute for Paralegal Studies,
Inc.
16699 Bagley Rd.
Cleveland 44130

American School of Technology
2100 Morse Rd.
Columbus 43229

Columbus Para Professional Institute
1077 Lexington Ave.
Columbus 43201

Columbus State Community College
550 East Spring St., P.O. Box 1609
Columbus 43216

Dyke College
112 Prospect Ave.
Cleveland 44115

Lakeland Community College
7700 Clocktower Dr.
Mentor 44060-7594

Lawrence County Joint Vocational School
Rte. 2 Getaway
Chesapeake 45619

Lima Technical College
4240 Campus Dr.
Lima 45804

Muskingum Area Technical College
1555 Newark Rd.
Zanesville 43701

Raedel College and Industrial Welding
School
137 Sixth St. NE
Canton 44702

Sawyer College of Business
3150 Mayfield Rd.
Cleveland Heights 44118

Sawyer College of Business-West
13027 Lorain Ave.
Cleveland 44111

Sinclair Community College
444 West Third St.
Dayton 45402

Technology Education Center
288 South Hamilton Rd.
Columbus 43213

Tri-County Vocational School
15675 St. Rte. 691
Nelsonville 45764

University of Akron-Main Campus
302 Buchtel Common
Akron 44325-4702

University of Cincinnati-Main Campus
2624 Clifton Ave.
Cincinnati 45221-0127

University of Toledo
2801 West Bancroft
Toledo 43606

OKLAHOMA

City College, Inc.
1370 North Interstate Dr.
Norman 73072

Oklahoma Junior College of Business
and Technology
3232 Northwest 65th
Oklahoma City 73116

Rogers State College
Will Rogers and College Hill
Claremore 74017

Rose State College
6420 Southeast 15th
Midwest City 73110

OREGON

College of Legal Arts
52M Southwest Hall
Portland 97201

Pioneer Pacific College
25195 Southwest Parkway Ave.
Wilsonville 97070

Portland Community College
P.O. Box 19000
Portland 97280-0990

Western Business College
505 Southwest Sixth Ave.
Portland 97204

PENNSYLVANIA

Academy of Medical Arts and Business
279 Boas St.
Harrisburg 17102

American Center for Technical Arts and
Sciences
100 East Lancaster Ave.
Wayne 19087

American Center for Technical Arts
1930 Chestnut St.
Philadelphia 19103

Central Pennsylvania Business School
107 College Hill Rd.
Summerdale 17093-0309

Community College of Allegheny County
800 Allegheny Ave.
Pittsburgh 15233-1895

Duffs Business Institute
110 Ninth St.
Pittsburgh 15222

Gannon University
109 West Sixth St.
Erie 16541

Harrisburg Area Community
College-Harrisburg Campus
One Hacc Dr.
Harrisburg 17110

Liberty Academy of Business
511 North Broad St.
Philadelphia 19123

Luzerne County Community College
1333 South Prospect St.
Nanticoke 18634

Manor Junior College
700 Fox Chase Rd.
Jenkintown 19046

Mount Aloysius College
One College Dr.
Cresson 16630-1999

Peirce Junior College
1420 Pine St.
Philadelphia 19102

Pennsylvania College of Technology
One College Ave.
Williamsport 17701

Pennsylvania State University-Main
Campus
201 Old Main
University Park 16802

Robert Morris College
Narrows Run Rd.
Coraopolis 15108-1189

Star Technical Institute-Kingston
212 Wyoming Ave.
Kingston 18704

Star Technical Institute-Whitehall
1541 Alta Dr.
Whitehall 18052

The Career Institute
1825 J F Kennedy Blvd.
Philadelphia 19103

The PJA School
7900 West Chester Pike
Upper Darby 19082

Western School of Health & Business
Careers
Rte. 22 and 3824 Northern Pike
Monroeville 15146

Western School of Health & Business
Careers
411 Seventh Ave.
Pittsburgh 15219

Westmoreland County Community
College
Youngwood 15697-1895

RHODE ISLAND

Johnson and Wales University
Abbott Park Place
Providence 02903-3376

Katharine Gibbs School
178 Butler Ave.
Providence 02906

SOUTH CAROLINA

Florence-Darlington Technical College
P.O. Box 100548
Florence 29501-0548

Greenville Technical College
Station B, P.O. Box 5616
Greenville 29606-5616

Midlands Technical College
P.O. Box 2408
Columbia 29202

Trident Technical College
P.O. Box 118067
Charleston 29423-8067

SOUTH DAKOTA

Kilian Community College
1600 South Menlo Ave.
Sioux Falls 57105

National College
321 Kansas City St.
Rapid City 57701

Nettleton Junior College
100 South Spring Ave.
Sioux Falls 57104

TENNESSEE

Chattanooga State Technical Community
College
4501 Amnicola Hwy.
Chattanooga 37406

Cleveland State Community College
P.O. Box 3570
Cleveland 37320-3570

Memphis State University
Memphis 38152

Pellissippi State Technical Community
College
P.O. Box 22990
Knoxville 37933-0990

State Technical Institute of Memphis
5983 Macon Cove
Memphis 38134

TEXAS

Austin Community College
5930 Middle Fiskville Rd.
Austin 78752

Center for Advanced Legal Studies
3910 Kirby
Houston 77098

Collin County Community College
2200 West University
McKinney 75070

Cooke County College
1525 West California
Gainesville 76240

Del Mar College
101 Baldwin
Corpus Christi 78404-3897

El Centro College
Main and Lamar
Dallas 75202

El Paso Community College
P.O. Box 20500
El Paso 79998

Grayson County College
6101 Grayson Dr.
Denison 75020

Houston Community College System
22 Waugh Dr., P.O. Box 7849
Houston 77270-7849

Midland College
3600 North Garfield
Midland 79705

National Career Institute
1209 Seventh St.
Harlingen 78550

North Harris Montgomery Community
College District
250 North Sam Houston Pkwy. E
Houston 77060

Phillips School of Business &
Technology
119 West Eighth St.
Austin 78701

San Antonio College
1300 San Pedro Ave.
San Antonio 78284

San Antonio Court Reporting Institute,
Inc.
5430 Fredericksburg Rd.
San Antonio 78229

Southern Career Institute, Inc.
2301 South Congress
Austin 78704

Southern Methodist University
6425 Boaz St.
Dallas 75275-0221

Southwestern Institutes
4888 Loop Central Dr.
Houston 77081

Tarrant County Junior College District
1500 Houston St.
Fort Worth 76102

Texas School of Business, Inc.
711 Airtex Dr.
Houston 77073

Texas School of Business-Southwest, Inc.
10250 Bissonnet
Houston 77036

Tyler Junior College
P.O. Box 9020
Tyler 75711

UTAH

Phillips Junior College-Salt Lake City
3098 Highland Dr.
Salt Lake City 84106

Utah Valley Community College
800 West, 1200 South
Orem 84058

Westminster College of Salt Lake City
1840 South, 1300 East
Salt Lake City 84105

VERMONT

Champlain College
163 South Willard St.
Burlington 05401

VIRGINIA

Commonwealth College
4160 Virginia Beach Blvd.
Virginia Beach 23452

Para-Legal Institute
95 24-A Lee Hwy.
Fairfax 22031

University of Richmond
Maryland Hall
Richmond 23173

WASHINGTON

Clark College
1800 East McLoughlin Blvd.
Vancouver 98663

Edmonds Community College
20000 68th Ave. W
Lynnwood 98036

Highline Community College
P.O. Box 98000
Des Moines 98198-9800

Phillips Junior College
North 1101 Fancher
Spokane 99212-1204

Pierce College
9401 Farwest Dr. SW
Tacoma 98498

Spokane Community College
North 1810 Greene Ave.
Spokane 99207

WEST VIRGINIA

Marshall University
400 Hal Greer Blvd.
Huntington 25755

The College of West Virginia
609 South Kanawha
Beckley 25802

The University of Charleston
2300 MacCorkle Ave. SE
Charleston 25304

West Virginia Business College
1052 Main St.
Wheeling 26003

West Virginia Business College
215 West Main St.
Clarksburg 26301

West Virginia Career College
148 Willey St.
Morgantown 26505

WISCONSIN

Chippewa Valley Technical College
620 West Clairemont Ave.
Eau Claire 54701

Lakeshore Vocational Training and Adult
Education System District
1290 North Ave.
Cleveland 53015

MBTI Business Training Institute
820 North Plankinton Ave.
Milwaukee 53203

Milwaukee Area Technical College
700 West State St.
Milwaukee 53233

Northeast Wisconsin Technical College
2740 West Mason St., P.O. Box 19042
Green Bay 54307-9042

WYOMING

Casper College
125 College Dr.
Casper 82601

Laramie County Community College
1400 East College Dr.
Cheyenne 82007

Library Assistant Technology

CALIFORNIA

Foothill College
12345 El Monte Rd.
Los Altos Hills 94022

Fresno City College
1101 East University Ave.
Fresno 93741

Palomar College
1140 West Mission
San Marcos 92069-1487

Sacramento City College
3835 Freeport Blvd.
Sacramento 95822

CONNECTICUT

Mohegan Community College
Mahan Dr., P.O. Box 629
Norwich 06360

ILLINOIS

City College of Chicago-Wright College
4300 North Narragansett
Chicago 60634

College of Du Page
Lambert Rd. and 22nd St.
Glen Ellyn 60137

NEW HAMPSHIRE

School for Lifelong Learning
25 Concord Rd., Dunlap Center
Durham 03824

Police Science and Law Enforcement Technology

ALABAMA

Community College of the Air Force
Maxwell Air Force Base
Montgomery 36112

Gadsden State Community College
P.O. Box 227
Gadsden 35902-0227

George C Wallace State Community
College-Hanceville
801 Main St. NW, P.O. Box 2000
Hanceville 35077-2000

John C Calhoun State Community
College
P.O. Box 2216
Decatur 35609-2216

ALASKA

University of Alaska-Southeast
11120 Glacier Hwy.
Juneau 99801

ARIZONA

Arizona Institute of Business and
Technology
925 South Gilbert Rd.
Mesa 85204

Arizona Western College
P.O. Box 929
Yuma 85366

Central Arizona College
8470 North Overfield Rd.
Coolidge 85228-9778

Glendale Community College
6000 West Olive Ave.
Glendale 85302

Mesa Community College
1833 West Southern Ave.
Mesa 85202

Phoenix College
1202 West Thomas Rd.
Phoenix 85013

Pima Community College
2202 West Anklam Rd.
Tucson 85709-0001

ARKANSAS

Capital City Junior College of Business
7723 Asher Ave.
Little Rock 72214

East Arkansas Community College
Newcastle Rd.
Forrest City 72335

Garland County Community College
100 College Dr.
Hot Springs 71913

CALIFORNIA

American Institute of Specialized Studies
8345 Reseda Blvd.
Northridge 91324

American Technical College for Career
Training
191 South East St.
San Bernardino 92401

California Security Training School
2458 West Lomita Blvd.
Lomita 90717

California Career Schools
392 West Cerritos Ave.
Anaheim 92805

Center for Employment Training-San
Jose-McGinness
1212 McGinness Ave.
San Jose 95127

Century Business College
3325 Wilshire Blvd.
Los Angeles 90010

Century Schools
2665 Fifth Ave.
San Diego 92103

Chaffey Community College
5885 Haven Ave.
Rancho Cucamonga 91737-3002

City College of San Francisco
50 Phelan Ave.
San Francisco 94112

Contra Costa College
2600 Mission Bell Dr.
San Pablo 94806

De Anza College
21250 Stevens Creek Blvd.
Cupertino 95014

Fresno City College
1101 East University Ave.
Fresno 93741

Fullerton College
321 East Chapman Ave.
Fullerton 92632-2095

Imperial Valley College
P.O. Box 158
Imperial 92251-0158

Lassen College
Hwy. 139, P.O. Box 3000
Susanville 96130

Martial Arts Security Service, Inc.
2024 North Broadway
Santa Ana 92706-2622

Mount San Antonio College
1100 North Grand
Walnut 91789

Napa Valley College
2277 Napa Vallejo Hwy.
Napa 94558

Palomar College
1140 West Mission
San Marcos 92069-1487

Professional Investigators Training
School
620 North Kenwood Place
Glendale 91206

Rancho Santiago College
17th at Bristol
Santa Ana 92706

Rio Hondo College
3600 Workman Mill Rd.
Whittier 90601-1699

Rouse School of Special Detective
Training
3410 G West McArthur Blvd.
Santa Ana 92704

Royal Security Training Academy
237 West Gage Ave.
Los Angeles 90003

Sacramento City College
3835 Freeport Blvd.
Sacramento 95822

Safety First Security Training Academy
156 North West Ave.
Fresno 93728

San Diego Miramar College
10440 Black Mountain Rd.
San Diego 92126-2999

San Joaquin Valley College
8400 West Mineral King Ave.
Visalia 93291

San Joaquin Valley College
201 New Stine Rd.
Bakersfield 93309

San Joaquin Valley College
3333 North Bond
Fresno 93726

Santa Rosa Junior College
1501 Mendocino Ave.
Santa Rosa 95401-4395

Shasta College
P.O. Box 496006
Redding 96049

Sierra College
5000 Rocklin Rd.
Rocklin 95677

Solano County Community College
District
4000 Suisun Valley Rd.
Suisun 94585

Southwestern College
900 Otay Lakes Rd.
Chula Vista 92010

Victor Valley College
18422 Bear Valley Rd.
Victorville 92392-9699

COLORADO

Aims Community College
P.O. Box 69
Greeley 80632

Colorado Mountain College
P.O. Box 10001
Glenwood Springs 81602

Delta-Montrose Area Vocational
Technical Center
1765 U.S. Hwy. 50
Delta 81416

Denver Business College
7350 North Broadway
Denver 80221

Morgan Community College
17800 County Rd. 20
Fort Morgan 80701

Nakazono Security Training
1780 South Bellaire St.
Denver 80222

Trinidad State Junior College
600 Prospect St.
Trinidad 81082

CONNECTICUT

Housatonic Community College
510 Barnum Ave.
Bridgeport 06608

Manchester Community College
60 Bidwell St., P.O. Box 1045
Manchester 06040-1046

Mattatuck Community College
750 Chase Pkwy.
Waterbury 06708

Mohegan Community College
Mahan Dr., P.O. Box 629
Norwich 06360

Northwestern Connecticut Community
College
Park Place E
Winsted 06098

Norwalk Community Technical College
188 Richards Ave.
Norwalk 06854

Tunxis Community College
Rtes. 6 and 177
Farmington 06032

DELAWARE

Delaware Technical and Community
College-Southern Campus
P.O. Box 610
Georgetown 19947

Delaware Technical Community College
Stanton-Wilmington
400 Stanton-Christiana Rd.
Newark 19702

DISTRICT OF COLUMBIA

PTC Career Institute
529 14th St. NW
Washington 20004

FLORIDA

Brevard Community College
1519 Clearlake Rd.
Cocoa 32922

Career City College
1317 Northeast Fourth Ave.
Fort Lauderdale 33304

Central Florida Community College
P.O. Box 1388
Ocala 34478

Chipola Junior College
3094 Indian Circle
Marianna 32446

Daytona Beach Community College
1200 Volusia Ave.
Daytona Beach 32114

Florida Community College at
Jacksonville
501 West State St.
Jacksonville 32202

Indian River Community College
3209 Virginia Ave.
Fort Pierce 34981

Lake City Community College
Rte. 3, P.O. Box 7
Lake City 32055

Lake County Area Vocational-Technical
Center
2001 Kurt St.
Eustis 32726

Lewis M Lively Area
Vocational-Technical Center
500 North Appleyard Dr.
Tallahassee 32304

Manatee Vocational-Technical Center
5603 34th St. W
Bradenton 34210

Miami-Dade Community College
300 Northeast Second Ave.
Miami 33132

North Florida Junior College
Turner Davis Dr.
Madison 32340

Palm Beach Community College
4200 Congress Ave.
Lake Worth 33461

Pasco-Hernando Community College
36727 Blanton Rd.
Dade City 33525-7599

Santa Fe Community College
3000 Northwest 83rd St.
Gainesville 32601

Sarasota County Technical Institute
4748 Beneva Rd.
Sarasota 34233-1798

Seminole Community College
100 Weldon Blvd.
Sanford 32773-6199

South Florida Community College
600 West College Dr.
Avon Park 33825

William T McFatter Vocational
Technical Center
6500 Nova Dr.
Davie 33317

Withlacoochee Technical Institute
1201 West Main St.
Inverness 32650

GEORGIA

Columbus College
4225 University Ave.
Columbus 31907-5645

Floyd College
P.O. Box 1864
Rome 30162-1864

Georgia Military College-Fort Gordon
Center
P.O. Box 7258
Fort Gordon 30905

Georgia Military College-Main Campus
201 East Greene St.
Milledgeville 31061-3398

Interactive Learning Systems
200 Cleveland Rd.
Bogart 30622

Interactive Learning Systems
2191 Northlake Pkwy.
Tucker 30084

Interactive Learning Systems
4814 Old National Hwy.
College Park 30337

PTC Career Institute
44 Broad St. NW
Atlanta 30303

HAWAII

Hawaii Community College
200 West Kawili St.
Hilo 96720-4091

Honolulu Community College
874 Dillingham Blvd.
Honolulu 96817

IDAHO

College of Southern Idaho
P.O. Box 1238
Twin Falls 83301

Eastern Idaho Technical College
1600 South, 2500 East
Idaho Falls 83404

Idaho State University
741 South Seventh Ave.
Pocatello 83209

North Idaho College
1000 West Garden Ave.
Coeur D'Alene 83814

Ricks College
Rexburg 83460-4107

ILLINOIS

Belleville Area College
2500 Carlyle Rd.
Belleville 62221

Black Hawk College-Quad-Cities
6600 34th Ave.
Moline 61265

City College of Chicago-Wright College
4300 North Narragansett
Chicago 60634

City College of Chicago-Harold
   Washington
30 East Lake St.
Chicago 60601

City College of Chicago-Richard J Daley
   College
7500 South Pulaski Rd.
Chicago 60652

College of Du Page
Lambert Rd. and 22nd St.
Glen Ellyn 60137

College of Lake County
19351 West Washington St.
Gray's Lake 60030-1198

Danville Area Community College
2000 East Main St.
Danville 61832

Illinois Central College
One College Dr.
East Peoria 61635

Illinois Valley Community College
2578 East 350th Rd.
Oglesby 61348

John A Logan College
Carterville 62918

Joliet Junior College
1216 Houbolt Ave.
Joliet 60436

Kankakee Community College
P.O. Box 888
Kankakee 60901

Kaskaskia College
27210 College Rd.
Centralia 62801

Lake Land College
5001 Lake Land Blvd.
Mattoon 61938

Lewis and Clark Community College
5800 Godfrey Rd.
Godfrey 62035

Lincoln Land Community College
Shepherd Rd.
Springfield 62194-9256

Moraine Valley Community College
10900 South 88th Ave.
Palos Hills 60465-0937

Morton College
3801 South Central Ave.
Cicero 60650

Northwestern University
633 Clark St.
Evanston 60208

Oakton Community College
1600 East Golf Rd.
Des Plaines 60016

Parkland College
2400 West Bradley Ave.
Champaign 61821

Pathfinder Enterprises, Inc.
19 East 21st St.
Chicago 60616

PTC Career Institute
11 East Adams St.
Chicago 60603

Rend Lake College
Rte. 1
Ina 62846

Richland Community College
One College Park
Decatur 62521

Rock Valley College
3301 North Mulford Rd.
Rockford 61114

Sauk Valley Community College
173 Rte. 2
Dixon 61021

Shawnee Community College
Shawnee College Rd.
Ullin 62992

South Suburban College
15800 South State St.
South Holland 60473

Southeastern Illinois College
3575 College Rd.
Harrisburg 62946

Southern Illinois University-Carbondale
Carbondale 62901

Triton College
2000 Fifth Ave.
River Grove 60171

Waubonsee Community College
Rte. 47 at Harter Rd.
Sugar Grove 60554-0901

William Rainey Harper College
1200 West Algonquin Rd.
Palatine 60067-7398

INDIANA

Indiana State University
210 North Seventh St.
Terre Haute 47809

Indiana University at Kokomo
2300 South Washington
Kokomo 46902

Indiana University at South Bend
1700 Mishawaka Ave.
South Bend 46615

Indiana University-Purdue University at
   Fort Wayne
2101 Coliseum Blvd. E
Fort Wayne 46805

Sawyer College-Merrillville Branch
3803 East Lincoln Hwy.
Merrillville 46410

Vincennes University
1002 North First St.
Vincennes 47591

IOWA

Des Moines Community College
2006 Ankeny Blvd.
Ankeny 50021

Hawkeye Institute of Technology
1501 East Orange Rd.
Waterloo 50704

Indian Hills Community College
525 Grandview
Ottumwa 52501

Iowa Lakes Community College
19 South Seventh St.
Estherville 51334

Iowa Valley Community College
P.O. Box 536
Marshalltown 50158

Iowa Western Community College
2700 College Rd., P.O. Box 4C
Council Bluffs 51502

Kirkwood Community College
P.O. Box 2068
Cedar Rapids 52406

North Iowa Area Community College
500 College Dr.
Mason City 50401

Western Iowa Technical Community
   College
4647 Stone Ave., P.O. Box 265
Sioux City 51102-0265

KANSAS

Barton County Community College
Rte. 3, P.O. Box 136Z
Great Bend 67530

Butler County Community College
901 South Haverhill Rd.
El Dorado 67042

Cowley County Community College
125 South Second St.
Arkansas City 67005

Garden City Community College
801 Campus Dr.
Garden City 67846

Hutchinson Community College
1300 North Plum St.
Hutchinson 67501

Johnson County Community College
12345 College Blvd.
Overland Park 66210-1299

Seward County Community College
P.O. Box 1137
Liberal 67905-1137

KENTUCKY

Eastern Kentucky University
Lancaster Ave.
Richmond 40475

Hopkinsville Community College
North Dr.
Hopkinsville 42240

Northern Kentucky University
University Dr.
Highland Heights 41099

University of Louisville
South Third St.
Louisville 40292-0001

LOUISIANA

Bossier Parish Community College
2719 Airline Dr. N
Bossier City 71111

Delgado Community College
615 City Park Ave.
New Orleans 70119

Delta Career College
4358 Hwy. 84 W
Vidalia 71373

Delta Career College
1900 Cameron St.
Lafayette 70506-1608

Delta Career College-Medical Support
   Division
1702 Hudson Ln.
Monroe 71201

Grambling State University
100 Main St., P.O. Drawer 607
Grambling 71245

Jefferson College
12 Westbank Expwy.
Gretna 70053

Louisiana State University-Eunice
P.O. Box 1129
Eunice 70535

Nicholls State University
University Station
Thibodaux 70310

Orleans Security Institute
Louisiana Superdome, P.O. Box 8383
New Orleans 70182

Southern University and A & M College
   at Baton Rouge
404 South Clark Building
Baton Rouge 70813

MAINE

Southern Maine Technical College
Fort Rd.
South Portland 04106

University of Maine at Augusta
University Heights
Augusta 04330-9410

University of Maine
Office of Institutional Studies
Orono 04469

MARYLAND

Allegany Community College
Willowbrook Rd.
Cumberland 21502

Anne Arundel Community College
101 College Pkwy.
Arnold 21012

Catonsville Community College
800 South Rolling Rd.
Catonsville 21228

Chesapeake College
P.O. Box 8
Wye Mills 21679-0008

Essex Community College
7201 Rossville Blvd.
Baltimore 21237

Hagerstown Junior College
11400 Robinwood Dr.
Hagerstown 21742-6590

Harford Community College
401 Thomas Run Rd.
Bel Air 21015

Investigative Training Institute
621 Ridgely Ave.
Annapolis 21401

Montgomery College of Rockville
51 Mannakee St.
Rockville 20850

Prince Georges Community College
301 Largo Rd.
Largo 23701-1243

PTC Career Institute
201 East Baltimore St.
Baltimore 21202

Wor-Wic Community College
1409 Wesley Dr.
Salisbury 21801-7131

MASSACHUSETTS

Becker College-Worcester
61 Sever St.
Worcester 01615-0071

Berkshire Community College
1350 West St.
Pittsfield 01201-5786

Bunker Hill Community College
New Rutherford Ave.
Boston 02129

Cape Cod Community College
Rte. 132
West Barnstable 02668

Dean Junior College
99 Main St.
Franklin 02038

Greenfield Community College
One College Dr.
Greenfield 01301-9739

Holyoke Community College
303 Homestead Ave.
Holyoke 01040

Massachusetts Bay Community College
50 Oakland St.
Wellesley Hills 02181

Massasoit Community College
One Massasoit Blvd.
Brockton 02402

Middlesex Community College
Springs Rd.
Bedford 01730

Mount Wachusett Community College
444 Green St.
Gardner 01440

North Shore Community College
One Ferncroft Rd.
Danvers 01923

Northeastern University
360 Huntington Ave.
Boston 02115

Northern Essex Community College
Elliott Way
Haverhill 01830-2399

Quincy College
34 Coddington St.
Quincy 02169

Quinsigamond Community College
670 West Boylston St.
Worcester 01606

Springfield Technical Community
College
Armory Square
Springfield 01105

MICHIGAN

Alpena Community College
666 Johnson St.
Alpena 49707

Delta College
University Center 48710

Grand Rapids Community College
143 Bostwick Ave. NE
Grand Rapids 49505

Jackson Community College
2111 Emmons Rd.
Jackson 49201

Kalamazoo Valley Community College
6767 West O Ave.
Kalamazoo 49009

Kellogg Community College
450 North Ave.
Battle Creek 49017

Kirtland Community College
10775 North Saint Helen Rd.
Roscommon 48653

Lake Michigan College
2755 East Napier
Benton Harbor 49022

Lake Superior State University
Sault Sainte Marie 49783

Lansing Community College
419 North Capitol Ave.
Lansing 48901-7210

Macomb Community College
14500 Twelve Mile Rd.
Warren 48093-3896

Madonna University
36600 Schoolcraft Rd.
Livonia 48150

Montcalm Community College
2800 College Dr.
Sidney 48885

Mott Community College
1401 East Court St.
Flint 48503

Muskegon Community College
221 South Quarterline Rd.
Muskegon 49442

Northern Michigan University
1401 Presque Isle
Marquette 49855

Northwestern Michigan College
1701 East Front St.
Traverse City 49684

Oakland Community College
2480 Opdyke Rd.
Bloomfield Hills 48304-2266

Schoolcraft College
18600 Haggerty Rd.
Livonia 48152

Suomi College
601 Quincy St.
Hancock 49930

Washtenaw Community College
P.O. D1
Ann Arbor 48016

West Shore Community College
3000 North Stiles
Scottville 49454

MINNESOTA

Alexandria Technical College
1601 Jefferson St.
Alexandria 56308

Fond Du Lac Community College Center
2101 14th St.
Cloquet 55720

Hibbing Community College
1515 East 25th St.
Hibbing 55746

Inver Hills Community College
5445 College Trail
Inver Grove Heights 55076

Lakewood Community College
3401 Century Ave. N
White Bear Lake 55110

Mankato State University
South Rd. and Ellis Ave.
Mankato 56001

Normandale Community College
9700 France Ave. S
Bloomington 55431

North Hennepin Community College
7411 85th Ave. N
Brooklyn Park 55445

Northland Community College
Hwy. 1 E
Thief River Falls 56701

Range Technical College-Hibbing
Campus
2900 East Beltline
Hibbing 55746

Rochester Community College
851 30th Ave. SE
Rochester 55904-4999

Willmar Community College
P.O. Box 797
Willmar 56201-0797

MISSISSIPPI

Mississippi Gulf Coast Community
College
Central Office, P.O. Box 67
Perkinston 39573

Queen City College
800 Hwy. 1 S
Greenville 38701

MISSOURI

Jefferson College
1000 Viking Dr.
Hillsboro 63050

Missouri Southern State College
3950 East Newman Rd.
Joplin 64801-1595

Missouri Western State College
4525 Downs Dr.
Saint Joseph 64507

Penn Valley Community College
3201 Southwest Trafficway
Kansas City 64111

Saint Louis Community College-Forest
Park
5600 Oakland Ave.
Saint Louis 63110

Three Rivers Community College
Three Rivers Blvd.
Poplar Bluff 63901

MONTANA

Dawson Community College
300 College Dr.
Glendive 59330

NEBRASKA

Metropolitan Community College Area
P.O. Box 3777
Omaha 68103

Northeast Community College
801 East Benjamin, P.O. Box 469
Norfolk 68702-0469

NEVADA

Community College of Southern Nevada
3200 East Cheyenne Ave.
Las Vegas 89030

Truckee Meadows Community College
7000 Dandini Blvd.
Reno 89512

Western Nevada Community College
2201 West Nye Ln.
Carson City 89703

NEW HAMPSHIRE

Hesser College
Three Sundial Ave.
Manchester 03103

NEW JERSEY

Atlantic Community College
5100 Black Horse Pike
Mays Landing 08330-2699

Barclay Career School
28 South Harrison St.
East Orange 07017

Bergen Community College
400 Paramus Rd.
Paramus 07652

Brookdale Community College
Newman Springs Rd.
Lincroft 07738-1599

Burlington County College
Rte. 530
Pemberton 08068

Camden County College
P.O. Box 200
Blackwood 08012

County College of Morris
214 Center Grove Rd.
Randolph 07869

Essex County College
303 University Ave.
Newark 07102

Gloucester County College
Tanyard Rd. & RR 4, P.O. Box 203
Sewell 08080

Mercer County Community College
1200 Old Trenton Rd.
Trenton 08690

Middlesex County College
155 Mill Rd., P.O. Box 3050
Edison 08818-3050

Ocean County College
College Dr.
Toms River 08753

Passaic County Community College
College Blvd.
Paterson 07509

PTC Career Institute-University Heights
200 Washington St.
Newark 07102

Raritan Valley Community College
P.O. Box 3300
Somerville 08876

Union County College
1033 Springfield Ave.
Cranford 07016

NEW MEXICO

Albuquerque Technical-Vocational
Institute
525 Buena Vista SE
Albuquerque 87106

New Mexico State University-Main
Campus
P.O. Box 30001
Las Cruces 88003

Santa Fe Community College
South Richards Ave., P.O. Box 4187
Santa Fe 87502-4187

University of New Mexico-Gallup Branch
200 College Rd.
Gallup 87301

NEW YORK

Adirondack Community College
Bay Rd.
Queensbury 12804

Broome Community College
P.O. Box 1017
Binghamton 13902

Canisius College
2001 Main St.
Buffalo 14208

Cayuga County Community College
Franklin St.
Auburn 13021

Clinton Community College
RR 3, P.O. Box 8A
Plattsburgh 12901

Columbia-Greene Community College
P.O. Box 1000
Hudson 12534

CUNY John Jay College Criminal Justice
899 Tenth Ave.
New York 10019

Dutchess Community College
Pendell Rd.
Poughkeepsie 12601

Erie Community College-North Campus
Main St. and Youngs Rd.
Williamsville 14221

Hilbert College
5200 South Park Ave.
Hamburg 14075-1597

Jamestown Community College
525 Falconer St.
Jamestown 14701

Marist College
290 North Rd.
Poughkeepsie 12601

Monroe Community College
1000 East Henrietta Rd.
Rochester 14623

Orange County Community College
115 South St.
Middletown 10940

Rockland Community College
145 College Rd.
Suffern 10901

Suffolk County Community
  College-Eastern Campus
Speonk Riverhead Rd.
Riverhead 11901

Suffolk County Community
  College-Western Campus
Crooked Hill Rd.
Brentwood 11717

Suffolk County Community
  College-Ammerman Campus
533 College Rd.
Selden 11784

Sullivan County Community College
Le Roy Rd., P.O. Box 4002
Loch Sheldrake 12759-4002

SUNY College of Technology at Canton
Canton 13617

SUNY College of Technology at
  Farmingdale
Melville Rd.
Farmingdale 11735

SUNY Westchester Commmunity College
75 Grasslands Rd.
Valhalla 10595

Superior Career Institute, Inc.
116 West 14th St.
New York 10011

Tompkins-Cortland Community College
170 North St.
Dryden 13053

NORTH CAROLINA

Alamance Community College
P.O. Box 8000
Graham 27253

American Institute of Applied Science
P.O. Box 639
Youngsville 27596

Asheville-Buncombe Technical
  Community College
340 Victoria Rd.
Asheville 28801

Beaufort County Community College
P.O. Box 1069
Washington 27889

Brunswick Community College
P.O. Box 30
Supply 28462

Cape Fear Community College
411 North Front St.
Wilmington 28401

Carteret Community College
3505 Arendell St.
Morehead City 28557

Catawba Valley Community College
2550 Hwy. 70 SE
Hickory 28602-0699

Central Carolina Community College
1105 Kelly Dr.
Sanford 27330

Central Piedmont Community College
P.O. Box 35009
Charlotte 28235

Cleveland Community College
137 South Post Rd.
Shelby 28150

Coastal Carolina Community College
444 Western Blvd.
Jacksonville 28546-6877

College of the Albemarle
P.O. Box 2327, 1208 North Road St.
Elizabeth City 27906-2327

Craven Community College
800 College Ct.
New Bern 28562

Davidson County Community College
P.O. Box 1287
Lexington 27293

Durham Technical Community College
1637 Lawson St.
Durham 27703

Fayetteville Technical Community
  College
2201 Hull Rd.
Fayetteville 28303

Forsyth Technical Community College
2100 Silas Creek Pkwy.
Winston-Salem 27103

Gaston College
Hwy. 321
Dallas 28034

Guilford Technical Community College
P.O. Box 309
Jamestown 27282

Halifax Community College
P.O. Drawer 809
Weldon 27890

Haywood Community College
Freedlander Dr.
Clyde 28721

James Sprunt Community College
P.O. Box 398
Kenansville 28349

Johnston Community College
P.O. Box 2350
Smithfield 27577-2350

Mayland Community College
P.O. Box 547
Spruce Pine 28777

Mitchell Community College
500 West Broad
Statesville 28677

Montgomery Community College
P.O. Box 787
Troy 27371

Pitt Community College
Hwy. 11 S, P.O. Drawer 7007
Greenville 27835-7007

Randolph Community College
P.O. Box 1009
Asheboro 27204

Richmond Community College
P.O. Box 1189
Hamlet 28345

Robeson Community College
P.O. Box 1420
Lumberton 28359

Rowan-Cabarrus Community College
P.O. Box 1595
Salisbury 28145-1595

Southeastern Community College
P.O. Box 151
Whiteville 28472

Stanly Community College
141 College Dr.
Albemarle 28001

Vance-Granville Community College
State Rd. 11, P.O. Box 917
Henderson 27536

Wake Technical Community College
9101 Fayetteville Rd.
Raleigh 27603-5696

Wayne Community College
P.O Box 8002
Goldsboro 27533-8002

Western Piedmont Community College
1001 Burkemont Ave.
Morganton 28655-9978

Wilson Technical Community College
902 Herring Ave.
Wilson 27893

NORTH DAKOTA

Minot State University
500 University Ave. W
Minot 58707

United Tribes Technical College
3315 University Dr.
Bismarck 58501

University of North Dakota-Lake Region
North College Dr.
Devils Lake 58301

OHIO

Brentley Institute, Inc.
11750 Shaker Blvd.
Cleveland 44120

Butler County JVS District-D Russel Lee
  Career Center
3603 Hamilton Middletown Rd.
Hamilton 45011

Central Ohio Technical College
1179 University Dr.
Newark 43055-1767

Columbus State Community College
550 East Spring St., P.O. Box 1609
Columbus 43216

Cuyahoga Community College District
700 Carnegie Ave.
Cleveland 44115-2878

Delaware Joint Vocational School District
1610 Rte. 521
Delaware 43015

Eastland Career Center
4465 South Hamilton Rd.
Groveport 43125

Edison State Community College
1973 Edison Dr.
Piqua 45356

Gallia Jackson Vinton JUSD
P.O. Box 157
Rio Grande 45674

Hocking Technical College
3301 Hocking Pkwy.
Nelsonville 45764

Jefferson Technical College
4000 Sunset Blvd.
Steubenville 43952-3598

Lakeland Community College
7700 Clocktower Dr.
Mentor 44060-7594

Lawrence County Joint Vocational School
Rte. 2 Getaway
Chesapeake 45619

Lima Technical College
4240 Campus Dr.
Lima 45804

Lorain County Community College
1005 North Abbe Rd.
Elyria 44035

Midwest Technical Schools, Inc.
7009 Taylorsville Rd.
Huber Heights 45424

Muskingum Area Technical College
1555 Newark Rd.
Zanesville 43701

North Central Technical College
2441 Kenwood Circle, P.O. Box 698
Mansfield 44901

Ohio University-Chillicothe Branch
P.O. Box 629
Chillicothe 45601

Owens Technical College-Findlay
  Campus
300 Davis St.
Findlay 45840

Owens Technical College
30335 Oregon Rd., P.O. Box 10000
Toledo 43699-1947

PTC Career Institute
1140 Euclid Ave.
Cleveland 44115

Sinclair Community College
444 West Third St.
Dayton 45402

Southern Hills Joint Vocational School
  District
9193 Hamer Rd.
Georgetown 45121

Terra Technical College
2830 Napoleon Rd.
Fremont 43420

University of Akron-Main Campus
302 Buchtel Common
Akron 44325-4702

University of Cincinnati-Main Campus
2624 Clifton Ave.
Cincinnati 45221-0127

University of Toledo
2801 West Bancroft
Toledo 43606

Youngstown State University
410 Wick Ave.
Youngstown 44555

OKLAHOMA

Cameron University
2800 Gore Blvd.
Lawton 73505

Central Oklahoma Area Vocational
Technical School
1720 South Main
Sapulpa 74030

Central Oklahoma Area Vocational
Technical School
Three Court Circle
Drumright 74030

Connors State College
Rte. 1, P.O. Box 1000
Warner 74469

Northeastern Oklahoma Agricultural and
Mechanical College
200 Eye St. NE
Miami 74354

Northern Oklahoma College
P.O. Box 310
Tonkawa 74653

Oklahoma State University-Oklahoma
City
900 North Portland
Oklahoma City 73107

Platt College
6125 West Reno
Oklahoma City 73127

Platt College
4821 South 72nd East Ave.
Tulsa 74145

Redland Community College
1300 South Country Club Rd., P.O. Box
370
El Reno 73036

Rogers State College
Will Rogers and College Hill
Claremore 74017

Rose State College
6420 Southeast 15th
Midwest City 73110

Tulsa Junior College
6111 East Skelly Dr.
Tulsa 74135

OREGON

Blue Mountain Community College
P.O. Box 100
Pendleton 97801

Clackamas Community College
19600 Molalla Ave.
Oregon City 97045

Lane Community College
4000 East 30th Ave.
Eugene 97405

Linn-Benton Community College
6500 Southwest Pacific Blvd.
Albany 97321

Pioneer Pacific College
25195 Southwest Parkway Ave.
Wilsonville 97070

Rogue Community College
3345 Redwood Hwy.
Grants Pass 97527

Southwestern Oregon Community
College
1988 Newmark Ave.
Coos Bay 97420

Treasure Valley Community College
650 College Blvd.
Ontario 97914

PENNSYLVANIA

Advanced Career Training
McClatchy Fl Southwest Corner 69th &
Market
Upper Darby 19082

American Center for Technical Arts
1930 Chestnut St.
Philadelphia 19103

Bucks County Community College
Swamp Rd.
Newtown 18940

Community College of Philadelphia
1700 Spring Garden St.
Philadelphia 19130

Community College of Allegheny County
800 Allegheny Ave.
Pittsburgh 15233-1895

Community College of Beaver County
One Campus Dr.
Monaca 15061

Delaware County Community College
901 South Media Line Rd.
Media 19063

Delaware County Institute of Training
615 Ave. of the States
Chester 19013

Harrisburg Area Community
College-Harrisburg Campus
One Hacc Dr.
Harrisburg 17110

Lackawanna Junior College
901 Prospect Ave.
Scranton 18505

Lehigh County Community College
4525 Education Park Dr.
Schnecksville 18078-2598

Lion Investigation Academy
434 Clearfield St.
Freemansburg 18017

Luzerne County Community College
1333 South Prospect St.
Nanticoke 18634

Mercyhurst College
501 East 38th St.
Erie 16546

Montgomery County Community College
340 Dekalb Pike
Blue Bell 19422

PTC Career Institute
40 North Second St.
Philadelphia 19106

Suburban Academy of Law Enforcement
3550 William Penn Hwy.
Pittsburgh 15235

Westmoreland County Community
College
Youngwood 15697-1895

York College Pennsylvania
Country Club Rd.
York 17405-7199

RHODE ISLAND

Community College of Rhode Island
400 East Ave.
Warwick 02886-1805

SOUTH CAROLINA

Central Carolina Technical College
506 North Guignard Dr.
Sumter 29150

Florence-Darlington Technical College
P.O. Box 100548
Florence 29501-0548

Horry-Georgetown Technical College
P.O. Box 1966
Conway 29526

Midlands Technical College
P.O. Box 2408
Columbia 29202

Orangeburg-Calhoun Technical College
3250 Saint Matthews Rd.
Orangeburg 29115

Piedmont Technical College
P.O. Drawer 1467
Greenwood 29648

Tri-County Technical College
P.O. Box 587
Pendleton 29670

Trident Technical College
P.O. Box 118067
Charleston 29423-8067

SOUTH DAKOTA

Western Dakota Vocational Technical
Institute
1600 Sedivy
Rapid City 57701

TENNESSEE

East Tennessee State University
P.O. Box 70716
Johnson City 37614

Roane State Community College
Patton Ln.
Harriman 37748

Shelby State Community College
P.O. Box 40568
Memphis 38174-0568

Tennessee Technological University
Dixie Ave.
Cookeville 38505

Walters State Community College
500 South Davy Crockett Pkwy.
Morristown 37813-6899

TEXAS

Alvin Community College
3110 Mustang Rd.
Alvin 77511

Austin Community College
5930 Middle Fiskville Rd.
Austin 78752

Bee County College
3800 Charco Rd.
Beeville 78102

Central Texas College
P.O. Box 1800
Killeen 76540-9990

Chenier
2816 Loop 306
San Angelo 76904

Chenier
6300 Richmond
Houston 77057

Cooke County College
1525 West California
Gainesville 76240

Del Mar College
101 Baldwin
Corpus Christi 78404-3897

El Centro College
Main and Lamar
Dallas 75202

El Paso Community College
P.O. Box 20500
El Paso 79998

Grayson County College
6101 Grayson Dr.
Denison 75020

Kilgore College
1100 Broadway
Kilgore 75662-3299

Lamar University-Beaumont
4400 Mlk, P.O. Box 10001
Beaumont 77710

Laredo Junior College
West End Washington St.
Laredo 78040

McLennan Community College
1400 College Dr.
Waco 76708

Navarro College
3200 West Seventh
Corsicana 75110

Northeast Texas Community College
P.O. Box 1307
Mount Pleasant 75456

Odessa College
201 West University
Odessa 79764

San Antonio College
1300 San Pedro Ave.
San Antonio 78284

San Jacinto College-Central Campus
8060 Spencer Hwy.
Pasadena 77505

San Jacinto College-North Campus
5800 Uvalde
Houston 77049

South Plains College
1401 College Ave.
Levelland 79336

Southwest Texas Junior College
2401 Garner Field Rd.
Uvalde 78801

Tarrant County Junior College District
1500 Houston St.
Fort Worth 76102

Texas Security Officers Institute
6906 Atwell
Houston 77081

Texas Southmost College
80 Fort Brown
Brownsville 78520

Trinity Valley Community College
500 South Prairieville
Athens 75751

Tyler Junior College
P.O. Box 9020
Tyler 75711

Wayland Baptist University
1900 West Seventh
Plainview 79072

Weatherford College
308 East Park Ave.
Weatherford 76086

UTAH

Bridgerland Applied Technology Center
1301 North, 600 West
Logan 84321

Salt Lake Community College
P.O. Box 30808
Salt Lake City 84130

Southern Utah University
351 West Center
Cedar City 84720

Weber State University
3750 Harrison Blvd.
Ogden 84408

VERMONT

Champlain College
163 South Willard St.
Burlington 05401

VIRGINIA

Central Virginia Community College
3506 Wards Rd.
Lynchburg 24502

Danville Community College
1008 South Main St.
Danville 24541

Germanna Community College
P.O. Box 339
Locust Grove 22508

J Sargeant Reynolds Community College
P.O. Box 85622
Richmond 23285-5622

John Tyler Community College
13101 Jefferson Davis Hwy.
Chester 23831-5399

Mountain Empire Community College
P.O. Drawer 700
Big Stone Gap 24219

New River Community College
P.O. Drawer 1127
Dublin 24084

Northern Virginia Community College
4001 Wakefield Chapel Rd.
Annandale 22003

Paul D Camp Community College
100 North College Dr., P.O. Box 737
Franklin 23851

Southside Virginia Community College
Rte. 1, P.O. Box 60
Alberta 23821

Southwest Virginia Community College
P.O. Box SVCC
Richlands 24641

Thomas Nelson Community College
P.O. Box 9407
Hampton 23670

Tidewater Community College
Rte. 135
Portsmouth 23703

Virginia Highlands Community College
P.O. Box 828
Abingdon 24210

Virginia School of Polygraph
7909 Brookfield Rd.
Norfolk 23518

Virginia Western Community College
3095 Colonial Ave.
Roanoke 24015

Wytheville Community College
1000 East Main St.
Wytheville 24382

WASHINGTON

Bellevue Community College
3000 Landerholm Circle SE
Bellevue 98007-6484

Columbia Basin College
2600 North 20th Ave.
Pasco 99301

Everett Community College
801 Wetmore Ave.
Everett 98201

Green River Community College
12401 Southeast 320th St.
Auburn 98002

Olympic College
1600 Chester Ave.
Bremerton 98310-1699

Shoreline Community College
16101 Greenwood Ave. N
Seattle 98133

Spokane Community College
North 1810 Greene Ave.
Spokane 99207

WEST VIRGINIA

Bluefield State College
219 Rock St.
Bluefield 24701

Fairmont State College
1201 Locust Ave.
Fairmont 26554

Southern West Virginia Community
College
P.O. Box 2900
Logan 25601

West Virginia State College
Rte. 25
Institute 25112

WISCONSIN

Blackhawk Technical College
P.O. Box 5009
Janesville 53547

Chippewa Valley Technical College
620 West Clairemont Ave.
Eau Claire 54701

Fox Valley Technical College
1825 North Bluemound Dr.
Appleton 54913-2277

Gateway Technical College
3520 30th Ave.
Kenosha 53144-1690

Good, Armstrong, and Associates, Ltd.
2142 South 55th St.
Milwaukee 53219

Lakeshore Vocational Training and Adult
Education System District
1290 North Ave.
Cleveland 53015

Mid-State Technical College-Main
Campus
500 32nd St. N
Wisconsin Rapids 54494

Milwaukee Area Technical College
700 West State St.
Milwaukee 53233

Nicolet Vocational Training and Adult
Education System District
P.O. Box 518
Rhinelander 54501

North Central Technical College
1000 Campus Dr.
Wausau 54401-1899

Northeast Wisconsin Technical College
2740 West Mason St., P.O. Box 19042
Green Bay 54307-9042

Waukesha County Technical College
800 Main St.
Pewaukee 53072

Western Wisconsin Technical College
304 North Sixth St., P.O. Box 908
La Crosse 54602-0908

Wisconsin Area Vocational Training and
Adult Education System District
Number Four
3550 Anderson St.
Madison 53704

Wisconsin Area Vocational Training and
Adult Education System-Moraine Park
235 North National Ave., P.O. Box 1940
Fond Du Lac 54936-1940

WYOMING

Casper College
125 College Dr.
Casper 82601

Sheridan College
P.O. Box 1500
Sheridan 82801

Public Administration Technology

ARIZONA

Phoenix College
1202 West Thomas Rd.
Phoenix 85013

CALIFORNIA

Allan Hancock College
800 South College Dr.
Santa Maria 93454

Antelope Valley College
3041 West Ave. K
Lancaster 93534

Butte College
3536 Butte Campus Dr.
Oroville 95965

Cabrillo College
6500 Soquel Dr.
Aptos 95003

Cerritos College
11110 Alondra Blvd.
Norwalk 90650

Chabot College
25555 Hesperian Blvd.
Hayward 94545

Citrus College
1000 West Foothill Blvd.
Glendora 91741-1899

College of Marin
Kentfield 94904

College of San Mateo
1700 West Hillsdale Blvd.
San Mateo 94402

College of the Sequoias
915 South Mooney Blvd.
Visalia 93277

College of the Canyons
26455 North Rockwell Canyon Rd.
Santa Clarita 91355

College of the Redwoods
7351 Tompkins Hill Rd.
Eureka 95501-9302

College of the Desert
43-500 Monterey St.
Palm Desert 92260

Cosumnes River College
8401 Center Pkwy.
Sacramento 95823-5799

Cuesta College
P.O. Box 8106
San Luis Obispo 93403-8106

Diablo Valley College
321 Golf Club Rd.
Pleasant Hill 94523

El Camino College
16007 Crenshaw Blvd.
Torrance 90506

Fresno City College
1101 East University Ave.
Fresno 93741

Fullerton College
321 East Chapman Ave.
Fullerton 92632-2095

Golden West College
15744 Golden West
Huntington Beach 92647

Grossmont College
8800 Grossmont College Dr.
El Cajon 92020

Hartnell College
156 Homestead Ave.
Salinas 93901

Long Beach City College
4901 East Carson St.
Long Beach 90808

Los Angeles Southwest College
1600 West Imperial Hwy.
Los Angeles 90047

Los Angeles Valley College
5800 Fulton Ave.
Van Nuys 91401

Mendocino College
P.O. Box 3000
Ukiah 95482

Merced College
3600 M St.
Merced 95348-2898

Merritt College
12500 Campus Dr.
Oakland 94619

Modesto Junior College
435 College Ave.
Modesto 95350-9977

Monterey Peninsula College
980 Fremont Blvd.
Monterey 93940-4799

Moorpark College
7075 Campus Rd.
Moorpark 93021

Mount San Jacinto College
1499 North State St.
San Jacinto 92383-2399

Pasadena City College
1570 East Colorado Blvd.
Pasadena 91106

Porterville College
100 East College Ave.
Porterville 93257

Rancho Santiago College
17th at Bristol
Santa Ana 92706

Riverside Community College
4800 Magnolia Ave.
Riverside 92506-1299

San Joaquin Delta College
5151 Pacific Ave.
Stockton 95207

Santa Monica College
1900 Pico Blvd.
Santa Monica 90405-1628

Southwestern College
900 Otay Lakes Rd.
Chula Vista 92010

Ventura College
4667 Telegraph Rd.
Ventura 93003

West Los Angeles College
4800 Freshman Dr.
Culver 90230

West Valley College
14000 Fruitvale Ave.
Saratoga 95070

Yuba College
2088 North Beale Rd.
Marysville 95901

COLORADO

Aims Community College
P.O. Box 69
Greeley 80632

Arapahoe Community College
2500 West College Dr.
Littleton 80160-9002

Colorado Northwestern Community
College
500 Kennedy Dr.
Rangely 81648-3598

Pikes Peak Community College
5675 South Academy Blvd.
Colorado Springs 80906-5498

Pueblo Community College
900 West Orman Ave.
Pueblo 81004

Red Rocks Community College
13300 West Sixth Ave.
Golden 80401

Trinidad State Junior College
600 Prospect St.
Trinidad 81082

CONNECTICUT

Connecticut Institute of Technology
Two Elizabeth St.
West Haven 06516

DELAWARE

Delaware Technical Community College
Stanton-Wilmington
400 Stanton-Christiana Rd.
Newark 19702

FLORIDA

Edison Community College
8099 College Pkwy. SW
Fort Myers 33906-6210

Florida Community College at
Jacksonville
501 West State St.
Jacksonville 32202

Indian River Community College
3209 Virginia Ave.
Fort Pierce 34981

Miami-Dade Community College
300 Northeast Second Ave.
Miami 33132

Pensacola Junior College
1000 College Blvd.
Pensacola 32504

Polk Community College
999 Ave. H NE
Winter Haven 33881

Seminole Community College
100 Weldon Blvd.
Sanford 32773-6199

HAWAII

Honolulu Community College
874 Dillingham Blvd.
Honolulu 96817

Maui Community College
310 Kaahumanu Ave.
Kahului 96732

IDAHO

Idaho State University
741 South Seventh Ave.
Pocatello 83209

ILLINOIS

Lake Land College
5001 Lake Land Blvd.
Mattoon 61938

INDIANA

Indiana University-Purdue University at
Indianapolis
355 North Lansing
Indianapolis 46202

Indiana University-Purdue University at
Fort Wayne
2101 Coliseum Blvd. E
Fort Wayne 46805

IOWA

Iowa Western Community College
2700 College Rd., P.O. Box 4C
Council Bluffs 51502

KENTUCKY

Kentucky Technical-West Kentucky
State Vocational Technical School
P.O. Box 7408
Paducah 42002-7408

LOUISIANA

Delgado Community College
615 City Park Ave.
New Orleans 70119

T H Harris Technical Institute
337 East South St., P.O. Box 713
Opelousas 70570

MAINE

University of Maine
Office of Institutional Studies
Orono 04469

MASSACHUSETTS

Hebrew College
43 Hawes St.
Brookline 02146

Lincoln Institute of Land Policy
113 Brattle St.
Cambridge 02138

Massasoit Community College
One Massasoit Blvd.
Brockton 02402

Quinsigamond Community College
670 West Boylston St.
Worcester 01606

Springfield Technical Community
College
Armory Square
Springfield 01105

University of Massachusetts at Lowell
One University Ave.
Lowell 01854

Wentworth Institute of Technology
550 Huntington Ave.
Boston 02115

MICHIGAN

Alpena Community College
666 Johnson St.
Alpena 49707

Ferris State University
901 South State St.
Big Rapids 49307

Grand Rapids Community College
143 Bostwick Ave. NE
Grand Rapids 49505

Henry Ford Community College
5101 Evergreen Rd.
Dearborn 48128

Lansing Community College
419 North Capitol Ave.
Lansing 48901-7210

Michigan Technological University
1400 Townsend Dr.
Houghton 49931-1295

MINNESOTA

Duluth Technical College
2101 Trinity Rd.
Duluth 55811

Saint Paul Technical College
235 Marshall Ave.
Saint Paul 55102

MISSISSIPPI

Northeast Mississippi Community
College
Cunningham Blvd.
Booneville 38829

MISSOURI

Mineral Area College
P.O. Box 1000
Flat River 63601

Park College
87 River Park Dr.
Parkville 64152-3795

MONTANA

College of Great Falls
1301 Twentieth St. S
Great Falls 59405-4996

NEW HAMPSHIRE

New Hampshire Technical Institute
11 Institute Dr.
Concord 03301

University of New Hampshire-Main
Campus
Thompson Hall
Durham 03824

NEW JERSEY

Mercer County Community College
1200 Old Trenton Rd.
Trenton 08690

Middlesex County College
155 Mill Rd., P.O. Box 3050
Edison 08818-3050

Ocean County College
College Dr.
Toms River 08753

Thomas A Edison State College
101 West State St.
Trenton 08608-1176

NEW MEXICO

Albuquerque Technical-Vocational
Institute
525 Buena Vista SE
Albuquerque 87106

NEW YORK

Broome Community College
P.O. Box 1017
Binghamton 13902

Columbia-Greene Community College
P.O. Box 1000
Hudson 12534

Corning Community College
Spencer Hill
Corning 14830

CUNY Bronx Community College
West 181st St. & University Ave.
Bronx 10453

CUNY College of Staten Island
2800 Victory Blvd.
Staten Island 10314

CUNY Hostos Community College
500 Grand Concourse
Bronx 10451

CUNY New York City Technical College
300 Jay St.
Brooklyn 11201

Erie Community College-City Campus
121 Ellicott St.
Buffalo 14203

Erie Community College-North Campus
Main St. and Youngs Rd.
Williamsville 14221

Finger Lakes Community College
4355 Lake Shore Dr.
Canandaigua 14424

Fulton-Montgomery Community College
2805 State Hwy. 67
Johnstown 12095

Genesee Community College
One College Rd.
Batavia 14020

Herkimer County Community College
Reservoir Rd.
Herkimer 13350-1598

Hudson Valley Community College
80 Vandenburgh Ave.
Troy 12180

Jefferson Community College
Outer Coffeen St.
Watertown 13601

Mater Dei College
Riverside Dr.
Ogdensburg 13669

Mohawk Valley Community College
1101 Sherman Dr.
Utica 13501

Monroe Community College
1000 East Henrietta Rd.
Rochester 14623

Nassau Community College
One Education Dr.
Garden City 11530

Niagara County Community College
3111 Saunders Settlement Rd.
Sanborn 14132

North Country Community College
20 Winona Ave., P.O. Box 89
Saranac Lake 12983

Onondaga Community College
Rte. 173
Syracuse 13215

Paul Smith's College of Arts and Science
New York 12970

Rochester Institute of Technology
One Lamb Memorial Dr.
Rochester 14623-0887

Saint John's University
8000 Utopia Pkwy.
Jamaica 11439

Schenectady County Community College
Washington Ave.
Schenectady 12305

SUNY College of Technology at
Farmingdale
Melville Rd.
Farmingdale 11735

SUNY College of Technology at Canton
Canton 13617

SUNY Ulster County Community College
Cottekill Rd.
Stone Ridge 12484

SUNY Westchester Commmunity College
75 Grasslands Rd.
Valhalla 10595

NORTH CAROLINA

Central Piedmont Community College
P.O. Box 35009
Charlotte 28235

Gaston College
Hwy. 321
Dallas 28034

Guilford Technical Community College
P.O. Box 309
Jamestown 27282

Wake Technical Community College
9101 Fayetteville Rd.
Raleigh 27603-5696

NORTH DAKOTA

North Dakota State College of Science
800 North Sixth St.
Wahpeton 58076

OHIO

Cincinnati Technical College
3520 Central Pkwy.
Cincinnati 45223

Clark State Community College
570 East Leffel Ln.
Springfield 45505

Columbus State Community College
550 East Spring St., P.O. Box 1609
Columbus 43216

Ohio University-Eastern Campus
National Rd. W
Saint Clairsville 43950

Ohio University-Ironton Branch
1804 Liberty Ave.
Ironton 45638

Ohio University-Main Campus
Athens 45701

Sinclair Community College
444 West Third St.
Dayton 45402

Stark Technical College
6200 Frank Ave. NW
Canton 44720

University of Akron-Wayne College
10470 Smucker Rd.
Orrville 44667

University of Akron-Main Campus
302 Buchtel Common
Akron 44325-4702

University of Cincinnati-Main Campus
2624 Clifton Ave.
Cincinnati 45221-0127

University of Toledo
2801 West Bancroft
Toledo 43606

Urbana University
College Way
Urbana 43078

OKLAHOMA

Platt College
4821 South 72nd East Ave.
Tulsa 74145

OREGON

Blue Mountain Community College
P.O. Box 100
Pendleton 97801

Clackamas Community College
19600 Molalla Ave.
Oregon City 97045

Oregon Institute of Technology
3201 Campus Dr.
Klamath Falls 97601-8801

PENNSYLVANIA

Bucks County Community College
Swamp Rd.
Newtown 18940

Harrisburg Area Community
College-Harrisburg Campus
One Hacc Dr.
Harrisburg 17110

Lehigh County Community College
4525 Education Park Dr.
Schnecksville 18078-2598

Pennsylvania College of Technology
One College Ave.
Williamsport 17701

Pennsylvania Institute of Technology
800 Manchester Ave.
Media 19063

Westmoreland County Community
College
Youngwood 15697-1895

RHODE ISLAND

Roger Williams University
One Old Ferry Rd.
Bristol 02809-2923

SOUTH CAROLINA

Florence-Darlington Technical College
P.O. Box 100548
Florence 29501-0548

Horry-Georgetown Technical College
P.O. Box 1966
Conway 29526

Spartanburg Methodist College
1200 Textile Dr.
Spartanburg 29301-0009

Spartanburg Technical College
Hwy. I-85, P.O. Drawer 4386
Spartanburg 29305

Trident Technical College
P.O. Box 118067
Charleston 29423-8067

University of South Carolina at Aiken
171 University Pkwy.
Aiken 29801

University of South Carolina at Lancaster
P.O. Box 889
Lancaster 29720

TENNESSEE

Pellissippi State Technical Community
College
P.O. Box 22990
Knoxville 37933-0990

TEXAS

San Antonio College
1300 San Pedro Ave.
San Antonio 78284

Tarrant County Junior College District
1500 Houston St.
Fort Worth 76102

Texarkana College
2500 North Robison Rd.
Texarkana 75501

VERMONT

Southern Vermont College
Monument Rd.
Bennington 05201

Vermont Technical College
Randolph Center 05061

VIRGINIA

J Sargeant Reynolds Community College
P.O. Box 85622
Richmond 23285-5622

New River Community College
P.O. Drawer 1127
Dublin 24084

Thomas Nelson Community College
P.O. Box 9407
Hampton 23670

Tidewater Community College
Rte. 135
Portsmouth 23703

WASHINGTON

Bates Technical College
1101 South Yakima Ave.
Tacoma 98405

Centralia College
600 West Locust St.
Centralia 98531

Spokane Community College
North 1810 Greene Ave.
Spokane 99207

Spokane Falls Community College
West 3410 Fort George Wright Dr.
Spokane 99204

Walla Walla Community College
500 Tausick Way
Walla Walla 99362

Yakima Valley Community College
P.O. Box 1647
Yakima 98907

WEST VIRGINIA

Bluefield State College
219 Rock St.
Bluefield 24701

WISCONSIN

Mid-State Technical College-Main
Campus
500 32nd St. N
Wisconsin Rapids 54494

Northeast Wisconsin Technical College
2740 West Mason St., P.O. Box 19042
Green Bay 54307-9042

Wisconsin Area Vocational Training and
Adult Education System District
Number Four
3550 Anderson St.
Madison 53704

Wisconsin Area Vocational Training and
Adult Education System-Moraine Park
235 North National Ave., P.O. Box 1940
Fond Du Lac 54936-1940

WYOMING

Laramie County Community College
1400 East College Dr.
Cheyenne 82007

Public Service Technology

ALABAMA

Samford University
800 Lakeshore Dr.
Birmingham 35229

CALIFORNIA

Phillips Junior College
8520 Balboa Blvd.
Northridge 91325

COLORADO

Parks Junior College
9065 Grant St.
Denver 80229

CONNECTICUT

Manchester Community College
60 Bidwell St., P.O. Box 1045
Manchester 06040-1046

FLORIDA

Daytona Beach Community College
1200 Volusia Ave.
Daytona Beach 32114

Valencia Community College
P.O. Box 3028
Orlando 32802

HAWAII

Denver Business College-Honolulu
1916 Young St.
Honolulu 96826

INDIANA

Indiana University-Purdue University at
   Indianapolis
355 North Lansing
Indianapolis 46202

IOWA

Des Moines Community College
2006 Ankeny Blvd.
Ankeny 50021

Iowa Valley Community College
P.O. Box 536
Marshalltown 50158

Kirkwood Community College
P.O. Box 2068
Cedar Rapids 52406

MAINE

University of Maine
Office of Institutional Studies
Orono 04469

MASSACHUSETTS

Berkshire Community College
1350 West St.
Pittsfield 01201-5786

Holyoke Community College
303 Homestead Ave.
Holyoke 01040

Lincoln Institute of Land Policy
113 Brattle St.
Cambridge 02138

Quinsigamond Community College
670 West Boylston St.
Worcester 01606

MICHIGAN

Delta College
University Center 48710

MINNESOTA

Minneapolis Community College
1501 Hennepin Ave.
Minneapolis 55403

North Hennepin Community College
7411 85th Ave. N
Brooklyn Park 55445

NEW MEXICO

University of New Mexico-Gallup Branch
200 College Rd.
Gallup 87301

NEW YORK

Cazenovia College
Cazenovia 13035

Corning Community College
Spencer Hill
Corning 14830

Fulton-Montgomery Community College
2805 State Hwy. 67
Johnstown 12095

Genesee Community College
One College Rd.
Batavia 14020

Herkimer County Community College
Reservoir Rd.
Herkimer 13350-1598

Hilbert College
5200 South Park Ave.
Hamburg 14075-1597

Hudson Valley Community College
80 Vandenburgh Ave.
Troy 12180

Jamestown Community College
525 Falconer St.
Jamestown 14701

Jefferson Community College
Outer Coffeen St.
Watertown 13601

Mater Dei College
Riverside Dr.
Ogdensburg 13669

Medaille College
18 Agassiz Circle
Buffalo 14214

Mohawk Valley Community College
1101 Sherman Dr.
Utica 13501

Monroe Community College
1000 East Henrietta Rd.
Rochester 14623

Niagara County Community College
3111 Saunders Settlement Rd.
Sanborn 14132

Onondaga Community College
Rte. 173
Syracuse 13215

Rochester Institute of Technology
One Lamb Memorial Dr.
Rochester 14623-0887

Schenectady County Community College
Washington Ave.
Schenectady 12305

Suffolk County Community
   College-Ammerman Campus
533 College Rd.
Selden 11784

SUNY College of Technology at Alfred
Alfred 14802

SUNY Empire State College
Two Union Ave.
Saratoga Springs 12866

SUNY Ulster County Community College
Cottekill Rd.
Stone Ridge 12484

SUNY Westchester Commmunity College
75 Grasslands Rd.
Valhalla 10595

Tompkins-Cortland Community College
170 North St.
Dryden 13053

Touro College
27-33 West 23rd St.
New York 10010

OHIO

Vocational Guidance Services
2239 East 55th St.
Cleveland 44103

OKLAHOMA

Kiamichi AVTS SD #7-Hugo Campus
107 South 15th, P.O. Box 699
Hugo 74743

Metro Tech Vocational Technical Center
1900 Springlake Dr.
Oklahoma City 73111

PENNSYLVANIA

Community College of Philadelphia
1700 Spring Garden St.
Philadelphia 19130

Sawyer School
717 Liberty Ave.
Pittsburgh 15222

TENNESSEE

Morristown State Area
   Vocational-Technical School
821 West Louise Ave.
Morristown 37813

Shelby State Community College
P.O. Box 40568
Memphis 38174-0568

TEXAS

Avalon Vocational Technical Institute
1407 Texas St.
Fort Worth 76102

Houston Community College System
22 Waugh Dr., P.O. Box 7849
Houston 77270-7849

WISCONSIN

Milwaukee Area Technical College
700 West State St.
Milwaukee 53233

Religious Occupations

CALIFORNIA

Booker T Crenshaw Christian College &
   School Ministry, Inc.
3134 Franklin Ave.
San Diego 92113

Golden Gate Baptist Seminary
Strawberry Point
Mill Valley 94941

International School of Theology
24600 Arrowhead Springs Rd.
San Bernardino 92414

Pacific Coast Baptist Bible College
1100 South Valley Center
San Dimas 91773

San Jose Christian College
790 South 12th St., P.O. Box 1090
San Jose 95108

The Master's College
21726 Placerita Cyn Rd.
Santa Clarita 91322-0878

The Salvation Army School for Officers'
   Training
30840 Hawthorne Blvd.
Rancho Palos Ve 90274

Trinity Life Bible College
5225 Hillsdale at Madison
Sacramento 95842

COLORADO

Nazarene Bible College
1111 Chapman Dr., P.O. Box 15749
Colorado Springs 80935

FLORIDA

Florida Baptist Theological College
5400 College Dr.
Graceville 32440

Florida Bible College
1701 Poinciana Blvd.
Kissimmee 34758

Florida Christian College, Inc.
1011 Bill Beck Blvd.
Kissimmee 34744

Gospel Crusade Institute of Ministry
1200 Glory Way Blvd., Rte. 2, P.O. Box
   279
Bradenton 34202

United Bible College & Seminary
P.O. Box 585284
Orlando 32858

Zoe College, Inc.
9570 One Regency Square Blvd.
Jacksonville 32225

GEORGIA

Beulah Heights Bible College
892-906 Berne St. SE
Atlanta 30316

IDAHO

Boise Bible College
8695 Marigold St.
Boise 83714

Northwest Nazarene College
623 Holly
Nampa 83686-5897

ILLINOIS

Lincoln Christian College and Seminary
100 Campus View Dr.
Lincoln 62656-2111

Moody Bible Institute
820 North Lasalle Blvd.
Chicago 60610

INDIANA

Indiana Wesleyan University
4201 South Washington St.
Marion 46953

IOWA

Emmaus Bible College
2570 Asbury Rd.
Dubuque 52001

KANSAS

Hesston College
P.O. Box 3000
Hesston 67062

Manhattan Christian College
1415 Anderson Ave.
Manhattan 66502

KENTUCKY

Clear Creek Baptist Bible College
300 Clear Creek Rd.
Pineville 40977

Kentucky Mountain Bible College
P.O. Box 10
Vancleve 41385

Southern Baptist Theological Seminary
2825 Lexington Rd.
Louisville 40280

LOUISIANA

New Orleans Baptist Theological
  Seminary
3939 Gentilly Blvd.
New Orleans 70126

World Evangelism Bible College and
  Seminary
P.O. Box 38000
Baton Rouge 70806

MARYLAND

Ner Israel Rabbinical College
Mount Wilson Ln.
Baltimore 21208

Washington Bible College
6511 Princess Garden Pkwy.
Lanham 20706

MASSACHUSETTS

Baptist Bible College East
950 Metropolitan Ave.
Hyde Park 02136

Gordon-Conwell Theological Seminary
130 Essex St.
South Hamilton 01982

MICHIGAN

Reformed Bible College
3333 East Beltline NE
Grand Rapids 49505

Sacred Heart Major Seminary
2701 Chicago Blvd.
Detroit 48206

MINNESOTA

Association Free Lutheran Bible School
3110 East Medicine Lake Blvd.
Plymouth 55441-3099

North Central Bible College
910 Elliot Ave.
Minneapolis 55404

Oak Hills Bible College
1600 Oak Hills Rd. SW
Bemidji 56601

MISSISSIPPI

Southeastern Baptist College
4229 Hwy. 15 N
Laurel 39440

MISSOURI

Baptist Bible College
628 East Kearney
Springfield 65803

Berean College
1445 Boonville Ave.
Springfield 65802

Central Bible College
3000 North Grant
Springfield 65803

Midwestern Baptist Theological Seminary
5001 North Oak St. Trafficway
Kansas City 64118

Ozark Christian College
1111 North Main St.
Joplin 64801

NEBRASKA

Grace College of the Bible
Ninth and Williams
Omaha 68108

Platte Valley Bible College
305 East 16th St., P.O. Box 1227
Scottsbluff 69361

NEW JERSEY

College of Saint Elizabeth
Two Convent Rd.
Morristown 07960-6989

NEW MEXICO

Nazarene Indian Bible College
2315 Markham Rd. SW, P.O. Box 12295
Albuquerque 87195

NEW YORK

Elim Bible Institute
7245 College St.
Lima 14485

Practical Bible Training School
400 Riverside Dr., P.O. Box 601
Bible School Park 13737-0601

Word of Life Bible Institute
Rte. 9
Pottersville 12860

NORTH CAROLINA

East Coast Bible College
6900 Wilkinson Blvd.
Charlotte 28214

Roanoke Bible College
714 First St.
Elizabeth City 27909-3926

Southeastern Baptist Theological
  Seminary
P.O. Box 1889
Wake Forest 27588-1889

OHIO

Cincinnati Bible College & Seminary
2700 Glenway Ave.
Cincinnati 45204-3200

Circleville Bible College
1476 Lancaster Pike
Circleville 43113

OKLAHOMA

Hillsdale Free Will Baptist College
P.O. Box 7208
Moore 73153

Oklahoma Baptist University
500 West University
Shawnee 74801

Southwestern College of Christian
  Ministries
P.O. Box 340
Bethany 73008

OREGON

Eugene Bible College
2155 Bailey Hill Rd.
Eugene 97405

Multnomah School of Bible
8435 Northeast Glisan St.
Portland 97220

Portland Bible College
9201 Northeast Fremont
Portland 97220

Western Baptist College
5000 Deer Park Dr. SE
Salem 97301

PENNSYLVANIA

Baptist Bible College and Seminary
538 Venard Rd.
Clarks Summit 18411

Lancaster Bible College
901 Eden Rd.
Lancaster 17601

Saint Charles Borromeo Seminary
1000 East Wynnewood Rd.
Overbrook 19096

Valley Forge Christian College
Charlestown Rd.
Phoenixville 19460

RHODE ISLAND

Zion Bible Institute
27 Middle Hwy.
Barrington 02806

SOUTH CAROLINA

Bob Jones University
Greenville 29614

Columbia Bible College and Seminary
7435 Monticello Rd., P.O. Box 3122
Columbia 29230

TENNESSEE

Emmanuel Bible College
610 Boscobel St.
Nashville 37206

Memphis School of Preaching
4400 Knight Arnold Rd.
Memphis 38118

Mid America Baptist Seminary
1255 Poplar Ave.
Memphis 38104

Tennessee Temple University
1815 Union Ave.
Chattanooga 37404

United Theological Seminary
  Scarritt-Bennett Center
19th Ave. S
Nashville 37203

TEXAS

International Christian Institute &
  Graduate School
P.O. Box 720405
Houston 71727

Texas Bible College
816 Evergreen
Houston 77023

VIRGINIA

Eastern Mennonite College and Seminary
1200 Park Rd.
Harrisonburg 22801-2462

The Catholic Home Study Institute
Nine Loudoun St. SE
Leesburg 22075-3012

WASHINGTON

Lutheran Bible Institute of Seattle
4221 228th SE
Issaquah 98027

Puget Sound Christian College
410 Fourth Ave. N
Edmonds 98020-3171

WEST VIRGINIA

Appalachian Bible College
P.O. Box ABC
Bradley 25818

Social Work and Recreation Technology

ALABAMA

Community College of the Air Force
Maxwell Air Force Base
Montgomery 36112

Lawson State Community College
3060 Wilson Rd. SW
Birmingham 35221

ARIZONA

Pima Community College
2202 West Anklam Rd.
Tucson 85709-0001

CALIFORNIA

Alexander Training Institute of San
  Francisco
30 Grant Ave.
San Francisco 94108

Allan Hancock College
800 South College Dr.
Santa Maria 93454

Diablo Valley College
321 Golf Club Rd.
Pleasant Hill 94523

Fresno City College
1101 East University Ave.
Fresno 93741

Imperial Valley College
P.O. Box 158
Imperial 92251-0158

COLORADO

Aims Community College
P.O. Box 69
Greeley 80632

FLORIDA

Charlotte Vocational-Technical Center
18300 Toledo Blade Blvd.
Port Charlotte 33948-3399

IDAHO

Ricks College
Rexburg 83460-4107

ILLINOIS

City College of Chicago-Kennedy-King
6800 South Wentworth Ave.
Chicago 60621

College of Du Page
Lambert Rd. and 22nd St.
Glen Ellyn 60137

Elgin Community College
1700 Spartan Dr.
Elgin 60123

Rock Valley College
3301 North Mulford Rd.
Rockford 61114

South Suburban College
15800 South State St.
South Holland 60473

INDIANA

Indiana University East
2325 Chester Blvd.
Richmond 47374

KANSAS

Allen County Community College
1801 North Cottonwood
Iola 66749

Cloud County Community College
2221 Campus Dr., P.O. Box 1002
Concordia 66901-1002

Colby Community College
1255 South Range
Colby 67701

Kansas City Area Vocational Technical
School
2220 North 59th St.
Kansas City 66104

Kaw Area Vocational-Technical School
5724 Huntoon
Topeka 66604

Neosho County Community College
1000 South Allen
Chanute 66720

North Central Kansas Area Vocational
Technical School
Hwy. 24, P.O. Box 507
Beloit 67420

Salina Area Vocational Technical School
2562 Scanlan Ave.
Salina 67401

Wichita Area Vocational Technical
School
428 South Broadway
Wichita 67202-3910

KENTUCKY

Hopkinsville Community College
North Dr.
Hopkinsville 42240

Jefferson Community College
109 East Broadway
Louisville 40202

Owensboro Community College
4800 New Hartford Rd.
Owensboro 42303

MASSACHUSETTS

Dean Junior College
99 Main St.
Franklin 02038

Massasoit Community College
One Massasoit Blvd.
Brockton 02402

Mount Ida College
777 Dedham St.
Newton Centre 02159

MICHIGAN

Delta College
University Center 48710

Grand Rapids Community College
143 Bostwick Ave. NE
Grand Rapids 49505

Macomb Community College
14500 Twelve Mile Rd.
Warren 48093-3896

Mott Community College
1401 East Court St.
Flint 48503

MINNESOTA

Inver Hills Community College
5445 College Trail
Inver Grove Heights 55076

Lakewood Community College
3401 Century Ave. N
White Bear Lake 55110

Willmar Community College
P.O. Box 797
Willmar 56201-0797

MISSISSIPPI

Mississippi Gulf Coast Community
College
Central Office, P.O. Box 67
Perkinston 39573

MISSOURI

Jefferson College
1000 Viking Dr.
Hillsboro 63050

Saint Louis Community College-Forest
Park
5600 Oakland Ave.
Saint Louis 63110

MONTANA

Blackfeet Community College
P.O. Box 819
Browning 59417

NEBRASKA

Metropolitan Community College Area
P.O. Box 3777
Omaha 68103

NEW JERSEY

Brookdale Community College
Newman Springs Rd.
Lincroft 07738-1599

Camden County College
P.O. Box 200
Blackwood 08012

Essex County College
303 University Ave.
Newark 07102

Hudson County Community College
901 Bergen Ave.
Jersey City 07306

Ocean County College
College Dr.
Toms River 08753

NEW MEXICO

Northern New Mexico Community
College
1002 North Onate St.
Espanola 87532

NORTH CAROLINA

Central Piedmont Community College
P.O. Box 35009
Charlotte 28235

Halifax Community College
P.O. Drawer 809
Weldon 27890

Wayne Community College
P.O. Box 8002
Goldsboro 27533-8002

OHIO

Clark State Community College
570 East Leffel Ln.
Springfield 45505

Columbus State Community College
550 East Spring St., P.O. Box 1609
Columbus 43216

Edison State Community College
1973 Edison Dr.
Piqua 45356

Washington State Community College
710 Colegate Dr.
Marietta 45750

OKLAHOMA

Caddo-Kiowa Area Vocational Technical
School
P.O. Box 190
Fort Cobb 73038

Connors State College
Rte. 1, P.O. Box 1000
Warner 74469

Francis Tuttle Area Vocational-Technical
Center
12777 North Rockwell Ave.
Oklahoma City 73142-2789

Metro Tech Vocational Technical Center
1900 Springlake Dr.
Oklahoma City 73111

OREGON

Chemeketa Community College
P.O. Box 14007
Salem 97309-7070

Lane Community College
4000 East 30th Ave.
Eugene 97405

Portland Community College
P.O. Box 19000
Portland 97280-0990

Rogue Community College
3345 Redwood Hwy.
Grants Pass 97527

PENNSYLVANIA

Community College of Allegheny County
800 Allegheny Ave.
Pittsburgh 15233-1895

Harrisburg Area Community
College-Harrisburg Campus
One Hacc Dr.
Harrisburg 17110

Keystone Junior College
P.O. Box 50
La Plume 18440-0200

Pennsylvania State University-Main
Campus
201 Old Main
University Park 16802

RHODE ISLAND

Community College of Rhode Island
400 East Ave.
Warwick 02886-1805

SOUTH CAROLINA

Denmark Technical College
P.O. Box 327
Denmark 29042

Florence-Darlington Technical College
P.O. Box 100548
Florence 29501-0548

Midlands Technical College
P.O. Box 2408
Columbia 29202

Piedmont Technical College
P.O. Drawer 1467
Greenwood 29648

Trident Technical College
P.O. Box 118067
Charleston 29423-8067

TEXAS

Austin Community College
5930 Middle Fiskville Rd.
Austin 78752

VERMONT

Champlain College
163 South Willard St.
Burlington 05401

WASHINGTON

Spokane Falls Community College
West 3410 Fort George Wright Dr.
Spokane 99204

WEST VIRGINIA

The College of West Virginia
609 South Kanawha
Beckley 25802

Teacher and Teacher's Aide Training

ALABAMA

Bishop State Community College
351 North Broad St.
Mobile 36690

Community College of the Air Force
Maxwell Air Force Base
Montgomery 36112

Gadsden State Community College
P.O. Box 227
Gadsden 35902-0227

John C Calhoun State Community
College
P.O. Box 2216
Decatur 35609-2216

Shoals Community College
P.O. Box 2545
Muscle Shoals 35662

ARIZONA

Berlitz Language Centers
3333 East Camelback Rd.
Phoenix 85018

Eastern Arizona College
Church St.
Thatcher 85552-0769

Mesa Community College
1833 West Southern Ave.
Mesa 85202

Navajo Community College
Tsaile 86556

Opportunities Industrialization
Center-Phoenix
39 East Jackson St.
Phoenix 85004

Pima Community College
2202 West Anklam Rd.
Tucson 85709-0001

ARKANSAS

Black River Technical College
Hwy. 304, P.O. Box 468
Pocahontas 72455

Quapaw Technical Institute
201 Vo-Tech Dr.
Hot Springs 71913

Red River Technical College
P.O. Box 140
Hope 71801

CALIFORNIA

Allan Hancock College
800 South College Dr.
Santa Maria 93454

Antelope Valley College
3041 West Ave. K
Lancaster 93534

Berlitz Language Centers
323 North Beverly Dr.
Beverly Hills 90210

Berlitz Language Centers
1475 South Bascom Ave.
Campbell 95008

Berlitz Language Centers
2061 Business Center Dr.
Irvine 92715

Berlitz Language Centers
3345 Wilshire Blvd.
Los Angeles 90010

Berlitz Language Centers
430 Cambridge Ave.
Palo Alto 94306

Berlitz Language Centers
600 South Lake Ave.
Pasadena 91106

Berlitz Language Centers
7801 Mission Center Ct.
San Diego 92108

Berlitz Language Centers
660 Market St.
San Francisco 94104

Berlitz Language Centers
501 Santa Monica Blvd.
Santa Monica 90401

Berlitz Language Centers
2355 Crenshaw Blvd., Park Del Amo
Torrance 90501

Berlitz Language Centers
1646 North California Blvd.
Walnut Creek 94596

Berlitz Language Centers
6415 Independence Ave.
Woodland Hills 91367

Bethesda Christian University
14300 Leffingwell Rd.
Whittier 90604

Cerritos College
11110 Alondra Blvd.
Norwalk 90650

Chaffey Community College
5885 Haven Ave.
Rancho Cucamonga 91737-3002

City College of San Francisco
50 Phelan Ave.
San Francisco 94112

College of Alameda
555 Atlantic Ave.
Alameda 94501

College of the Canyons
26455 North Rockwell Canyon Rd.
Santa Clarita 91355

Columbia College-Columbia
P.O. Box 1849
Columbia 95310

Compton Community College
1111 East Artesia Blvd.
Compton 90221

D-Q University
Rd. 31, P.O. Box 409
Davis 95617-0409

El Camino College
16007 Crenshaw Blvd.
Torrance 90506

Golden West College
15744 Golden West
Huntington Beach 92647

Hartnell College
156 Homestead Ave.
Salinas 93901

Imperial Valley College
P.O. Box 158
Imperial 92251-0158

Long Beach City College
4901 East Carson St.
Long Beach 90808

Mira Costa College
One Barnard Dr.
Oceanside 92056-3899

Modesto Junior College
435 College Ave.
Modesto 95350-9977

Monterey Institute of International Studies
425 Van Buren
Monterey 93940

Montessori Training Center of San Diego
4544 Pocahontas Ave.
San Diego 92117

Montessori Western Teacher Training
Program
5856 Belgrove
Garden Grove 92645

Mount Saint Mary's College
12001 Chalon Rd.
Los Angeles 90049

Napa Valley College
2277 Napa Vallejo Hwy.
Napa 94558

Pasadena City College
1570 East Colorado Blvd.
Pasadena 91106

Phillips Junior College-Condie Campus
One West Campbell Ave.
Campbell 95008

Rowland Heights Montessori Institute
18760 East Colima Rd.
Rowland Heights 91748

Rudolf Steiner College
9200 Fair Oaks Blvd.
Fair Oaks 95628

San Diego City College
1313 12th Ave.
San Diego 92101

Santa Monica College
1900 Pico Blvd.
Santa Monica 90405-1628

Santa Monica Montessori Institute
1909 Colorado Ave.
Santa Monica 90404

Santa Rosa Junior College
1501 Mendocino Ave.
Santa Rosa 95401-4395

Shasta College
P.O. Box 496006
Redding 96049

Sierra College
5000 Rocklin Rd.
Rocklin 95677

Southwestern College
900 Otay Lakes Rd.
Chula Vista 92010

Saint Giles Language Teaching Center
One Hallidie Plaza
San Francisco 94102

Ventura College
4667 Telegraph Rd.
Ventura 93003

Vista College
2020 Milvia St.
Berkeley 94704-1183

Yuba College
2088 North Beale Rd.
Marysville 95901

COLORADO

Berlitz Language Centers
55 Madison St.
Denver 80206

College of the Canons
Forge Rd. Industrial Park, P.O. Box 1180
Canon City 81212

CONNECTICUT

Berlitz Language Centers
3001 Summer St.
Stamford 06905

Berlitz Language Centers
125 Main St.
Westport 06880

Berlitz Language Centers
61 South Main St.
West Hartford 06107

Manchester Community College
60 Bidwell St., P.O. Box 1045
Manchester 06040-1046

DELAWARE

Berlitz Language Centers
One Rodney Square
Wilmington 19801

DISTRICT OF COLUMBIA

Berlitz Language Centers
1050 Connecticut Ave. NW
Washington 20036

The Washington Montessori Institute
2119 South St. NW
Washington 20008

FLORIDA

Berlitz Language Centers
396 Alhambra Circle
Coral Gables 33134

Berlitz Language Centers
2455 East Sunrise Blvd.
Fort Lauderdale 33304

Berlitz Language Centers
100 North Biscayne Blvd.
Miami 33132

Berlitz Language Centers
100 West Kennedy Blvd.
Tampa 33602

GEORGIA

Andrew College
College St.
Cuthbert 31740-1395

Berlitz Language Centers
3400 Peachtree Rd. NE
Atlanta 30326

Covered Bridge Montessori School
NCME-Atlanta
2175 Norcross Tucker Rd.
Norcross 30071

Dekalb Technical Institute
495 North Indian Creek Dr.
Clarkston 30021

Reinhardt College
P.O. Box 128
Waleska 30183

South College
709 Mall Blvd.
Savannah 31406

HAWAII

Brigham Young University-Hawaii
Campus
55-220 Kulanui St.
Laie 96762

Hawaii Community College
200 West Kawili St.
Hilo 96720-4091

IDAHO

College of Southern Idaho
P.O. Box 1238
Twin Falls 83301

North Idaho College
1000 West Garden Ave.
Coeur D'Alene 83814

Ricks College
Rexburg 83460-4107

ILLINOIS

Berlitz Language Centers
Two North Lasalle
Chicago 60602

Berlitz Language Centers-Water Tower
Place
845 North Michigan
Chicago 60611

Berlitz Language Centers
201 East Ogden Ave.
Hinsdale 60521

Berlitz Language Centers
1821 Walden Office Square
Schaumburg 60173

Berlitz Language Centers
950 Green Bay Rd.
Winnetka 60093

Montessori Education Center Associated
302 South Grant
Hinsdale 60521

Spanish Coalition for Jobs, Inc.
2011 West Pershing Rd.
Chicago 60609

INDIANA

Ancilla Domini College
P.O. Box 1
Donaldson 46513

Anderson University
1100 East Fifth St.
Anderson 46012-3462

Berlitz Language Centers
8888 Keystone Crossing
Indianapolis 46240

Indiana University-Purdue University at
Fort Wayne
2101 Coliseum Blvd. E
Fort Wayne 46805

Vincennes University
1002 North First St.
Vincennes 47591

IOWA

Kirkwood Community College
P.O. Box 2068
Cedar Rapids 52406

KANSAS

Allen County Community College
1801 North Cottonwood
Iola 66749

Barton County Community College
Rte. 3, P.O. Box 136Z
Great Bend 67530

Butler County Community College
901 South Haverhill Rd.
El Dorado 67042

Cloud County Community College
2221 Campus Dr., P.O. Box 1002
Concordia 66901-1002

Coffeyville Community College
400 West 11th St.
Coffeyville 67337

Colby Community College
1255 South Range
Colby 67701

Cowley County Community College
125 South Second St.
Arkansas City 67005

Dodge City Community College
2501 North 14th Ave.
Dodge City 67801

Fort Scott Community College
2108 South Horton
Fort Scott 66701

Garden City Community College
801 Campus Dr.
Garden City 67846

Highland Community College
P.O. Box 68
Highland 66035-0068

Hutchinson Community College
1300 North Plum St.
Hutchinson 67501

Independence Community College
Brookside Dr. and College Ave.
Independence 67301

Kansas City Kansas Community College
7250 State Ave.
Kansas City 66112

Pratt Community College
Hwy. 61
Pratt 67124

Seward County Community College
P.O. Box 1137
Liberal 67905-1137

KENTUCKY

Midway College
512 Stephens St.
Midway 40347-1120

LOUISIANA

Delgado Community College
615 City Park Ave.
New Orleans 70119

Southern University Shreveport-Bossier
City Campus
3050 Martin L King Dr.
Shreveport 71107

MAINE

University of Maine at Farmington
86 Main St.
Farmington 04938

MARYLAND

Allegany Community College
Willowbrook Rd.
Cumberland 21502

Anne Arundel Community College
101 College Pkwy.
Arnold 21012

Berlitz Language Centers
Two North Charles St.
Baltimore 21201

Berlitz Language Centers
11300 Rockville Pike
Rockville 20852

Catonsville Community College
800 South Rolling Rd.
Catonsville 21228

Chesapeake College
P.O. Box 8
Wye Mills 21679-0008

Dundalk Community College
7200 Sollers Point Rd.
Dundalk 21222

Essex Community College
7201 Rossville Blvd.
Baltimore 21237

Frederick Community College
7932 Opossumtown Pike
Frederick 21702

Hagerstown Junior College
11400 Robinwood Dr.
Hagerstown 21742-6590

Harford Community College
401 Thomas Run Rd.
Bel Air 21015

Howard Community College
Little Patuxent Pkwy.
Columbia 21044

Montgomery College of Rockville
51 Mannakee St.
Rockville 20850

Prince Georges Community College
301 Largo Rd.
Largo 23701-1243

MASSACHUSETTS

Aquinas College at Newton
15 Walnut Park
Newton 02158

Bay Path College
588 Longmeadow St.
Longmeadow 01106

Becker College-Worcester
61 Sever St.
Worcester 01615-0071

Berlitz Language Centers
437 Boylston St.
Boston 02116

Berlitz Language Centers
40 Washington St.
Wellesley Hills 02181

Bristol Community College
777 Elsbree St.
Fall River 02720

Cape Cod Community College
Rte. 132
West Barnstable 02668

Dean Junior College
99 Main St.
Franklin 02038

Endicott College
376 Hale St.
Beverly 01915

Fisher College
118 Beacon St.
Boston 02116

Greenfield Community College
One College Dr.
Greenfield 01301-9739

Hebrew College
43 Hawes St.
Brookline 02146

Lasell College
1844 Commonwealth Ave.
Newton 02166

Middlesex Community College
Springs Rd.
Bedford 01730

Mount Wachusett Community College
444 Green St.
Gardner 01440

North Shore Community College
One Ferncroft Rd.
Danvers 01923

Quinsigamond Community College
670 West Boylston St.
Worcester 01606

Springfield Technical Community
College
Armory Square
Springfield 01105

Wheelock College
200 the Riverway
Boston 02215

MICHIGAN

Alpena Community College
666 Johnson St.
Alpena 49707

Berlitz Language Centers
30700 Telegraph Rd.
Bingham Farms 48025

Delta College
University Center 48710

Ferris State University
901 South State St.
Big Rapids 49307

Gogebic Community College
East 4946 Jackson Rd.
Ironwood 49938

Grand Rapids Community College
143 Bostwick Ave. NE
Grand Rapids 49505

Kalamazoo Valley Community College
6767 West O Ave.
Kalamazoo 49009

Monroe County Community College
1555 South Raisinville Rd.
Monroe 48161

Muskegon Community College
221 South Quarterline Rd.
Muskegon 49442

Schoolcraft College
18600 Haggerty Rd.
Livonia 48152

Southwestern Michigan College
58900 Cherry Grove Rd.
Dowagiac 49047-9793

MINNESOTA

Berlitz Language Centers
6600 France Ave. S
Minneapolis 55435

College of Saint Catherine-Saint Mary's
Campus
2500 South Sixth St.
Minneapolis 55454

Rochester Community College
851 30th Ave. SE
Rochester 55904-4999

MISSISSIPPI

Coahoma Community College
3240 Friars Point Rd.
Clarksdale 38614

Mary Holmes College
Hwy. 50 W
West Point 39773

Mississippi Gulf Coast Community
College
Central Office, P.O. Box 67
Perkinston 39573

Northeast Mississippi Community
College
Cunningham Blvd.
Booneville 38829

Northwest Mississippi Community
College
Hwy. 51 N
Senatobia 38668

MISSOURI

Berlitz Language Centers
200 South Hanley Rd.
Saint Louis 63105

Crowder College
601 Laclede
Neosho 64850

Saint Charles County Community College
4601 Mid Rivers Mall Dr.
Saint Peter's 63376

NEBRASKA

Central Community College-Grand Island
P.O. Box 4903
Grand Island 68802

Northeast Community College
801 East Benjamin, P.O. Box 469
Norfolk 68702-0469

NEW HAMPSHIRE

Hesser College
Three Sundial Ave.
Manchester 03103

NEW JERSEY

Bergen Community College
400 Paramus Rd.
Paramus 07652

Berlitz Language Centers
One Palmer Square
Princeton 08540

Berlitz Language Centers
40 West Ridgewood Ave.
Ridgewood 07450

Berlitz Language Centers
47 Maple St.
Summit 07901

Brookdale Community College
Newman Springs Rd.
Lincroft 07738-1599

Cumberland County College
College Dr., P.O. Box 517
Vineland 08360

Essex County College
303 University Ave.
Newark 07102

Gloucester County College
Tanyard Rd. & RR 4, P.O. Box 203
Sewell 08080

NEW MEXICO

New Mexico Junior College
5317 Lovington Hwy.
Hobbs 88240

University of New Mexico-Gallup Branch
200 College Rd.
Gallup 87301

NEW YORK

Berlitz Language Centers
41 Mineola Blvd.
Mineola 11501

Berlitz Language Centers
61 Broadway
New York 10006

Berlitz Language Centers
40 West 51st St.
New York 10020

Berlitz Language Centers
36 Main St. W
Rochester 14614

Berlitz Language Centers
One North Broadway
White Plains 10601

Cazenovia College
Cazenovia 13035

CUNY Borough of Manhattan
Community College
199 Chambers St.
New York 10007

CUNY Bronx Community College
West 181st St. & University Ave.
Bronx 10453

CUNY Hostos Community College
500 Grand Concourse
Bronx 10451

CUNY Kingsborough Community
College
2001 Oriental Blvd.
Brooklyn 11235

Iona College
715 North Ave.
New Rochelle 10801

Maria College of Albany
700 New Scotland Ave.
Albany 12208

Mater Dei College
Riverside Dr.
Ogdensburg 13669

Siena College
Rte. 9
Loudonville 12211

Trocaire College
110 Red Jacket Pkwy.
Buffalo 14220

Villa Maria College-Buffalo
240 Pine Ridge Rd.
Buffalo 14225-3999

NORTH CAROLINA

Berlitz Language Centers
5821 Fairview Rd.
Charlotte 28209

Berlitz Language Centers
5974A Six Forks Rd.
Raleigh 27609

Campbell University, Inc.
P.O. Box 97
Buies Creek 27506

Chowan College
Murfreesboro 27855

Isothermal Community College
P.O. Box 804
Spindale 28160

Vance-Granville Community College
State Rd. 1126, P.O. Box 917
Henderson 27536

OHIO

Berlitz Language Centers
156 South Main St.
Akron 44308

Berlitz Languages Centers
503 Race St.
Cincinnati 45202

Berlitz Language Centers
815 Superior
Cleveland 44115

Bowling Green State University-Firelands
901 Rye Beach Rd.
Huron 44839

Cuyahoga Community College District
700 Carnegie Ave.
Cleveland 44115-2878

Lorain County Community College
1005 North Abbe Rd.
Elyria 44035

Montessori Teacher Education
Collaborative
11424 Bellflower Rd. NE
Cleveland 44106

Sinclair Community College
444 West Third St.
Dayton 45402

University of Akron-Main Campus
302 Buchtel Common
Akron 44325-4702

University of Rio Grande
North College St.
Rio Grande 45674

OKLAHOMA

Bacone College
2299 Old Bacome Rd.
Muskogee 74403-1597

Carl Albert State College
1507 South McKenna
Poteau 74953-5208

Connors State College
Rte. 1, P.O. Box 1000
Warner 74469

Eastern Oklahoma State College
1301 West Main St.
Wilburton 74578

Northeastern Oklahoma Agricultural and
Mechanical College
200 Eye St. NE
Miami 74354

Northern Oklahoma College
P.O. Box 310
Tonkawa 74653

Pontotoc Skill Development Center
601 West 33rd
Ada 74820

Redland Community College
1300 South Country Club Rd., P.O. Box
370
El Reno 73036

Rogers State College
Will Rogers and College Hill
Claremore 74017

Rose State College
6420 Southeast 15th
Midwest City 73110

Seminole Junior College
P.O. Box 351
Seminole 74868

Tulsa Junior College
6111 East Skelly Dr.
Tulsa 74135

Western Oklahoma State College
2801 North Main St.
Altus 73521-1397

OREGON

Montessori Institute Northwest
P.O. Box 771
Oregon City 97045

Portland Community College
P.O. Box 19000
Portland 97280-0990

PENNSYLVANIA

Berlitz Language Centers
1608 Walnut St.
Philadelphia 19103

Berlitz Language Centers
355 Fifth Ave.
Pittsburgh 15222

Berlitz Language Centers
230 Sugartown Rd.
Wayne 19087

Bucks County Community College
Swamp Rd.
Newtown 18940

Butler County Community College
College Dr. Oak Hills
Butler 16003-1203

Community College of Philadelphia
1700 Spring Garden St.
Philadelphia 19130

Community College of Allegheny County
800 Allegheny Ave.
Pittsburgh 15233-1895

Delaware County Community College
901 South Media Line Rd.
Media 19063

Harrisburg Area Community
College-Harrisburg Campus
One Hacc Dr.
Harrisburg 17110

Keystone Junior College
P.O. Box 50
La Plume 18440-0200

Lehigh County Community College
4525 Education Park Dr.
Schnecksville 18078-2598

Luzerne County Community College
1333 South Prospect St.
Nanticoke 18634

Manor Junior College
700 Fox Chase Rd.
Jenkintown 19046

Montgomery County Community College
340 Dekalb Pike
Blue Bell 19422

Northampton County Area Community
College
3835 Green Pond Rd.
Bethlehem 18017

Reading Area Community College
P.O. Box 1706
Reading 19603

RHODE ISLAND

Community College of Rhode Island
400 East Ave.
Warwick 02886-1805

TENNESSEE

Hiwassee College
225 Hiwassee College Dr.
Madisonville 37354

Jackson State Community College
2046 North Pkwy.
Jackson 38301

TEXAS

Amarillo College
P.O. Box 447
Amarillo 79178

Angelina College
P.O. Box 1768
Lufkin 75902-1768

Berlitz Language Centers
8400 North Mopac
Austin 78759

Berlitz Language Centers
17194 Preston Rd.
Dallas 75248

Berlitz Language Centers
1555 Merrimac Circle
Fort Worth 76107

Berlitz Language Centers
3100 Richmond Ave.
Houston 77098

Berlitz Language Centers
5815 Callaghan Rd.
San Antonio 78228

Cisco Junior College
Rte. 3, P.O. Box 3
Cisco 76437

College of the Mainland
1200 Amburn Rd.
Texas City 77591

Del Mar College
101 Baldwin
Corpus Christi 78404-3897

El Paso Community College
P.O. Box 20500
El Paso 79998

Frank Phillips College
P.O. Box 5118
Borger 79008-5118

Galveston College
4015 Ave. Q
Galveston 77550

Grayson County College
6101 Grayson Dr.
Denison 75020

Hill College
P.O. Box 619
Hillsboro 76645

Houston Montessori Center
9601 Katy Fwy.
Houston 77024-1330

Howard County Junior College District
1001 Birdwell Ln.
Big Spring 79720

Kilgore College
1100 Broadway
Kilgore 75662-3299

King's Way Missionary Institute
401 South Kings Hwy.
McAllen 78501

McLennan Community College
1400 College Dr.
Waco 76708

Navarro College
3200 West Seventh
Corsicana 75110

North Harris Montgomery Community
   College District
250 North Sam Houston Pkwy. E
Houston 77060

Panola College
West Panola St.
Carthage 75633

Richland College
12800 Abrams Rd.
Dallas 75243-2199

San Jacinto College-Central Campus
8060 Spencer Hwy.
Pasadena 77505

San Jacinto College-North Campus
5800 Uvalde
Houston 77049

Southwest Texas Junior College
2401 Garner Field Rd.
Uvalde 78801

Temple Junior College
2600 South First St.
Temple 76504-7435

Texas Southmost College
80 Fort Brown
Brownsville 78520

Trinity Valley Community College
500 South Prairieville
Athens 75751

Tyler Junior College
P.O. Box 9020
Tyler 75711

Weatherford College
308 East Park Ave.
Weatherford 76086

Wharton County Junior College
911 Boling Hwy.
Wharton 77488

UTAH

Dixie College
225 South, 700 East
Saint George 84770

VERMONT

Champlain College
163 South Willard St.
Burlington 05401

Community College of Vermont
P.O. Box 120
Waterbury 05676

VIRGINIA

Berlitz Language Centers
2070 Chain Bridge Rd.
Vienna 22182

J Sargeant Reynolds Community College
P.O. Box 85622
Richmond 23285-5622

Northern Virginia Community College
4001 Wakefield Chapel Rd.
Annandale 22003

Saint Paul's College
406 Windsor Ave.
Lawrenceville 23868

Southern Virginia College for Women
One College Hill Dr.
Buena Vista 24416

Tidewater Community College
Rte. 135
Portsmouth 23703

Virginia Western Community College
3095 Colonial Ave.
Roanoke 24015

WASHINGTON

Berlitz Language Centers
400 112th Ave. NE
Bellevue 98009

Berlitz Language Centers
1525 Fourth Ave.
Seattle 98101

WEST VIRGINIA

Opportunities Industrialization
   Center-North Centerl West Virginia
120 Jackson St.
Fairmont 26554

WISCONSIN

Berlitz Language Centers
111 East Wisconsin Ave.
Milwaukee 53202

Milwaukee Area Technical College
700 West State St.
Milwaukee 53233

North Central Technical College
1000 Campus Dr.
Wausau 54401-1899

Opportunities Industrialization Center
2835 North 32nd St.
Milwaukee 53210

Waukesha County Technical College
800 Main St.
Pewaukee 53072

WYOMING

Casper College
125 College Dr.
Casper 82601

Central Wyoming College
2660 Peck Ave.
Riverton 82501

Eastern Wyoming College
3200 West C St.
Torrington 82240

Laramie County Community College
1400 East College Dr.
Cheyenne 82007

Northwest Community College
231 West Sixth St.
Powell 82435

Sheridan College
P.O. Box 1500
Sheridan 82801

Western Wyoming Community College
P.O. Box 428
Rock Springs 82902

Index

All jobs mentioned in this volume are listed and cross-referenced in the index. Some main entries appear in all capital letters; these relate to jobs that have separate occupational profiles. For example, ADULT EDUCATION WORKER, ARMED SERVICES CAREER, BORDER PATROL AGENT, and so on are profiles in this volume. Main entries that are not capitalized refer either to jobs that do not have a separate profile, but for which information is given, or to relevant career topics.

Under some capitalized entries there is a section entitled "Profile includes." This lists jobs that are mentioned in the main-entry profile. So, in the case of ADULT EDUCATION WORKER, jobs that are included in the profile are: Administrator and Continuing education teacher.

Some main entries are followed by a list of related job profiles. These appear in parentheses after the page numbers on which they can be found. Using the BORDER PATROL AGENT profile as an example, a related job that is profiled in this volume is (Federal government worker).

Accountant: 48 (Federal government worker); 102, 103 (Internal revenue service worker)
Acquisitions librarian, 109 (Librarian, public)
Activities director, 84 (Youth organization worker)
Administrative assistant, 89 (City manager)
Administrative worker, 48 (Federal government worker)
Administrator: 75 (Institutional child care worker); 88 (Adult education worker); 88–90 (City manager); 91 (College student personnel worker); 92 (Criminologist); 118 (Parole officer); 128 (School counselor); 137 (Teacher, elementary and preschool); 138 (Teacher, secondary school); 145 (Vocational counselor)
ADULT EDUCATION WORKER, 87–88; Profile includes: Administrator, Continuing education teacher
Agent: 39–40 (Border patrol agent); 95–96 (FBI special agent)
Agricultural quarantine inspector, 101 (Government inspector and examiner)
Aide: 52–53 (Geriatric aide); 79–80 (Paralegal aide); 82–84 (Teacher's aide)
Alcohol and tobacco tax inspector, 101 (Government inspector and examiner)
Ambassador, 98 (Foreign service worker)
Ammunition handler, 37 (Armed service career)
Apprenticeship, 49 (Federal government worker)
ARMED SERVICES CAREER, 37–39
Armor reconaissance specialist, 37 (Armed service career)
Art museum librarian, 114 (Librarian, special)
Assistant city manager, 89 (City manager)
Assistant fund raiser, 100 (Fund raiser)
Assistant operator, 61 (Power plant worker)
Assistant principal, 139 (Teacher, secondary school)

Assistant professor, 133 (Teacher, college)
Associate, 105 (Lawyer)
Associate professor, 133 (Teacher, college)
Attorney: 77–78 (Legal assistant, corporate); 79 (Paralegal aide); 104–106 (Lawyer)
Aviation safety officer, 101 (Government inspector and examiner)

Ballistics technician, 69 (Crime laboratory technician)
Battalion chief, 52 (Fire fighter)
Bilingual teacher: 136 (Teacher, elementary and preschool); 139 (Teacher, secondary school)
Biologist, 48 (Federal government worker)
Bodyguard, 72 (Detective)
Boiler operator, 60, 61 (Power plant worker)
Bookmobile librarian, 109 (Librarian, public)
BORDER PATROL AGENT, 39–40; 48 (Federal government worker)
Bouncer, 72 (Detective)
Brother, 124 (Religious vocation)
Budget examiner, 101 (Government inspector and examiner)
BUILDING CUSTODIAN, 41–42
Building custodian supervisor, 41–42 (Building custodian)

Cable splicer, 46, 47 (Electric power transmission and distribution worker)
Cadet: 57 (Police officer); 66 (State police officer)
Captain: 52 (Fire fighter); 57, 58 (Police officer); 67 (State police officer)
Case supervisor, 132 (Social worker)
Caseworker, 131 (Social worker)
Cataloger, 109 (Librarian, public)
Chaplain, 124 (Religious vocation)
Chauffeur, 48 (Federal government worker)
Chemical and physical analysis technician, 69 (Crime laboratory technician)
Chemist, 48 (Federal government worker)

Chief of detectives, 73 (Detective)
Chief of fire protection, 88 (City manager)
Chief of police, 73 (Detective)
Chief probation officer, 121 (Probation officer)
Chief social worker, 132 (Social worker)
Child care worker, 74–75 (Institutional child care worker)
Children's librarian, 109 (Librarian, public)
CITY MANAGER, 88–90
Claim examiner, 101 (Government inspector and examiner)
Clean-up worker, 61 (Power plant worker)
Clerk, 48 (Federal government worker)
College admissions officer, 90 (College student personnel worker)
College and university librarian, 111–112 (Librarian, school)
College placement counselor: 90 (College student personnel worker); 143 (Vocational counselor)
College president: 91 (College student personnel worker); 134 (Teacher, college)
COLLEGE STUDENT PERSONNEL WORKER, 90–91; Profile includes: College admissions officer, College placement counselor, Dean of students, Financial aid officer, Foreign student adviser, Registrar, Student center staff member, Student counselor
College teacher: 130 (School media specialist); 133–135 (Teacher, college)
Communications and records assistant, 97 (Foreign service worker)
Construction inspector, 101 (Government inspector and examiner)
Consultant: 89 (City manager); 99 (Fund raiser); 107 (Lawyer, public service); 118–120 (Political consultant); 122 (Rehabilitation counselor); 133 (Teacher, college); 145 (Vocational counselor)
Continuing education teacher, 87, 88 (Adult education worker)

Control room operator, 61 (Power plant worker)

Corporal, 67 (State police officer)

Corporate lawyer, 106–107 (Lawyer, corporate)

Corporate legal assistant, 77–78 (Legal assistant, corporate)

Corporate lobbyist, 118–120 (Political consultant)

Corporate paralegal aide, 77–78 (Legal assistant, corporate)

Corrections captain, 43 (Corrections officer)

CORRECTIONS OFFICER, 42–44

Counsel, 104–106 (Lawyer)

Counselor: 115–116 (Marriage and family counselor); 122–123 (Rehabilitation counselor); 124 (Religious vocation); 127–129 (School counselor); 138, 139 (Teacher, secondary school)

Court reporter: 37 (Armed service career); 80–81 (Shorthand reporter)

Court stenographer, 48 (Federal government worker)

Crime investigator, 69 (Crime laboratory technician)

CRIME LABORATORY TECHNICIAN, 69–70; Profile includes: Ballistics technician, Chemical and physical analysis technician, Documents technician, Fingerprint technician, Instruments technician, Photography technician, Polygraph technician

Crime scientist, 69 (Crime laboratory technician)

Criminal lawyer, 104 (Lawyer)

CRIMINOLOGIST, 92–93; 69 (Crime laboratory technician)

Custodian, 41–42 (Building custodian)

Customs agent, 94 (Customs worker)

Customs inspector, 94 (Customs worker)

CUSTOMS WORKER, 94–95; Profile includes: Customs agent, Customs inspector, Import specialist

Day camp counselor, 84 (Youth organization worker)

DAY CARE WORKER, 70–71

Deacon, 124 (Religious vocation)

Dean of students: 90, 91 (College student personnel worker); 133 (Teacher, college)

Dental hygienist, 37 (Armed service career)

Department head: 102 (Government inspector and examiner); 118 (Parole officer); 134 (Teacher, college); 139 (Teacher, secondary school)

Deputy keeper, 43 (Corrections officer)

DETECTIVE, 72–73; 58 (Police officer); 69 (Crime laboratory technician); Profile includes: Bodyguard, Bouncer, House detective, Plainclothes detective, Police detective, Private investigator, Store detective

Director of curriculum or media planning, 130 (School media specialist)

Director of fund-raising programs, 100 (Fund raiser)

Director of probation department, 121 (Probation officer)

Director of rehabilitation programs, 122 (Rehabilitation counselor)

Director of research department, 92 (Criminologist)

Director of special educational projects, 137 (Teacher, elementary and preschool)

Distribution clerk, 58, 59 (Postal service worker)

District attorney: 105 (Lawyer); 108 (Lawyer, public service)

District representative, 44, 45 (Electric power service worker)

Documents technician, 69 (Crime laboratory technician)

Driver, 50 (Fire fighter)

Drug therapist, 117 (Parole officer)

Economist, 48 (Federal government worker)

Electric meter repairer, 44, 45 (Electric power service worker)

ELECTRIC POWER SERVICE WORKER, 44–46; Profile includes: District representative, Electric meter repairer, Meter installer, Meter tester, Service representative

ELECTRIC POWER TRANSMISSION AND DISTRIBUTION WORKER, 46–48; Profile includes: Cable splicer, Ground helper, Line installer and repairer, Load dispatcher, Substation operator, Troubleshooter

Elementary school librarian, 111 (Librarian, school)

Elementary school teacher, 136, 137 (Teacher, elementary and preschool)

Employment counselor, 143–145 (Vocational counselor)

Employment interviewer, 144 (Vocational counselor)

Engineer, 48 (Federal government worker)

Environmental lawyer, 107–108 (Lawyer, public service)

ESL (English as a second language) teacher: 136 (Teacher, elementary and preschool); 139 (Teacher, secondary school)

Estate tax attorney, 102, 103 (Internal revenue service worker)

Examiner, 101–102 (Government inspector and examiner)

Family counselor, 115–116 (Marriage and family counselor)

FBI SPECIAL AGENT, 95–96

FEDERAL GOVERNMENT WORKER, 48–50

Federal law enforcement worker, 39–40 (Border patrol agent)

Federal school administrator, 125, 126 (School administrator)

Financial aid officer, 91 (College student personnel worker)

Fingerprint technician, 69 (Crime laboratory technician)

Fire chief, 52 (Fire fighter)

FIRE FIGHTER, 50–52; Profile includes: Driver, Fire inspector, Fire science specialist, Hose operator, Pump operator, Tiller

Fire inspector, 51 (Fire fighter)

Fire science specialist, 51 (Fire fighter)

First sergeant, 67 (State police officer)

Food and drug inspector, 101 (Government inspector and examiner)

Food service worker, 48 (Federal government worker)

Foreign service officer, 97 (Foreign service worker)

Foreign service reserve officer, 97 (Foreign service worker)

Foreign service staff member, 97 (Foreign service worker)

FOREIGN SERVICE WORKER, 97–99; Profile includes: Foreign service officer, Foreign service reserve officer, Foreign service staff member

Foreign student adviser, 91 (College student personnel worker)

Freelance reporter, 81 (Shorthand reporter)

Full professor, 133 (Teacher, college)

FUND RAISER, 99–100

General reporter, 81 (Shorthand reporter)

Geologist, 48 (Federal government worker)

GERIATRIC AIDE, 52–53

GOVERNMENT INSPECTOR AND EXAMINER, 101–102; Profile includes: Agricultural quarantine inspector, Alcohol and tobacco tax inspector, Aviation safety officer, Budget examiner, Claim examiner, Construction inspector, Food and drug inspector, Grain inspector, Meat grader

Government lawyer, 107 (Lawyer, public service)

Government page, 48 (Federal government worker)

Government worker, 48–50 (Federal government worker)

Grain inspector, 101 (Government inspector and examiner)

Ground helper, 46, 47 (Electric power transmission and distribution worker)

Guard, 64–66 (Security guard)

Guidance counselor, 127–129 (School counselor)

Head housekeeper, 76 (Institutional housekeeper)

Head librarian: 112 (Librarian, school); 114, 115 (Librarian, special)

Hearing reporter, 81 (Shorthand reporter)

Heavy equipment operator, 63 (Refuse worker)

Helicopter repairer, 37 (Armed service career)

Helper, 61 (Power plant worker)

High school teacher, 138 (Teacher, secondary school)

Highway inspector, 55 (Highway maintenance worker)

HIGHWAY MAINTENANCE WORKER, 54–55

Homebound teacher: 136 (Teacher, elementary and preschool); 139 (Teacher, secondary school)

Hose operator, 50 (Fire fighter)

Hotel detective, 72 (Detective)

House detective, 72 (Detective)

House parent, 74 (Institutional child care worker)

Housekeeper, 76–77 (Institutional housekeeper)

Import specialist, 94 (Customs worker)

Incinerator operator, 62, 63 (Refuse worker)

Inspector: 58 (Police officer); 101–102 (Government inspector and examiner)

INSTITUTIONAL CHILD CARE WORKER, 74–75

INSTITUTIONAL HOUSEKEEPER, 76–77

Instructional teacher's aide, 82 (Teacher's aide)

Instructor, 133 (Teacher, college)

Instruments technician, 69 (Crime laboratory technician)